Brandeis meets Gutenberg

Res Publica

ÖFFENTLICHES UND INTERNATIONALES RECHT

Herausgegeben von Udo Fink, Dieter Dörr
und Rolf Schwartmann

Band 15

PETER LANG
Frankfurt am Main · Berlin · Bern · Bruxelles · New York · Oxford · Wien

Dieter Dörr / Udo Fink /
Russel Weaver / Tobias Keber
(eds.)

Brandeis meets Gutenberg

German-American Conversations on Law,
1991-2011

PETER LANG
Internationaler Verlag der Wissenschaften

Bibliographic Information published by the Deutsche Nationalbibliothek
The Deutsche Nationalbibliothek lists this publication in the Deutsche Nationalbibliografie; detailed bibliographic data is available in the internet at http://dnb.d-nb.de.

ISSN 1614-838X
ISBN 978-3-631-63182-9

www.peterlang.de

Table of Contents

Foreword: Honoring and Remembering theJohannes Gutenberg Faculty of Law - University of Louisville Louis D. Brandeis School of Law Exchange Relationship

by Russell L. Weaver, Eckart Klein,** Dieter Dörr,*** Udo Fink*****

As we celebrate the twentieth anniversary of the exchange between Johannes Gutenberg Faculty of Law and the University of Louisville's Louis D. Brandeis School of Law, it is worthwhile to reflect on how the exchange came into being, and some of the many connections that have developed over the years.

In 1990, when this exchange began, the University of Louisville's Louis D. Brandeis School of Law had only one active academic exchange relationship: with the University of Leeds School of Law. This exchange had existed since the 1950s, and there had been many fruitful exchanges. Indeed, many current and former faculty had participated in the Leed's exchange, including Professor Robert L. Stenger, Professor David Leibson and Professor Russell L. Weaver. However, the Leeds-Louisville relationship was built on a model that contemplated year-long exchanges of faculty. By the early 1990s, this model was still viable, but was becoming more difficult to sustain. Few faculty, especially those with children, could go away for an entire year. Moreover, the University of Louisville found it difficult to raise the money to support a year-long exchange. As a result, Professor Russell Weaver conceived the idea of shorter (2-3 week) academic exchanges designed to facilitate more frequent academic exchanges, and the ability to maintain closer contacts between faculties on an ongoing basis.

---

* Professor of Law & Distinguished University Scholar, University of Louisville, Louis D. Brandeis School of Law.

** Professor Emeritus. Eckart Klein held the chair for Public Law, International Law European law at the Johannes Gutenberg-University from 1981-1994 and at the Potsdam University (1994-1998).

*** Chair for Public Law, International and European Law, Media Law, Johannes Gutenberg University Mainz

**** Chair for Public Law, European and International Law, International Trade Law, Johannes Gutenberg-University Mainz.

As this new exchange model was being developed, it was logical to try to extend it to other universities besides Leeds. Johannes Gutenberg University and the University of Montpellier were likely targets for the establishment of such exchange links. Both universities are located in sister cities of Louisville (Johannes Gutenberg University being located in Mainz, Germany, and the University of Montpellier being located in Montpellier, France), and there were support structures that could help support and nourish exchange relationships. As a result, the University of Louisville decided to send Professor Russell L. Weaver to both cities to conduct discussions and attempt to bring exchange relationships to fruition.

Sister Cities of Louisville and the Mainz Friendship Circle were instrumental in helping establish the exchange relationship. In particular, Frau Gerlinde Brautszch played a critical role. Frau Brautszch was a tireless advocate for the Mainz-Louisville Sister City relationship. Interestingly, at that time, although the City of Louisville had officially designated the City of Mainz as a "Sister City," Mainz had only designated Louisville as a "friendship city." This difficulty was rectified a few years later when Mainz officially declared Louisville as a Sister City. Frau Brautszch deserves some credit for the finalization of the relationship because she worked incessantly to bring it to fruition.

Frau Brautszch was also instrumental in the development of the law school exchange. She an ever present friend to the many Louisvillians who visited Mainz, and she established a "Friendship Circle" designed to help nurture and facilitate the relationship. Inevitably, as he sought to develop the exchange link, Professor Weaver learned about Frau Brautszch, and contacted her about how to best make contact with Johannes Gutenberg University. Frau Brautszch immediately took charge of the situation. Within days, she had contacted Professor Dr. Eckart Klein and Professor Dr. Alexander Böhm, and arranged a meeting during Professor Weaver's proposed visit. At that meeting, a decision was taken to establish the exchange link, and Dr. Professor Klein came to Louisville the following September as the first exchangee.

In the early years of the exchange, Frau Brautszch provided invaluable assistance to the Louisvillians who came to Mainz. Using her Friendship Circle, she would always arrange accommodation with a family. She also arranged numerous excursions and events for visitors from Louisville, as well as visits to the Gutenberg Museum, Rhine River boat tours, free bus passes, dinners and lunches. These home stays were very interesting for the Louisvillian visitors. Not only did the Louisvillians get the opportunity to interact more closely with Mainzers, they came away with many interesting stories. Professor Eades stayed with a family where the man, who was getting up in years, had been a prisoner of war in the United States during World War II. Professor Weaver stayed with a man who had fought under Field Marshall Rommel in World War II, who could recount the devastation of post-World War II Germany, and whose family had owned Kupferburg Wineries (which they were able to visit as special guests). In addition, visitors to Mainz heard many interesting stories.[1] The early Louisvillians who went to Mainz have a very strong affection for Frau Brautszch who helped introduce them to her beloved city.

Over the years, many Louisville and Mainz faculty have participated in the exchange. From the Louisville side, Professor Ronald Eades (now retired), Professor Robert Stenger (now retired), Professor Russell Weaver, Professor John Cross, former Dean Donald Burnett, Professor Susan Duncan, Professor Judy Fisher and Professor Lisa Nicholson. From Mainz, participants have included Professor Dr. Eckart Klein (now retired), Professor Dr. Walter Rudolf (now retired), Professor Dr. Dieter Dörr, Professor Dr. Udo Fink, Prof. Dr. Frank Peter Schuster, Professor Dr. Mark Cole (now with Luxembourg University), Dr. Tobias Keber, Dr. Heiner Baab, Jessica Sänger and Ines Gillich.

Today, as the Johannes Gutenberg University- University of Louisville law exchange approaches the beginning of its third decade, the bond between the two law schools is stronger than ever. Although Professor Klein has moved on to Potsdam, Professor Dieter Dörr and Professor Udo Fink have stepped forward to nourish and manage the exchange on the Mainz side, and have taken the exchange to new levels. Professor Weaver now speaks regularly at the Mainz Media Institute's annual media symposium, and he teaches a course for the Institute each year. In addition, Professor Weaver, Professor Dörr and Professor Fink

1 During the following years, Professor Weaver became particularly close friends with Herr Eckart Schneider-Reuter (unfortunately, now deceased), a former merchant in Mainz who was later President of the Friendship Circle. Herr Schneider-Reuter told Professor Weaver about his recollections of World War II, and in particular the night that Mainz was bombed during February of 1945. During the bombing, some ninety percent of the city was obliterated, and Herr Schneider-Reuter (who had just turned 15), who was subject to induction into Hitler's army, took advantage of the situation to quietly slip off to live with relatives under the war was over. On another occasion, Herr Schneider-Reuter invited Professor Weaver to dinner at his house (in fact, Professor Weaver was there with his young kids, and Herr Schneider-Reuter in an extraordinary gesture of kindness and good will had moved out for the week so that Professor Weaver and his family could use the house), and told Professor Weaver that a "genealogist" would be coming to dinner that night. Professor Weaver, in an attempt to make conversation, tried to engage the "genealogist" in conversation about his work. However, the "genealogist" seemed absolutely clueless about genealogy. Turned out that he was a "gynecologist" and Professor Weaver decided not ask a lot of questions about his work.

have hosted a free speech discussion forum in Mainz, and will co-host the Privacy Discussion Forum in 2011. In addition, various faculty have co-written articles together.

For many Louisvillians, frequent trips to Mainz have simply become a regular and enjoyable part of life. For law school faculty, not only are the trips enjoyable, but they are intellectually, academically, and professionally rewarding.

Learning on International Faculty Exchange

*by Robert L. Stenger**

As a professor emeritus now, I reflect upon thirty-five years of teaching law and forty-six years of teaching in colleges and universities. In retrospect you realize how people and events shaped one's personal and professional development. Experiences stand out and blend together as you realize how they contributed to and structured your career. One significant dynamic for me was faculty exchanges.

I began law school after eight years of college and university teaching of theology, philosophy and ethics. When I graduated from law school, Louisville was initiating a philosophically-based introductory course in law. They were seeking a faculty member with philosophical training. I was hired and began teaching "Law, Language and Ethics" and Torts; I soon expanded into Family Law, Constitutional Law, Jurisprudence and Decedents' Estates and Trusts.

When I began law teaching, I did not expect that I would also become a world traveler. But Louisville had regular year-long exchanges with the faculty of Law at the University of Leeds. While faculty from Leeds were regularly visiting Louisville, no one had gone to Leeds for some years. In 1979-1980 Geoff Hoon [later MEP,MP and member of Tony Blair's cabinet] came to Louisville and we planned my visit to Leeds After I received tenure, we [my wife and sons, then three and six] went to Leeds in August, 1981, for a year-long stay.

I lectured in Family Law and conducted tutorials (a new teaching method for me at the time) in Trusts. I learned how to read English statutes, where bits and pieces from existing statutes remained in force while modified by recent statutes [some of which may not go into effect immediately]. I worked to construct holdings from the speeches of five law lords. I struggled to find an appropriate adjective--it was not English law for it usually applied also in Wales and Northern Ireland. Scotland often had its own law which may not even be common law but civil law. And companies located on Jersey or Guernsey to enjoy their favorable business and revenue laws.

One of my colleagues, who had written a textbook on property, asked "Do you have legal future interests in Kentucky? “ When I replied "Yes" his response

---

* Professor Emeritus. On February 12th 2010, Bob Stenger retired from 46 years of college and university teaching; thirty-five of those were at the University of Louisville Brandeis School of Law.

was "Only the Irish do that!" As I attended the lectures and read the textbooks in Trusts I deepened my knowledge and appreciation of equity jurisprudence. In my first article after I returned to Louisville I followed Lord Denning's use of the constructive trust to give equity to litigants, especially women, whose non-marital cohabitation would produce no legal claims to property. I was privileged to visit Lord Denning's court in London during his final year on the bench and to appreciate his belief that equity was not beyond the age for childbearing. Geoff Hoon and I debated about rights in our offices and in classes as Geoff claimed that "We have more rights than you do" for the rights of English persons know no limits while you have only the rights listed in the Constitution or civil rights statutes. [That debate became moot after the UK codified rights in the Human Rights Act.]

I returned to Leeds for teaching and research visits in 1994, 1997 and 2008. I wrote articles on the 1990 Human Fertilisation and Embryology Act regulating assisted reproduction procedures in the United Kingdom, which had been prompted by the birth of Louise Brown, the first-child born as a result of in vitro fertilization in 1978. I urged similar legislation for the United States where the field remains quite unregulated. A later article compared medical decisions by parents for adolescents as both countries attempted to recognize the gradual maturation of teenagers and to articulate an appropriate role for them in medical decisions. It became obvious how the legislative process in Parliament was enriched by reports compiled by leading scientists, philosophers, and appropriate experts followed by papers commissioned by Parliament.

I found upon my return to Louisville how my thinking and teaching practices had been enriched by a year in England. I knew that English common law was our heritage--Kentucky law began with "the law of Kentucky is the law of Virginia" and Virginia law began with "the law of Virginia is the law of England in the fourth year of James I" [the settlement at Jamestown in 1607]. But living under the parliamentary system and working daily with English law made the historical backdrop a rich presence. The year in West Yorkshire immersed us in English life in ways well beyond the few days in central London which was the experience most visitors from the United States had had. [We often told our English friends, "You haven't been to the United States; you've been to Disney World."]

Faculty exchanges with Leeds continued but it was only at the end of the nineteen eighties that horizons broadened. Because of the vision and initiatives of my colleague, Russ Weaver, faculty exchanges were developed literally around the world. Over the years many of my colleagues have visited foreign law schools and our faculty and students have been enriched by presentations from foreign visitors. During the nineties a rather provincial university and law school in Louisville opened itself and reached out to universities elsewhere. The global vision was basic to the leadership of University President John Shumaker and Law Dean Don Burnett.

The exchange relationship between Mainz and Louisville was initiated in 1990 with the visit of Professor Eckart Klein to Louisville. In classes and talks to and with faculty he broadened our understanding of federalism. We learned how the German Constitution granted basic powers to the “Länder” and limited the role of the central government. The tearing down of the Berlin Wall and the reunion of East and West Germany had been foreseen by the framers and their reunion took place with no constitutional changes. From both a constitutional and jurisprudential perspective we examined how nations and their governments fit together into a transnational political and monetary union. [During my year in Leeds I had had the opportunity to accompany a busload of students to the European Parliament in Luxemburg, the European Court of Human Rights in Strasbourg, and the various offices in Brussels.] I remember Professor Klein's being asked in the faculty common room "Will Bonn remain the capital of Germany?" He smiled and replied, as though no explanation were necessary, "Berlin is the capital of Germany."

The following year I visited Mainz. Through the generosity of the mayor's office I found accommodation with a family in Mainz-Finthen. The husband sang in a chorus for Karneval and they introduced me to marvelous church music with a Czech choir at St. Peter's and a Mozart Mass in the Dom. The wife volunteered to make me breakfast if I helped her with her English homework; she wanted to speak to their son-in-law's family in Raleigh, North Carolina. I agreed, if she would help me decipher the Frankfurt paper which arrived in the morning.

As a student of medieval theology, philosophy, law and history, I was delighted to be in Mainz, the Chancery of the Empire, and to visit its many historical sites, especially the artifacts in the historical museum. I came to appreciate Gutenberg and what printing meant in the cultural development of the West. The Dom with its unique elevations for the emperor and the bishop was a striking visualizion of the sacerdotium-imperium relationship. I saw seats physically being moved in the parliament to reflect the changes in representation resulting from a recent election. I was astounded to find faculty members campaigning to become head of the university, because the current head was to become minister of education. In the United States university presidents are hired by the trustees or regents with little, if any, faculty input. I was happy to find such an enduring contribution of the medieval universities.

During my first visit to Mainz in 1991 I focused on Constitutional Law and attempted to relate the constitutions of Germany and the United States. In attempting to teach equal protection I used the example of age discrimination. When I asked "How old must one be in Germany to consume alcoholic beverages?" I got only confused looks in response. "We didn't know there was an age" they responded, "wine and beer are on the table and you drink whenever your parents say you can." I came to gender equality and asked why all around campus were posters "Die Frauen an der Spitze" when gender equality was to be the norm. As we say in English, there was always "an elephant in the room" as we discussed constitutions and law. The issues of property rights in slaves and the slave trade on one side and the Final Solution and the holocaust on the other. I had similar experiences only in South Africa and the building of a constitutional structure after the experience of apartheid.

During my second and third visits to Mainz I made presentations on law, medicine and bioethics. I found that students in Mainz as well as the European students I had in Turku had difficulty comprehending the pay-for-service health care delivery system in the United States. Students expected medical care to be provided as needed; there would be no questioning whether the patient has (or hasn't) medical insurance or other financial means. The issue became clearer when my colleagues in Mainz explained that Germany is a both a "Rechtsstaat" and a "Sozialstaat". European documents include not only declarations of human rights but also covenants on both civil and political and social and cultural rights. In the United States rule of law is emphasized while social matters such as health care, education, retirement and unemployment benefits, are the result of statutes [often called "welfare law"]. While the patria potestas power enables and requires the governments in the United States to provide for individuals who cannot care for themselves, social services and welfare remain matters of governmental choice and largesse. Thus, people in the United States have difficulty understanding the recent social unrest and demonstrations in the United Kingdom, France, Greece and elsewhere as fees were imposed upon students and social benefits and services were reduced in the need for reducing budget deficits. They do not understand claims that such matters are rights, not privileges.

Similar questions came from European students who asked "Why do you kill people?" They knew that the death penalty did not exist in Europe and was judged inappropriate in modern times. The argument that the prohibition on "cruel and unusual punishment" in the Eighth Amendment to the Constitution of the Unite States did not prohibit the death penalty, which was not uncommon when the Bill of Rights was adopted in 1791, made little impression.

On substantive matters of law and medicine, however, we found considerable agreement concerning medical treatment at the end of life, the forbidding of assisted suicide (with exceptions in Europe in the Netherlands and Switzerland and in the United States in Oregon and Washington), and the respect owed to prenatal human life during its developmental stages. The highest courts in both Germany and the United States had focused on the value of fetal life as they considered the constitutionality of abortion. While the federal government and the individual states in the United States have little regulation of assisted reproduction technologies, there is much more regulation in Europe, where nations and the European Union attempt to provide boundaries and direction to scientists and fertility specialists who are developing and providing reproductive services. The recently developed field of bioethics rests in the United States, as it does elsewhere, in the Nuremberg Code (appended to the decision of the court in its judgment condemning Nazi physicians who conducted medical experiments with no consent from the subjects) and in the Code of Helsinki adopted by the World Health Organization.

Visitors from Mainz to Louisville have provided valuable insight into a number of legal issues. I have frequently questioned the meaning of "Deutsche Volk." My grandfather was born near Saarbrücken, one great grandfather came from Baden-Württemberg and another from Alsace (whose family considered themselves German and went to the German parish church). Walter Rudolph explained the provision in the United Nations Charter about "self-determination of peoples." He pointed out how many "peoples" there are in Europe. Groups with their own language, customs and traditions struggle today to retain their identities in the face of growing legal and extralegal pressures for conformity and homogeneity. Other visitors explored how environmental regulations touch not only nations but also local regions, e.g. legislation concerning the Rhine involves all the local governments in different nations along the river.

A particular focus of the Mainz-Louisville exchange has been freedom of speech (the First Amendment in the United States Constitution). Because many recent visitors have come from the Media Law group on the law faculty in Mainz (Udo Fink, Dieter Dörr, Mark Cole, Tobias Keber) and because of the interest of Louisville professors (Russ Weaver, Bob Stenger) in constitutional law, limits to speech have frequently been explored. From my first visit to Mainz when I bought a German Constitution I noted the central and powerful role of dignity [Würde] in constitutional language and interpretation. That word rarely appears in constitutional discourse or decisions of courts in the United States. Recent efforts to criminalize hate speech are met with First Amendment "slippery slope" arguments--"Legal limits to speech anywhere endanger free speech everywhere."

Professors from Mainz presented a number of powerful arguments which suggest a more significant role for the notion of dignity alongside the right of freedom of speech. One is recognition of the cumulative social evil which hateful words can produce. Centuries of anti-semitic speech seem to lead almost inevitably to the holocaust. It becomes easier for the less powerful to become marginalized and victimized when their very humanity is denied so often and so publically. In medical ethics it becomes less possible to assert the inviolability of every patient without a Kantian appreciation that "no one is a means to another's ends." Legally and jurisprudentially an emphasis upon human rights in international declarations and covenants and in their implementation requires recognition of the centrality of the human dignity of every individual.

The opportunity to visit law faculty and students around the world and to have them visit us has opened doors and expanded understanding. Visiting Paris and Poitiers introduced me not only to the administrative structure of government in France but also to research in civil law. In faculty discussions and in time spent in law libraries I learned how to work with a civil code. In legal education we frequently stress reason, the reasonable person, and how law produces reasonable results. It is also important to learn that reasonable people do things differently and both remain reasonable. One example I remember is visiting a criminal trial in France and watching a fair trial without cross examination by a defense attorney or trial by jury. In Finland I met with professors in Criminal Law who explained how sentences which are far shorter than those commonly employed in the United States yet work to result in a much smaller percentage of incarcerated people.

My experience of teaching in Louisville and Leeds made the summer session I taught in Sydney much more challenging. I was there at a time when the students asked in my first class in Jurisprudence "Do Americans think less of us because our Queen happens also to be Queen of other nations?" I replied that Americans don't think about that. The students were considering whether Australia would be better off with a President. Being in Sydney was interesting because their history, like Kentucky's, was about two hundred years from the arrival of early colonists. Later I learned that the voters had chosen not to change the constitutional structure or the flag. Just as visits to Turku introduced me to Baltic La , so in Australia I became aware of Pacific Basin Law. Legal systems must be responsive to their physical environments as well as the political and economic realities of their neighbors. In Finland I was told that there was little emphasis or spending on defense--"What use is defense when you have Sweden on one side and Russia on the other?"

In China I visited law schools in Shanghai and Beijing and lectured in Kunming. It was easier to communicate with junior faculty, many of whom had studied in Europe or the United States. I was introduced to a legal system which holds together the largest population of any nation. As a professor of Jurisprudence, I met a modern legal system which incorporated age-old traditions, ethics and culture. In Japan I visited a law school in Tokyo and lectured in Takamatsu. The constitution, influenced by the presence of people from the United States after the Second World War, engrafted a modern constitution upon an enduring culture. Discussions and proposals concerning nuclear weapons are forever changed after a visit to the memorials at Hiroshima.

Finally, the opportunity to visit South Africa and to teach in Pietermaritzburg was unique. I began by visiting Capetown and Nelson Mandela's cell on Robbins Island. In Pietermaritzburg I saw the statute of Ghandi, who arrived there as a young barrister. Not only were there landmarks of constitutional law in the efforts to create one nation from many languages and peoples and to bring together the influences of British, Dutch and indigenous laws and legal traditions, but also the effort to move from apartheid to a new social and political reality. I write this as we in the United States celebrate Martin Luther King weekend by reflecting on how much law owes to the Ghandis, Mandelas and Kings of recent history.

In conclusion, as I look back on faculty exchanges to law schools on five continents and to their visitors to Louisville, I am struck by one remark I heard frequently: "Law schools, law faculties and law students are the same everywhere." It is true that they share many of the same ideals and values, their teaching and research are amazingly similar, and their physical surroundings could not be more alike. Yet only by visiting different places and meeting other faculty and students can one appreciate how cultural and religious traditions and historical developments and setbacks have produced different legal structures, institutions and content. What looks similar is animated by such different currents. The similarities make it possible for us to live together; the differences make living together rich and beneficial.

A Global Theatre of American Justice? O. J. Simpson and Gutenberg's Second Wave

*by Don Burnett**

When my wife Karen and I came to Mainz in the summer of 1995, we received gracious hospitality in a wonderfully amiable flow of small-group gatherings. We were welcomed by the Mainz-Louisville Friendship Circle; by the Mayor's staff and Sister City volunteers (cheerfully energized by the remarkable Gerlinde Brautzsch); by the hosts of intimate receptions and musical recitals within the city and out in the country; by boat companions on the Rhine; by business and civic leaders who invited us to dinner at the downtown Deutsche Bank; by diverse clusters of law and economics faculty engaged in collegial discourse along the academic hallways and in their homes at Mainz and Bonn; and by the students who came, in bands of 15 to 30 at a time, to hear my comparative law lectures. Earnest and smiling, the students listened intently at first, but soon they began demonstrating impressive skills in Socratic dialogue and analysis on issues ranging from federalism and environmental law to civil and criminal procedure – and then, politely rapping the table and shaking hands with me when our conversations had concluded.[1]

---

* Dean and Foundation Professor of Law, University of Idaho College of Law, 2002 – present. Professor of Law, Louis D. Brandeis School of Law at the University of Louisville, 1990 – 2002 (Dean, 1990 – 2000). A.B. degree magna cum laude, Harvard University; J.D. degree, University of Chicago; LL.M. degree, University of Virginia.

1 For a brief overview of perceived differences and similarities in German and American law class interactions during the 1990s, see *Eckart Klein*, Legal Education in Germany, Symposium: Winds of Change – A Global Look at Legal Education, 72 Oregon Law Review 953 (1993). The adaptability and responsiveness of the Mainz students, as well as the collegiality of the professoriate and the community, had been noted by Louisville faculty who participated before me in the Mainz exchange. As the dean I encouraged and gave priority support to faculty participation in all of our exchanges. Through the efforts of Professor Russell Weaver and other faculty colleagues, the University of Louisville School of Law (which became the Louis D. Brandeis School of Law at the University of Louisville in 1997) had established a rich array of academic relationships around the world, including connections with the University of Montpellier, the University of Natal, Daito Bunka University, Macquarie University, and other institutions, in addition to a long-standing relationship with the University of Leeds. Faculty at these universities as well as at the Johannes Gutenberg Universitat/Mainz enjoyed a distinctive set of shared experiences in Louisville, establishing friendships with the Brandeis

The small groups were memorable. There was an intriguing exception, however, to this small-group experience. During the evening of 21 June 1995, I made the introductory presentation in a panel discussion entitled, "O. J. Simpson – Is Television Coverage of the Courtroom Desirable?" For this program I had expected an audience somewhat larger than my usual classes, perhaps reaching as many as 50 - 75 persons. In fact, the program drew an audience roughly ten times that large -- more than 700 people. The reason was due in part to the splendid academic and professional credentials of others on the panel: Prof. Dr. Jórg Lucke (whose subsequent passing we still mourn), a scholar in public law; Prof. Dr. Andreas Roth, a scholar in the history of law and civil law; Hans Seeliger, the Leading Prosecuting Attorney of Mainz; Peter Doebel, ZDF (Second Public Channel) television court reporter; and Rainer Hastrich, Head of the Legal Department of Sat 1 (Private Channel) in Mainz.

But there was a reason beyond credentials for the large assemblage. It was the fact that even as the panelists spoke, a worldwide audience was following the O. J. Simpson criminal trial as it unfolded before a bank of cameras in a courtroom at Los Angeles, California. There were 12 jurors seated in that courtroom, charged with the duty of listening attentively to all of the proceedings and of making a decision guided by law. Yet the cameras were carrying sounds and images, usually edited for attention-grabbing value and framed by urgent commentary, to a global "13th juror." This "juror" – the international community of television drama consumers fascinated by a daily high-stakes drama – was charged with no duty other than to satisfy a wavering attention span and a self-directed impulse to join a chorus of popular opinion, unburdened by any responsibility to weigh all of the evidence or to apply the judge's instructions. The 12 jurors in Los Angeles eventually would be called to render a verdict on whether the prosecution had proven the guilt of the accused beyond a reasonable doubt, but the global "13th juror" would make a broader judgment, for better or worse, about the American criminal justice system.

As the panelists in our program examined the Simpson case, several of us mentioned the symbolism of witnessing, as we gathered that evening at a university named for Johannes Gutenberg, a shift in power and influence from the print medium to electronic media – a second wave of information technology arguably as profound as the transition nearly five hundred years earlier from individually handwritten books to publications produced in mass quantities on Mr.

---

faculty and with each other. During my time at Louisville, none of these friendships was stronger or warmer than the personal and institutional relationship between members of the faculties in Louisville and Mainz.

Gutenberg's type-piece press. In both eras of change, technology had made the dissemination of public information faster and cheaper; but the participants in our panel discussion were left with the question of why this second wave of technology seemed to produce a more discernible and controversial impact on American criminal justice than on justice elsewhere. Why – other than the celebrity of the defendant, a famous African American football player, movie actor, and media personality – did this American criminal trial seem to generate much more popular interest in Germany than, say, criminal trials in Germany?

Although culture differences may supply part of the answer, the question points to an underlying element of the American legal system: the use of a lay jury, composed of persons drawn from all walks of life to perform a civic task and to resume their ordinary lives when the task is done. The lay jury is a cornerstone of the American legal process, even though the vast majority of cases are settled rather than tried. The Sixth Amendment to the United States Constitution protects a criminal defendant's right to a "speedy and public trial, by an impartial jury ...." The Seventh Amendment also recognizes the right to a jury trial in a civil case, on issues triable to juries under the common law. Lay juries drawn from the local community, unlike the panels of jurists and trained civil servants found in Germany and other civil law countries, embody an American tradition of populism and cautious skepticism about officially reposed expertise. The juries also are creatures of history, interposing the judgment of a cross-section of the community against perceived excesses of authoritarian rule, whether exercised by a British monarch in the colonial era or by overreaching prosecutors in today's legal setting.[2]

The American requirement for a "public" trial includes the right of the public, or representatives of the public, to attend a trial.[3] The guaranty of a public trial in the United States is not substantially different from the German requirement. What is distinctively American, however, is the synergy of the public trial and the lay jury, coupled with the methods employed to present a case to such a jury. The lay jury engaged in one-time service ordinarily does not see a case in the context of a past stream of cases presented by the same prosecutors and defense counsel; nor do lay jurors move through evidence with the adeptness of a

---

2 See, e.g., *Laura G. Dooley*, Our Juries, Our Selves: The Power, Perception, and Politics of the Civil Jury, 80 Cornell Law Review 325 (1995).

3 *Richmond Newspapers, Inc. v. Virginia*, 448 U.S. 555 (1980). The Supreme Court earlier held in *Sheppard v. Maxwell*, 384 U.S. 333 (1966), that persons or the media can be excluded from a trial if necessary to protect the right to a fair trial. The Richmond decision did not overturn that principle.

practiced routine or with the shared understandings of professionals collaborating in a practiced task. Instead, they make sense of a case individually, especially complex matters, by developing in their minds a narrative – a story line – that "connects the dots" of the evidence presented. The lawyers' challenge is to furnish the jury a persuasive narrative that fits the evidence and leads to a desired conclusion under the law.[4] In meeting this challenge, lawyers in America have a greater role in questioning witnesses and presenting non-testimonial evidence than is generally true of their civil law counterparts.

The lay juror's propensity to develop a narrative, the lawyers' efforts to present evidence in a way that laypersons can interpret in the context of a narrative, and the openness of a public trial, coalesce with the modern "story model" of journalism. Indeed, the American jury trial has the ingredients of an entertaining television show, which can be marketed successfully if it is trimmed and tailored to the audience's attention span and if the dynamic tension of the "plot" can be reinforced through a running commentary, coupled with recurrent emphasis upon emotive topics and with attention paid to especially sympathetic or alienating personality traits of the participants. The trial becomes a form of theatre – at least as it is depicted on television.

This has been a matter of concern for decades, even before television. Early worries about the presence of media in the courtroom tended to focus on the potential for disruption of the proceedings, distraction of the participants, or the creation of a "circus" atmosphere that would deprive the accused of a fair trial and bring the judicial process into disrepute. These concerns were heightened in the infamous Lindbergh infant kidnapping and murder case, State v. Hauptmann,[5] where a trial was conducted with 141 newspaper reporters and photographers, 125 telegraph operators, and 40 messengers in the courtroom. Hauptmann was convicted, and his conviction was not overturned; but later, in the politically sensational case of Billy Sol Estes, a financier who was charged with fraud and who allegedly had links to President John F. Kennedy and Vice President Lyndon B. Johnson, the U.S. Supreme Court held that the media had so disrupted and tainted the proceedings that Estes was denied a fair trial.[6] In particu-

---

4 Lawyers may not introduce false evidence in support of a proposed narrative. Under Rule 3.8 of the American Bar Association Rules of Professional Conduct for Lawyers, a prosecutor is a "minister of justice" whose duty is to see that justice is done, not merely to secure a conviction. Under Rule 3.3, both the prosecutor and the defense counsel are prohibited from presenting evidence known to be false.

5 180 A. 809, cert. denied 296 U.S. 649 (1935).

6 *Estes v. Texas*, 381 U.S. 532 (1965).

lar, the Court held that the intrusive presence of cameras in the courtroom had violated due process.[7] The Court reached this decision only by a 5-4 vote, with the deciding fifth vote coming from Justice Harlan, who observed that if and when television technology became more sophisticated and less intrusive in the future, a due process analysis might yield a different outcome.

Justice Harlan's observation proved prophetic, as the Court later held, in the lower-profile case of Chandler v. Florida, that cameras in the courtroom were not a *per se* violation of due process, and that they had not impermissibly impacted the proceedings in that particular case. The Court in *Chandler* did not go, nor has it since gone, to the other end of the spectrum and declared – as some have urged it to do -- that it would a deprivation of due process for the accused or for the prosecution, or that it would be a violation of the public's right to know under the First Amendment, if a court did *not* allow cameras in the courtroom. The Supreme Court has, in essence, taken a "federalism" approach, leaving the question of cameras in the courtroom for the various states to address as a matter of judicial *policy* rather than of constitutional law.

The Court itself has yet to approve cameras in the federal system, although in 2011 a limited three-year experiment with in-court cameras was approved by the Judicial Conference of the United States (a special body that develops administrative policy for the federal courts, subject to ultimate Supreme Court review). In contrast, nearly all of the American states now allow cameras in the courtroom in some circumstances, although they generally preserve the authority of a judge to preclude cameras if s/he believes they present a substantial likelihood of materially prejudicing the proceeding.[8]

The policy arguments in favor of allowing cameras include enhancing the transparency of the courts, educating the public, making the courts accountable through the most immediate and understandable public access to judicial proceedings, giving electronic reporters the same access as print reporters, and pro-

7 The issue of cameras in the courtroom is related to, but distinguishable from, the question of prejudice resulting from pervasive pretrial publicity that deprives the accused of a fair trial; see. e.g., *Sheppard v. Maxwell*, supra note 3.

8 This constitutional standard – substantial likelihood of materially prejudicing the proceeding – is drawn from the case of *Gentile v. State Bar of Nevada*, 501 U.S. 1030 (1991), where the Supreme Court struck down, on First Amendment grounds, a general prohibition against out-of-court statements by attorneys during the pendency of a case. The Court found the prohibition to be overbroad, but the Court held that there is a compelling governmental interest in fair and impartial judicial proceedings and, therefore, restrictions more narrowly tailored to achieve this interest are permissible.

viding an empirical basis to test the accuracy of descriptions by court observers – including "real-time bloggers" – of events in the courtroom. These arguments are not universally accepted, however, as evidenced by the reluctance of German courts to allow cameras in the courtroom.[9]

The opposing arguments include a concern that cameras – even if they have evolved to the point of being physically unobtrusive – do not merely "report" what happens in the courtroom; rather, they materially affect the behavior of the judges (especially judges who are elected, as are many in the United States), lawyers, witnesses, and jurors; and the impact of cameras on behavior is more profound that the impact of print reporters taking notes in the gallery. Opponents also express concern about the degree of editing and commentary that characterize market-driven television broadcasts. They worry about the enhanced capacity of television, combined with the Internet, to create and inflame constituencies, and they worry about the electronic media's potential for casting a criminal defendant in such a negative light that even if the trial results in an acquittal, the defendant's face is recognizable everywhere and s/he may be unable to resume a normal life.[10]

This brings us back to O. J Simpson. At the end of the panel discussion on 21 June 1995, the issue of cameras in the courtroom had not been resolved, but at least it had been explored collegially. The Simpson case did not end on such a collegial note. The trial went on until early October, pitting a prosecutorial narrative of guilt revealed by scientific and circumstantial evidence against the defense narrative of a police department that had jumped to a conclusion of guilt and had compounded the error with biased and clumsy investigatory work. The jury returned a widely televised verdict of not guilty, much to the consternation of viewers who had long since made up their minds about the case. Many of the viewers comprising the "13th juror" were unimpressed by the notion that the role of a juror is not simply to form a belief about a defendant's guilt, but rather to

9 See generally, *Peer Zumbansen*, Federal Constitutional Court Affirms Ban of TV-Coverage of Court Proceedings, German Law Journal, vol. 2, no. 3 (15 February 2001).

10 This concern may be illustrated by the recent case of *Florida v. Casey Anthony*, in which a mother was accused of murdering her child Caylee. The case received a level of television publicity nearly as extensive as the O. J. Simpson case, plus a deluge of commentary on the Internet. The "Nancy Grace" show on the HLN television network (previously known as CNN Headline News) kept a "Justice for Caylee" focus on the case throughout the investigation and pretrial phases, and during the trial. When the jury returned a surprise verdict of not guilty, the host of the show opined that the defendant was guilty and that she "got away with murder." The defendant has been released and apparently is living in seclusion, to the extent possible.

determine whether guilt has been proven, in light of the full record, beyond a reasonable doubt. (The importance of the burden of proof became manifest when, in a subsequent, civil action brought by the family of one of the murder victims, a jury found Simpson liable in damages. The standard of proof in that case was a preponderance of the evidence.)

The outcome of the criminal case was vexing. A Gallup Poll conducted several days after the verdict showed the American public as a whole to be evenly divided regarding the verdict, with 47% saying it was correct on the evidence, 44% saying it was wrong, and 9% expressing no opinion. The racial breakdown showed a sharper division, with 42% of whites saying the verdict was correct on the evidence and 78% of blacks sharing that view, but 49% of whites thinking it was wrong and only 10% of blacks agreeing. The respondents were about evenly divided on whether Simpson would have been convicted if he were white (41% yes, 45% no); but a strong majority (73%) thought he likely would have been convicted had he not been rich and able to afford a "dream team" of defense counsel.

Today, we are left to grapple with the implications of that last question. We cannot blame cameras in the courtroom for a nagging doubt that the American legal system is living up to its high standard of *equal* justice under law. Therein lies an issue for another day and, in academies and courtrooms on both sides of the Atlantic, a noble cause worthy of a life in the law.

Gutenberg and Mass Communication*

*by Russell L. Weaver***

Given the rapid advances in technology over the last twenty years, with the development of the Internet (and a whole host of related technologies including Twitter, text messaging, etc.), it is easy to underestimate the historical importance of Johannes Gutenberg to freedom of expression. For those who have visited the Gutenberg Museum,[1] the Gutenberg press seems relatively quaint, slow and inefficient. In order to create a single page, a printer was required to handset the page, apply ink and paper, and then crank the large press down so that it made an ink impression on the paper.[2] In order to create multiple copies of a single page from a single page that had been handset, the printer had to apply new ink and paper, and re-crank the press, for each copy to be printed. In order to print other pages of a book, each had to be individually set and the remainder of the process continued for each page. It is no exaggeration to say that a great deal of effort, and a great deal of effort, was required to print an entire book. That is part of the reason that the Gutenberg Bible (to be found at the Gutenberg Museum) is such a marvel.

Given the crudeness of his invention, one might wonder why Gutenberg is so famous that the City of Mainz has established a museum in his honor, that a German university has been named after him, and that his statute stands prominently in downtown Mainz. The answer lies partly in the fact that, despite its slowness and inefficiencies, the Gutenberg printing press was remarkably quick compared to the technologies that preceded it. Prior to Gutenberg's invention in the fifteenth century, much communication was oral. Gutenberg's fellow citizens could talk to others, or could communicate by giving speeches. However, oral communication was inherently limiting because it could only reach a small

---

** Professor of Law & Distinguished University Scholar, University of Louisville, Louis D. Brandeis School of Law.

1 For those who have not visited the Gutenberg Museum, it is well worth the time. For more information about the museum, see http://www.gutenberg-museum.de/

2 See *Peter Linzer*, From the Gutenberg Bible to Net Neutrality – How Technology Makes Law and Why English Majors Need to Understand It, 39 McGeorge L. Rev. 1, 4-5 (2008) ("Some time around 1450, building on existing machines, Johannes Gutenberg invented the printing press and movable type. Because of the printing press, mass communication became more than talking to a crowd or a church congregation.").

number of people. People could, of course, draft and circulate letters, circulars and petitions. However, since there was no special technology (other than quill pens and parchment) for preparing or reproducing writings, written documents had to be laboriously prepared by hand, and it was extremely time consuming to create mass copies. Moreover, because distribution methods were limited, ordinary people would have found it difficult to mass disseminate their writings (even if they had been able to mass produce them). As a result, mass communication was understandably difficult (if not virtually impossible) for the average person.

Of course, Gutenberg did not invent books. They existed prior to his invention. The difficulty was that most books were created by laborious hand-written methods, and it would require far more time to create a single page. Moreover, most of those who created handwritten works were monks who wrote in Latin and focused on creating religious texts.[3] Handwritten processes were so slow that it might take years to create a single copy of a work,[4] and twenty to fifty years to create sixty to create one hundred and fifty books.[5] The printing press was as much as 50 times faster than prior methods and therefore made mass production of books possible for the first time.

Gutenberg's invention was also important because it made mass communication possible. As noted, most books were created at the time by monks who wrote in Latin, and who prepared primarily religious texts.[6] Since few people spoke or read Latin, those few written works that existed were inaccessible to

---

3 See *Katie Lula*, Neither Here Nor There But Fair: Finding an International Copyright Legal System Between East and West, Past and Present, 8 Asian-Pac. L. & Policy J. 96, 101 (2006); *Jay H. Perlman & Lawrence T. Greenberg*, The Internet Reformation: Gutenberg and Martin Luther on Wall Street, 4 Wall Street Lawyer 9 (2000).

4 See *Peter K. Yu*, Of Monks, Medieval Scribes and Middlemen, 2006 Mich. St. L. Rev. 1, 7 ("Notwithstanding the Church's active participation, the production of knowledge remained parochial. The copying of books was also slow, tedious, and very time- consuming; it took years for a scribe to complete "a particularly fine manuscript with colored initials and miniature art work.").

5 See *Yu*, supra note 4, at 7 ("When Bishop Leofric took over the Exeter Cathedral in 1050, he found only five books in its library. Despite immediately establishing a scriptorium of skilled workers, his crew managed to produce only sixty-six books in the twenty-two years before the bishop's death in 1072. Likewise, although the Library of Cambridge University had a remarkable collection of 122 books in 1424, it 'labored for a half-century to increase the number to 330.'").

6 See *Rogelio Lasso*, From the Paper Chase to the Digital Chase: Technology and the Challenge of Teaching 21st Century Law Students, 43 Santa Clara L. Rev. 1, 4 n.2. See Lasso, supra, note 3, at 4 n.2.

most people.[7] With the printing press, it was now possible for private individuals to mass communicate in their own languages. As a result, publications and books were no longer the reserve of the clergy or just those who had the ability to read Latin. In other words, the printing press revolutionized communication because it allowed non-clergy to mass produce written works in their own languages, and ultimately to communicate much more easily with their fellow citizens.

Gutenberg's invention led to a flowering of ideas and publications. The technology spread quickly and had broad influence. Indeed, by 1499, some 2,500 European cities had printing presses, and some 15 million books (representing some thirty thousand book titles) had been printed.[8] The ability to communicate more broadly through the written word allowed great thinks and writers to communicate through the written word. Indeed, some have credited Gutenberg's invention as a factor in bringing about the Renaissance, the Scientific Revolution, and the Protestant Reformation.[9]

Of course, many governments did not welcome the new invention, but instead regarded it as a threat.[10] After Gutenberg invented the printing press, governments did not willingly or readily embrace its potential in the hands of pri-

---

7 See id.

8 *Joseph Karl Grant*, Shattering and Moving Beyond the Gutenberg Paradigm: The Dawn of the Electronic Will, 42 U. Mich. J. L. Reform 105, 111-112 (2008).

9 See *Lasso*, supra, note 6, at 4 n.2. ("Printing changed every aspect of the human condition--from thinking, learning, and language, to science, religion, and government." "The 17th century became known as 'the century of genius' in large part due to the explosion of creativity and new ideas fueled by printing. Creativity is often the result of a combination of intellectual activities. For example, reading two books on separate topics and combining their themes in one mind produces a creative interaction. Increased output of printed works led first to the combination of old ideas, and later to the creation of entirely new systems of thought."); *George Paul & Jason Baron*, Information Inflation: Can the Legal System Adapt?, 13 Rich. J. L. & Tech. 1, 8 (2007) ("There has been only one transformative advance in the original writing technology. Circa 1450 Johannes Gutenberg invented the movable type printing press, which dramatically lowered the cost of producing written records. The printing press allowed mass production of information and thus contributed to the Renaissance, the Scientific Revolution, and the Protestant Reformation.").

10 See *Elizabeth Townsend Gard*, Conversations with Renowned Professors on the Future of Copyright, 12 Tul. J. Tech. & Intell. Prop. 35, 101 (2009) ("From monks transcribing Aristotle, to Gutenberg's printing press, to the photocopier, to the Betamax, we have seen striking similarities in the way various societies have feared the effects of new technologies and then created law in reaction to these fears.").

vate citizens who could use it to communicate with each other. On the contrary, many governments feared the potential of the printing press, and sought to restrain the potential "evils" that might result.[11] Restrictions on the printing press took various forms. For example, in addition to limiting the total number of presses that could exist,[12] the English government sought to restrain the content of printing through licensing schemes.[13] Under the Printing Act of 1662, Parliament 'prescribed what could be printed, who could print, and who could sell."[14] In particular, the British licensing scheme prohibited the publication of any book or pamphlet without a license, and required those who wished to publish to submit their work for review as a condition of obtaining a license.[15] Of course, if a proposed publication contained material that the censor deemed objectionable, the license could be denied.[16] Licensing expired in the late eighteenth century, but was a motivating factor that led the American colonists to demand protection for free expression in the United States Constitution.[17]

---

11 See *First National Bank of Boston v. Bellotti*, 435 U.S. 765, 800-801 (1978) ("Soon after the invention of the printing press, English and continental monarchs, fearful of the power implicit in its use and the threat to Establishment thought and order-political and religious-devised restraints, such as licensing, censors, indices of prohibited books, and prosecutions for seditious libel, which generally were unknown in the pre-printing press era. Official restrictions were the official response to the new, disquieting idea that this invention would provide a means for mass communication."); see also *William T. Mayton*, Seditious Libel and the Lost Guarantee of a Freedom of Expression, 84 Colum. L. Rev. 91, 97-98 (1984); *Norman L. Rosenberg*, Protecting the Best Men: An Interpretive Theory of the History of Libel (U. N. Carolina Press, 1986); *M. Lindsay Kaplan*, The Culture of Slander in Early Modern England (Cambridge U. Press 1997).

12 See *Edward Lee*, Guns and Speech Technologies: How the Right to Bear Arms Affects Copyright Regulations of Speech Technologies, 17 Wm. & Mary Bill Rights J. 1037, 1072 (2009).

13 See *Thomas v. Chicago Park District*, 534 U.S. 316, 320 (2002).

14 Id. (quoting *William T. Mayton*, Toward a Theory of First Amendment Process: Injunctions of Speech, Subsequent Punishment, and the Costs of the Prior Restraint Doctrine, 67 Cornell L. Rev. 245, 248 (1982).

15 See *Thomas v. Chicago Park District*, 534 U.S. 316, 320 (2002); see also *F. Siebert*, Freedom of the Press in England, 1476-1776 240 (1952).

16 See *Lovell v. City of Griffin*, 303 U.S. 444. 451 (1938); see also *City of Lakewood v. Plain Dealer Publishing*, Co., 486 U.S. 750, 757 (1988); *Lowe v. Securities & Exchange Commission*, 472 U.S. 181, 205 (1985).

17 See *Thomas v. Chicago Park District*, 534 U.S. 316, 320 (2002).

In 1606, England also created the crime of seditious libel[18] in the Star Chamber's decision in *de Libellis Famosis.*[19] That decision replaced, in part, the crime of constructive treason,[20] and made it a crime to criticize the government or governmental officials (and, at one point, the clergy as well).[21] The crime was enforced by "threats of punishment, litigation costs, and stigma,"[22] and was justified by the notion that criticism of the government "inculcated a disrespect for public authority."[23] "Since maintaining a proper regard for government was the goal of this new offense, it followed that truth was just as reprehensible as falsehood" and therefore was not a defense.[24] Indeed, truthful criticisms were punished more severely because it was assumed that true criticisms were potentially more damaging to the government.[25]

These governmental fears may have been well-founded. On this side of the Atlantic, the printing press had a profound effect on the course of society, and played a decisive role in the American Revolution. Not that the British did not try to impose speech restrictions in the American colonies. The colonial government in New York attempted to prosecute John Peter Zenger for seditious libel.[26] The prosecution was based on the fact that Zenger had published stories mocking the royal Governor and his administration.[27] Among other things, his publications included "anti-British song-sheets and mock advertisements de-

---

18 For a thorough discussion of the history of seditious libel, see Law Commission Working Paper No. 72, Treason, Sedition and Allied Offences (1977); *Judith Schenck Koffler & Bennett L. Gershman*, The New Seditious Libel, 69 Cornell L. Rev. 816 (1984); see also *Jeffrey K. Walker*, A Poisen in Ye Commonwealthe: Seditious Libel in Hanoverian London, 25 Anglo-Am. L. Rev. 1996, 25(3), 341-366.

19 77 Eng.Rep. 250 (Star Chamber 1606).

20 See *Mayton*, supra note 345, at 98.

21 Id. Indeed, in de Libellis Famosis, the defendants had ridiculed high clergy.

22 Id.

23 Id. at 103; see also *Matt J. O'Laughlin*, Exigent Circumstances: Circumscribing the Exclusionary Rule in Response to 9/11, UMKC L. Rev. 707,720-21 (2002) (referring to the seditious libel prosecution of John Wilkes during the reign of George III: (1760-64) LJ 426, (1761-64) CJ 674). See further *LOUIS KRONENBERGER*, THE EXTRAORDINARY MR WILKES (London: New English Library, 1974)

24 Id; see also *William R. Glendon*, The Trial of John Peter Zenger, 68 N.Y. St. B.J. 48, 49 (1996).

25 See *Stanton D. Krauss*, An Inquiry into the Right of Criminal Juries to Determine the Law in America, 89 J. Crim. L. & Criminology 111, 183 n.290 (1998); see also *Glendon*, supra note 358, at 48.

26 See *William R. Glendon*, The Trial of John Peter Zenger, 68 N.Y. St. B.J. 48, 49 (1996).

27 See id.

scribing an associate of the royal governor as 'a large Spaniel, of about 5 feet 5 inches high . . . lately strayed from his kennel with his mouth full of fulsome panegyricks,' and a 'monkey . . . lately broke from his chain and run into the country.'"[28] After three unsuccessful attempts, the Governor managed to indict Zenger for seditious libel. Zenger languished in jail for 10 months awaiting trial, and the Governor arranged for the disbarment of his lawyers for stating exceptions on Zenger's behalf.[29] When the case was finally tried, Zenger's lawyer admitted that Zenger had published the allegedly libelous statements, and offered to concede the libel if the prosecution could prove that the allegations were false. When the prosecution declined, Hamilton offered to prove that the statements were true. Although the court disallowed the evidence, on the then valid legal basis that truth was immaterial to libel, Zenger was acquitted in what is an early and significant exercise of jury nullification.[30]

The printing itself deeply influenced the American Revolution in several important respects. For one thing, printed ideas from Europe strongly influenced the thinking of the drafters of Declaration of Independence and the United States Constitution. These ideas, originally printed in Europe, included the writings of John Locke[31] and Baron de Montesqieu.[32] In the Declaration of Independence, itself, which was widely distributed thanks to the printing press, Thomas Jefferson provides a compelling justification for breaking away from English colonial rule. One must remember that, at the time, the idea of a rebellion against a monarch was considered highly inappropriate. Kings (so the theory went) were placed on their thrones by God, and their actions reflected the divine. As a result, how could ordinary people presume to question the actions of a King much less to rebel against them? In the Declaration of Independence, Thomas Jefferson skillfully articulates the rights of man:

"When in the Course of human events it becomes necessary for one people to dissolve the political bands which have connected them with another and to assume among the powers of the earth, the separate and equal station to which the Laws of Nature and of Nature's God entitle them, a decent respect to the

---

28 See *Elizabeth I. Haynes*, United States v. Thomas: Pulling the Jury Apart, 30 CONN. L. REV. 731 (1998).

29 See *Cohen v. Hurley*, 366 U.S. 117, 140 (1961) (Black, J., dissenting).

30 See *Elizabeth I. Haynes*, United States v. Thomas: Pulling the Jury Apart, 30 CONN. L. REV. 731 (1998).

31 *XI Baron Montesquieu*, The Spirit of the Laws 202 (1977).

32 *John Locke*, The Second Treatise of Government 81 (1952).

opinions of mankind requires that they should declare the causes which impel them to the separation.

We hold these truths to be self-evident, that all men are created equal, that they are endowed by their Creator with certain unalienable Rights, that among these are Life, Liberty and the pursuit of Happiness. — That to secure these rights, Governments are instituted among Men, deriving their just powers from the consent of the governed, — That whenever any Form of Government becomes destructive of these ends, it is the Right of the People to alter or to abolish it, and to institute new Government, laying its foundation on such principles and organizing its powers in such form, as to them shall seem most likely to effect their Safety and Happiness.[1]

And, of course, the printing press was used to disseminate Jefferson's ideas far and wide.

The printing press also played an important role during the constitutional drafting process. The Federalist Papers provided one method of commentary on the constitutional process, and the printing press allowed those ideas to be reproduced and distributed widely.

Today, the technologies that we use may have changed and improved. However, the fundamental commitment to the rights of man, as articulated and reflected in Thomas Jefferson's Bill of Rights, continues to influence us. The values were so deeply held that, when the Framers of the United States Constitution produced a draft that did not contain a Bill of Rights (including, among other things, protection for freedom of expression), it rapidly became clear that the Constitution would not be ratified without one.[34]

In the final analysis, even though the Gutenberg press was relatively slow and inefficient compared to modern methods of communication, Gutenberg's invention transformed society in important and fundamental ways.

---

33 U.S. Declaration of Independence (July 4, 1776).

34 *R. Weaver, C. Hancock, D. Lively & J. Knechtle*, The First Amendment: Cases, Prob lems & Materials 4 (3d ed. 2011).

The Tension between Ensuring and Protecting Personal Reputation and Cherishing Free Speech: Comparative Perspectives - An Overview of the Constitutional Court's position under consideration of Art. 10 ECHR

*by Dieter Dörr**

I. Introduction

The German legal approach to questions of hate speech is somewhat different to regulations in other countries and from my point of view especially to the situation in the US. Whereas it may not be unusual in the US to see open display of Nazi memorabilia, e.g. on private campgrounds or on Internet Auction sites, this is strictly forbidden in Germany, where the Criminal Code includes a general prohibition of display of symbols of the Third Reich era. Also, there are rules to stop race discrimination or agitation of the People e.g. by inciting hatred against segments of the population. Irrespective of these rules in the Criminal Code the highly rated so-called communication human rights of the Basic Law, which is our Constitution, in effect mean that we do have demonstrations with at least doubtable display of flags or similar, because the Courts often decide in favour of the right to demonstrate or freely express your opinion and by doing so risk violation of Criminal Code regulations.

In my short presentation I would like to give an overview of the way the Federal Constitutional Court in Germany has balanced the two conflicting positions of the important right to have, express and disseminate one's own opinion and the right of others not to be harmed by these expressions. As in so many areas of the law in Germany and other European countries today, this cannot be understood without a short account of the rules in the European Charter of Human Rights, a covenant which every Member State of the European Council – which needs to be differentiated from the European Union – has to ratify and adhere to.

* Chair for Public Law, International and European Law, Media Law, Johannes Gutenberg University Mainz (www.jura.uni-mainz.de/doerr, email: ddoerr@uni-mainz.de) and Director Mainz Media Institute (www.mainzer-medieninstitut.de, email: doerr@mainzer-medieninstitut.de).

II. The rules in the German Constitution and interpretation by the Constitutional Court

1. General

The Federal Constitutional Court in Germany has the right to finally interpret our Constitution. So if the contents of any right or its connection to other rights is doubtful then it is in the authority of the Court to set the outlines. This has proven necessary in regard to the freedom of opinion and speech in many ways. I will only mention its stance in terms of defining the structure of the dual system of broadcasting in Germany which cannot be overrated. A similarly important role it has played in explaining the following words of Art. 5 para. 1 Basic Law (GG):

> „Everyone has the right to freely express and disseminate his opinion in speech, writing, and pictures and to freely inform himself from generally accessible sources. Freedom of the press and freedom of reporting by means of broadcasts and films are guaranteed. There will be no censorship."

Even more so it has itself developed an extensive right of personal honour and set this into a frame with the aforementioned right.

2. Freedom of speech

a) Extent of the right

Due to its extremely important role in upholding a functioning democracy the Constitutional Court understands the right of freedom of speech very extensively and includes also negative opinions and also opinions that are relevant in terms of criminal law. Especially in political contexts one has the right to express even most severe criticism, also in satirical ways. The Court has also included an objective aspect in Article 5 according to which the free press and other media as institution are protected.

b) Limitations to the right

Like all other basic rights there are limitations to the freedom of speech, they are regulated in paragraph 2 of Art. 5. This provision sets the legal norms that protect children and youth and the ones to protect personal honour and additionally the so-called "general laws" as borders to free speech. In order to protect the youth there are strict rules dealing with pornography or indecent content e.g. in television programmes which in a constitutional way limit Art. 5's freedoms. "General laws" and laws protecting the right of personal honour are the mentioned Criminal Act provisions and also the rules on defamation. However, the limiting rules as such are not sufficient in an actual case. The always applicable rule that limitations have to be reasonable is especially important in the context of freedom of opinion. In a specific case the right only has to step back if the protection of the other legal norm is clearly more important and if the limitation stays within reasonable limits itself: in dubio pro libertate also works for free speech in the German constitutional context.

In deciding on the limitations of the right one has to differentiate whether someone is expressing a factual claim or a value judgement. Usually, one has to consider expressions to be subjective and including an evaluation but if they are merely about facts the right to free expression is more limited. For example, it is not protected to disseminate untruthful facts in a way that you can speak in critical terms about something. Certain facts cannot be denied publicly because that is a violation even of Criminal Law standards: this has been especially significant concerning the denial of the existence of the Holocaust. A well-known Neo-Nazi who is trying to historically claim that the Holocaust didn't happen, has been sentenced several times for this lie.

3. The right of honour

Because of the above described situation of giving the freedom of speech a priority, the Constitutional Court has been – in my point of view wrongly – criticised for not weighing the significance of the right of honour enough. There have been several spectacular cases in the previous years which resulted in massive criticism because of the results, even though the Court carefully prolonged its long-standing case law. Before I mention a couple of these cases let me briefly give an overview of the right of honour. It is not explicitly mentioned in our Constitution and although there are rules in different laws that amount to a sufficient protection it would be different if this right had no foundation in the constitution. The Constitutional Court – again in a profoundly visionary way – developed and bit by bit differentiated a right to the protection of one's own honour and personality by deriving it from Art. 1, the utmost important provision of the Constitution on human dignity and Art. 2 which gives the right to freely behave and do as one wants. This results in having the right to be left alone within the private sphere and can decide by oneself how and if one wants to be presented in public. Obviously, there are different measurements set for public figures such as politicians or stars and private people.

Generally one can say that if the use of free speech endangers the human dignity of another person that person's right to personal honour has priority. Especially in public debates, however, there is a general tendency in favour of free speech.

4. Some important cases in recent years

Criticism of the Constitutional Court was especially strong when it ruled that claiming "Soldiers are murderers", which is a citation by Kurt Tucholsky, does not infringe the personal honour of individual soldiers and therefore violate the prohibition of defamation but instead is covered by the freedom of expression, because it is a value judgement on the profession of soldiers.

A long series of decisions in reference to the royal family of Monaco, especially Princess Caroline and recently also her husband Prince Ernst August, have outlined a system of balancing the rights of public figures to a certain amount of privacy and the interest of the public in receiving information on celebrities. According to the reasoning of the cases the press (and other media) have the right to extensively observe and cover stories about the royal family, as long as certain limits are respected, e.g. not to take pictures if the whole family (including the kids) is moving in an obviously secluded area and behaves clearly in expectation of the general public being cut off from insights into this scene. On the other hand, if the press disseminates untrue stories the right of reply is extensive also for Caroline which in result once meant that the reply had to be published on the title page of a magazine because that was where originally the headline that gave reason for the reply was positioned. Also the European Court of Human Rights had to give a judgement referring Princess Caroline. I will come to that in a minute.

I myself am along with many scholars convinced that another controversial decision of the Court was quite clearly wrong: a right-wing party was using the image of a famous social democrat, i.e. politically left-wing, mayor of Bremen in a electoral tv spot claiming that this person – he is dead since quite a long time – today would vote for this right-wing party if he were still alive. The Court decided against the lawsuit of his daughter not accepting that there was a violation of the right to decide oneself how one wants to appear in public, in this case of the post mortem personality right. This is a strange decision because from my point of view it would have fitted better into the general system of the Court if it had decided the other way round, because usually human dignity of a person is an absolute limit to the freedom of expression and in this case one can argue that the element of dignity combined with the right to free decision about the presentation of the personality in public – also after one has deceased – was infringed.

Finally, one last decision needs to be mentioned that has manifested the importance of the freedom of press and free speech in a convincing way. The clothing company of Benetton is known for their advertisements in print magazines and on posters with shock-images such as the blood-soaked shirt of a killed soldier or the picture of a male seat with the word "H.I.V. POSITIVE" tattooed onto. A publishing company had originally been prosecuted because of printing this advertisement but the Constitutional Court rejected this because the freedom of press includes advertisements that include political statements or ones referring to social circumstances. There is no violation of human dignity because as a statement the advertisement actually wants to provoke people to think about the treatment of ill people and not hurt their dignity.

5. Consequences when balancing the opposing rights

Before talking about the European influence one can summarise as follows:

- As an absolute right at the top of the constitutional value system the right to human dignity (as it is founded in Art. 1 Basic Law) cannot be balanced against other rights. It stands absolutely and any infringement of its area of protection equals an illegal violation. This is a clear difference to other legal systems where the right to human dignity is just one right amongst others between which a balancing has to take place. In our system human dignity allows no compromise. However, and this needs to be stated, too, violations of human dignity are seldom, because there is only a limited area in which this right actually comes into action. It is an element of human dignity in our understanding that oneself can decide about the contents of one's own dignity and therefore human dignity only protects against extreme intrusions into the private sphere or personal integrity. The right to dignity strengthens the right to personal honour in its core.

- There is a general priority for the right of free speech so that in doubtful cases the Constitutional Court tends to uphold this right against the right to personal honour. The principle "in dubio pro libertate" in this context is more than a mere saying, the Court really adheres to it and therefore has decided in favour of freedom of speech in several occasions. This has a long tradition and goes back to an early decision about the right to call for a boycott of a film that was made by a director who had close connections to the Nazi regime (so-called "Lueth"-Decision). On the other hand, the – democratic – fight about conflicting positions is only legitimate if it is committed with mental means. It is illegal if economic power is used to suppress an opinion, e.g. if a boycott was called out by a dominating publication company that at the same time threatens the newspaper agents not to deliver them anymore if they don't support the call for boycott (similarly decided in the early so-called "Blinkfuer"-Decision).

- Further limits to the right of free speech can be derived from the kind of utterance one makes. If it is a value judgement it is more protected and can also include harsh criticism of the opponent, if it is a factual claim one needs to consider certain rules on finding out the truth about something one claims. This is especially important if one cites someone else's words: a citation must be correct, there is no protection for a claim that someone said something, if this is untrue, even if one purports that the person could have said something of the kind (so-called "Boell"-Decision).

III. The influence of Art. 10 ECHR

As already mentioned, an important final look needs to be aimed at the European Convention on Human Rights. This is a Human Rights Covenant that all Member States of the Council of Europe have ratified and that is binding for all signatory states. Germany as all other European States is not only bound to this Convention but there is also an obligatory jurisdiction, the European Court of Human Rights. Its decisions are binding and need to be respected. If an individual brings a lawsuit to the Court in Strasbourg and is successful, the Member State that violated his rights deriving from the Convention is ruled to pay compensation and end the breech if it is still ongoing.

In Art. 10 ECHR the right to free speech with all its components is protected. The range of protection and the limitations have been established by the Court in a very similar way to the one the German Constitutional Court has in the above described way. Also here there is a rule that in general the right to free speech has priority over other affected rights such as the right to personal honour. In numerous decisions in the past years the Court has confirmed this, e.g. very recently it has found that it was a violation by France to sentence a publisher and journalist to a fine because of critically reporting on the King of another state. Moreover, Art. 10 according to this "Colombani"-Decision in line with long-standing practice can only be limited if it is justified and necessary in a democratic society which was not the case here because the journalists had not disregarded the necessity to thorough research before publishing the article.

This means that the criticism against the jurisdiction of the German Constitutional Court is narrow-minded: had the Court chosen to follow a different line as it has in the past decades, Germany would have lost numerous lawsuits before the European Court of Human Rights. As it is, at least in view of Art. 10 ECHR, Germany is alongside the European Court and in my point of view they both sufficiently protect the right of honour of individuals in specific cases and at the same time maintain the immeasurable significance of free speech for a functioning democracy.

But there is an important difference between the rulings of the European Court and the German Constitutional Court. Like the German Constitutional Court the European Court of Human Rights attaches vital importance to the question of proportionality.

In this context, the court recently made the following remarks:

> "The adjective "necessary", within the meaning of Article 10 § 2, implies the existence of a "pressing social need". The Contracting States have a certain margin of appreciation in assessing whether such a need exists, but it goes hand in hand with a European supervision, embracing both the legislation and the decisions applying it, even those given by an independent court. The Court is therefore empowered to give the final ruling on whether a "restriction" is reconcilable with freedom of expression as protected by Article 10[1]. In exercising its supervisory jurisdiction, the Court must look at the impugned interference in the light of the case as a whole, including the content of the remarks held against the applicant and the context in which he made them. In particular, it must determine whether the interference in issue was "proportionate to the legitimate aims pursued" and whether the reasons adduced by the national authorities to justify it are "relevant and sufficient" [2]. In doing so, the Court has to satisfy itself that the national authorities applied standards which were in conformity with the principles embodied in Article 10 and, moreover, that they based themselves on an acceptable assessment of the relevant facts[3].

Within the framework of limitations of article 10, section 2 ECHR, according to the jurisprudence of the European Court of Human Rights, freedom of expression applies also to utterances which injure, shock, or disturb the recipi-

---

1 ECHR, Coll. 1999-I, no. 30 = NJW 1999, 1318 = JuS 1999, 1011 – *Janowski/Poland.*

2 ECHR, 1979, Series A, vol. 30, no. 62 – *Sunday Times/United Kingdom* (no. 1); ECHR, 1986, Series A, vol. 103, no. 40 – *Lingens/Austria*; ECHR, 1989, Series A, vol. 149, no. 28 – *Barfod/Denmark*; coll. 1999-I, no. 30 = NJW 1999, 1318 = JuS 1999, 1011 – *Janowski/Poland*; coll. 2000-I, Nr. 52 – *News-Verlags GmbH u. Co KG/Austria.*

3 ECHR, 1994, Series A, vol. 298, no. 31 – *Jersild/Denmark.*

ent, because a tolerant, "democratic society" is only possible if such speech is permitted[4]. In particular, press and broadcasters must be able to address information an ideas concerning questions of public interest within certain limits[5] in order to fulfil their duties within a democratic society, and in doing so, they must be permitted to resort to exaggeration and provocation[6]. Freedom of expression also applies to the publication of photographies, whereas, according to the opinion of the European Court of Human Rights, this is an area in which the "protection of the reputation and rights of others" as mentioned in article 10, section 2 ECHR, is particularly relevant. Regarding photographies, it might be important to have a look at the words which correspond to the photographies. To this issue I will come back in a minute.

In its considerations concerning proportionality, the court, in contrast to the German Federal Constitutional Court, makes a distinction depending on whether the opinions voiced make any contribution to a current debate on a question of general public interest, or not[7]. Because debates on questions of public interest flare up and die down, the answer to the question whether an utterance is relevant to such a debate, may change over time. The need for protection of the individual stating an opinion might gradually decrease in weight compared to the public interest[8].

Therefore, the court makes a fundamental distinction between reporting on facts and persons of the political sphere pertaining to matters of public interest, and reports about details concerning private individuals who do not perform any official function, even when they are acting in a representative function. The press and broadcasters are only in a "watchdog" role where their coverage promotes the exchange of information and ideas concerning questions of general public interest. The right of the general public to information is considered to extend to aspects of the private life of individuals, especially where politicians are concerned.

---

4 EGMR, 1976, Serie A, Bd. 24, S. 23 Nr. 49 – *Handyside/Vereinigtes Königreich.*

5 ECHR, 1991, Series A, vol. 216, p. 29-30 no. 59 – *Observer und Guardian/United Kingdom*; coll. 1999-III = NJW 2000, 1015 = JuS 2000, 805 no. 59 – *Bladet Tromsø und Stensaas/Norway.*

6 ECHR, 1995, Series A, vol. 313, p. 19 no. 38 – *Prager and Oberschlick/Austria.*

7 The latest example is ECHR, coll. 2001-I, nos. 59 ff., in particular. 65 f. – *Tammer/Estonia.*

8 This was the reason given by the ECHR for deciding that the prolonged prohibition of divulging information from the medical record of the meanwhile deceased French President Mittérand amounted to a violation of article 10 ECHR, cf. ECHR, coll. 2004, no. 53 – *Plon [Societé]/France* (available only in French).

In this regard the European Court of Human Rights also gave a judgement referring the royal family of Monaco, thus Princess Caroline and her husband. Therein, the Court had to balance the right to Respect for Private and Family Life out of Article 8 ECHR and the right to Freedom of Expression, Article 10 ECHR. Beforehand, the German Federal Constitutional Court decided that the protection of the privacy in Germany is not wide enough. For the assessment of the acceptance of photographies' publication of celebrities in their private spare time, the European Court of Human Rights has the opinion that these photos in question have to make any contribution to a current debate on a question of general public interest, as said before. Today, the German Courts follow the European Court's opinion. Thus, in March 2007, the German Federal Court of Justice had to judge about several cases referring Princess Caroline and her husband. Herein, the Court set out a couple of guidelines: Therefore the report's value of information is an essential criterion for the acceptance of photographies, published in this context. Contrary to that judgement, a couple of month ago, the German Federal Constitutional Court decided in the constitutional complaint referring the Federal Court of Justice's judgement that the protection of the personal rights in parts is too wide. The Federal Constitutional Court set out that for the assessment if photographies may be published the corresponding words have to be considered. One has to wait, how the European Court of Human Rights would decide, if such a case submits to Court again. The several judgements referring Princess Caroline show in an exemplary way the conjunction to the above mentioned European and German Courts.

In a final summary, we may say the following: Where coverage of questions of public interest is concerned, the European Court of Human Rights will usually give priority to freedom of opinion and information above other conflicting aspects such as the reputation and rights of other individuals. This is also true for polemic, disparaging, and satirical criticism. This fact became particularly evident in the Oberschlick case, where a journalist ventured to name the Austrian politician Haider a "fool" in a headline in reference to statements Haider had made beforehand. The journalist's conviction for criminal insult was considered a violation of freedom of opinion by the European Court of Human Rights. Accordingly, the Member States of the Council of Europe must respect the far-reaching right to freedom of opinion and information. They violate freedom of information if they attempt to limit or prevent reception of such utterances of opinion from foreign countries. This way, in the end, the court is safeguarding the community of values in Europe, because all Member States of the Council of Europe profess to uphold Human Rights as the basis for democracy and the rule of law. Without comprehensive and unchecked flow of information, without dispute with the weapons of the mind, there is no free opinion making. And this freedom is a vital ingredient for rule of law and democracy anywhere.

The Atlantic or Pacific(a) Divide: On Regulating Broadcast Indecency in the U.S. from a Comparative European Perspective

*by Mark D. Cole**

I. Introduction: The same and just so different...

It is generally recognized that there are significant differences in the approach to free speech cases in the U.S. and most European states, namely Germany. This is evident in view of hate speech cases in which e.g. the difference in approach to racist or Nazi-related speech is obvious and based *inter alia* on historical reasons. Also, the fundamental role the protection of human dignity – and with it personality rights – plays in the European and namely the German constitution, requires a different approach to the U.S. idea in which the broadest possible use of free speech rights is based on the nearly unlimited prohibition of restrictions to free speech in the First Amendment ("...no law ..."). Numerous books and articles have been published analyzing this difference and it has been a recurring theme in the Louisville-Mainz exchanges in which this topic has not only been debated but also attempts have been made to make the approach of the other more easily understandable.[1]

However, the differences are not limited to hate speech and the protection of an individual person's reputation.[2] Moreover, and this is going to be the topic of

* The author is Associate Professor for the Law of New Information Technologies, Media and Communications Law at the University of Luxembourg. He used to work at the Johannes Gutenberg University of Mainz and still teaches in the LL.M. Media Law-programme there as guest lecturer. During his time as research associate in Mainz he visited Louisville and gave guest lectures on comparative free speech, constitutional and international law topics several times.

1 Cf. only the Mainz Media Forum series held regularly on free speech comparative topics http://www.mainzer-medieninstitut.de/veranstaltungen/archiv.php.

2 On the first e.g. *Brugger*, The Treatment of Hate Speech in German Constitutional Law (Part I), 3 German Law Journal (2002), http://www.germanlawjournal.com/index.php?-pageID=11&artID=212 and Part II, 4 German Law Journal 1 (2003), http://www.-germanlawjournal.com/index.php?pageID=11&artID=225, on the latter e.g. the contributions in the forthcoming collection reproducing the papers of the Privacy Forum 2011 (ed. by Weaver/Dörr). All Internet sources were last accessed on August 15, 2011.

this contribution, in recent years it has become evident that media-related content regulation, namely the supervision of broadcasting by competent authorities, shows significant divergence and has resulted in several important cases on both sides of the Atlantic. Especially the question of what kind of content restrictions are needed to safeguard the development of minors seems to lead to completely different answers even though the actual content is the same, not the least because many U.S. television shows and series are screened in Europe and Germany, too. The topic is of continuous interest because in view of new technological developments and phenomena (e.g. new television shows, new media usage such as the phenomenon of "sexting"[3] or cyberbullying) one has to re-evaluate whether the balance between freedom of speech and protection of minors is rightly struck.

In this sense, there is a fairly recent development in the realm of protection of minors in Germany that may serve as an introductory blueprint for the comparison. Last year, German language television viewers were "treated" to *Tatort Internet,* a reality show based upon the programmes popular in the U.S. and U.K., there titled *To Catch a Predator,* wherein alleged paedophiles are confronted with video cameras as they attempt to seduce (supposedly) under-aged youths they have previously "met" on the Internet. The programme sparked a large controversy in German legal circles as it had happened in the U.S., although there it seems there was a much stronger support of the position focussing on the anger towards the predators.

Civil libertarian groups, child protection groups and the German Justice Minister derided the show as counter-productive and dangerous to civil liberties: "There is the danger that innocents will be put in the stocks and damage caused, and the rule of law will be thrown out of balance" said Justice Minister *Leutheusser-Schnarrenberger*.[4] The show is formatted much the same way the American and British counterparts were. A therapist and actor pose online as a child under the age of consent. The team engages in online conversations with would-be-molesters and arrange a meeting, presumably to consummate the ill-conceived relationship. At the appointed time and place, the individual is confronted while the cameras role.

In the U.S., the series ran from 2004 to 2007. There were twelve episodes in total and the series was cancelled only after a subject committed suicide while

3 On this *Schmitz/Siry*, Teenage Folly or Child Abuse? State Responses to "Sexting" by Minors in the U.S. and Germany, Policy & Internet: Vol. 3 (2011): Iss. 2, Article 3, http://www.psocommons.org/policyandinternet/vol3/iss2/art3.

4 Cf. http://www.spiegel.de/kultur/tv/0,1518,723995,00.html.

the cameras were rolling. The individual, who was an assistant prosecutor in a county adjacent to Dallas, Texas, was identified as a person who pursued what he believed to be a minor on the Internet. When he did not show up at the arranged location to meet the minor, police and an NBC camera crew went to his home. As the police entered the suspect's home, he fatally shot himself. The family sued NBC for intentional infliction of emotional distress and violation of civil rights. In response to NBC's motion to dismiss, the trial judge ruled that the case could go forward, finding that NBC's actions pushed the

> "police to engage in tactics that were unnecessary and unwise, solely to generate more dramatic footage for a television show. […] A reasonable jury could find that by doing so, NBC created a substantial risk of suicide or other harm, and that it engaged in conduct so outrageous and extreme that no civilized society should tolerate it."[5]

In light of this ruling, the parties settled the case and shortly thereafter, the show was cancelled by NBC.[6] The show has also run in local variations in the U.K., Australia and New Zealand under the same title.

Differences in the formats of the show concern the involvement of the police, which were an integral part of the investigations in the U.S. format as well as the anonymity of the suspect. In the German version, the name of the subject was not revealed and the face was pixelated[7], whereas the U.S. production showed the subject's image and name, thus potentially impacting the right to a fair trial.

This is just one example showing how differently television content is perceived and discussed in the two States in question. Now we will turn to examples where media authorities or courts had to take a decision on "restriction or not" and how this differs in the U.S. and Europe. In doing so, the U.S. approach will be analyzed to which then some comparative views will be added.

---

5 *Conradt v. NBC Universal*, Opinion 07 Civ. 6623 (DC) of Feb. 26, 2008, U.S. Dist. Court, Southern Distr. of New York, Chin, J., esp. p. 2 *et seq.* and 34, decision retrievable at http://online.wsj.com/public/resources/documents/conradt.pdf.

6 Cf. on the complete background http://latimesblogs.latimes.com/showtracker/2008/06/-nbc-resolves-la.html.

7 Although media authorities saw a violation of personality rights by insufficient pixelation in the first two episodes without the competent body initiating enforcement proceedings, cf. http://www.die-medienanstalten.de/pressecenter/pressemitteilungen/-detailansicht/article/zak-pressemitteilung-162010-zak-beanstandet-zwei-folgen-von-tatort-internet-moegliche-taet.html.

II. The U.S. approach to "indecent" content

1. Some rules concerning the First Amendment and broadcasting

Without being able to address the issue in detail in this contribution, the constitutional rule guiding the monitoring of broadcast including television content is the broad protection speech enjoys under the First Amendment of the U.S. constitution. Generally spoken, restrictions of speech by government are only admissible to a very limited extent and need to be justified by legitimate interests respecting both the no prior restraints- and content neutrality-rules.[8]

On the other hand, certain categories of speech fall outside of the realm of protection by the First Amendment, because they are worthless as a contribution to the search for truth on the marketplace of ideas, because they create harm or actually obstruct the development of free speech.[9] These categories include child pornography and obscenity.[10] However, merely indecent speech which does not quite reach the standard of obscenity is *within* the First Amendment's protection. Unsurprisingly therefore, courts in the U.S. have been struggling to define the borderline between the two.

Complicating the issue further, due to the nature of broadcast, government in the U.S. has also the right to regulate (and thereby restrict) television and oth-

---

8 A general overview on the free speech rules can be found in *Weaver/Lively*, Understanding the First Amendment, 3rd ed. 2009 or in more detail in *Weaver/Hellmann*, The First Amendment: Cases, Materials and Problems, 2002, the two issues mentioned above are treated in the latter in ch. 5 and 7.

9 A concise summary of the bill of rights in its application by Courts can be found in the Analysis and Interpretation of the Constitution, Annotations of Cases Decided by the Supreme Court of the United States, Senate Document No. 108-17, 2002 Edition, accessible at http://www.gpoaccess.gov/constitution/browse2002.html#04supp. The part of interest in our context is at pp. 1220 *et seq.* Supplements of 2004, 2006 and 2008 are to be found at the same website.

10 The Supreme Court has held in *Roth v. United States*, 354 U.S. 476 (1957) in *Miller v. California*, 413 U.S. 15 (1973) that the state could restrict obscene material, which has been defined in *Roth* at 487 *et seq.* as "material which deals with sex in a manner appealing to prurient interest" whereby the standard to establish this is "whether to the average person, applying contemporary community standards, the dominant theme of the material taken as a whole appeals to prurient interest". Material appealing to prurient interest was defined as "material having a tendency to excite lustful thoughts" and the prurient interest as "a shameful or morbid interest in nudity, sex, or excretion".

er broadcast content more extensively than speech uttered in other ways.[11] As a result, certain speech that is normally protected may be found to be restricted if aired on broadcast and it is exactly the category of "indecent" in which this problem arises frequently. And although restrictions need to be "narrowly tailored to further a substantial governmental interest"[12], the general assumption that U.S. protection of free speech is wider than the one afforded by other nations around the world, proves erroneous in the case of sexually expressive or other "indecent" material to which the U.S. is less permissive and regulation much stricter. As will be shown in the following, in broadcasting content is much more readily suppressed than in other context and currently federal courts in the U.S. have begun to revisit the topic of indecency on broadcast media. The cases, which call into question the continued validity of the seminal case of *Pacifica Foundation v. FCC*[13] fall into two categories: "fleeting explicatives" and "fleeting nudity".

Like elsewhere the increased use of airways necessitated the need for frequency management and in the U.S. the Congress created an independent regulatory agency to control and regulate the airways and thereby oversee the nation's broadcast system. The Federal Communications Commission (FCC) was introduced by the Communications Act of 1934[14] and was charged with the responsibility of overseeing the limited resource of the broadcast spectrum. The scarcity of available spectrum was the argument to require users of this spectrum to serve the interest of the public. Therefore, the FCC could introduce a licensing system, which enabled the imposition of rules restricting content on the party profiting of the assigned frequency. However, in view of the First Amendment an obvious limitation to imposing rules is the prohibition of any form of censoring by the FCC.[15]

According to the Supreme Court interpretation, the First Amendment does not protect every form of speech. For this reason the statutory prohibition of ob-

---

11 Therefore also licensing requirements for broadcast stations do not constitute a violation of First Amendment standards although they are a form of prior restraint, cf. *NBC v. United States*, 319 U.S. 190 (1943); *Red Lion Broadcasting Co. v. FCC*, 395 U.S. 367 (1969); *FCC v. National Citizens Comm. for Broadcasting*, 436 U.S. 775 (1978).

12 *FCC v. League of Women Voters*, 468 U.S. 364 (1984), at 380 where the Court did not require the interest to be compelling, but regarded it sufficient if it was substantial; cf. also generally outside of FCC domain *Arkansas Writers' Project, Inc. v. Ragland*, 481 U.S. 221, 231 (1987).

13 *Pacifica Foundation v. FCC*, 438 U.S. 726 (1978).

14 Codified as Chapter 5 of 47 U.S.C., starting with § 151.

15 Cf. also § 326 of the Communications Act 1934.

scene content applies to any form of programmes, whether on radio or television and whether disseminated via terrestrial – in the U.S. terminology "broadcast television or radio" –, cable or satellite.[16] Violations of this rule can result in criminal prosecution but also lead to FCC administrative proceedings against the provider of the programme. And although the FCC's competencies expand for certain questions also to cable television and post-licensing matters in direct satellite broadcasting, for the decisive matter here this is not the case: indecent content is not prohibited as such, but speech protected by the First Amendment. Any restriction of dissemination of such content therefore needs a special justification.

Because satellite and cable television require an individual contract of the subscriber, the situation was and is regarded differently than with broadcast television (and radio).[17] With the latter, the argument of pervasiveness gives – in the understanding of the FCC and the Courts until now – a justification for more restrictions especially concerning indecent content. As broadcast airwaves are publicly available – obviously under the condition of having an appropriate device reproducing sound and picture – these come potentially surprising to the television viewer or radio listener because he or she has not entered into a contract covering specific content on channels known in advance.[18] The stronger argument may be that this kind of content is also easily available for children.[19] In the words used by the Supreme Court in the *FCC v. Pacifica Foundation* case:

---

16 Cf. Chapter 71 of 18 U.S.C., specifically § 1464 and 1468 (the basic rule being added by the second to clarify extension to any form of dissemination such as cable or satellite) as well as obscenity laws in the different states.

17 Also for content disseminated via the Internet restrictions like with broadcast are not possible, cf. e.g. *Reno v American Civil Liberties Union*, 521 U.S. 844 (1997) and also *Ashcroft v ACLU*, 542 U.S. 656 (2004), although space limitations prohibit further analysis of this issue in this contribution.

18 This was the argument of the complainant that lead to the *Pacifica* case, he had just tuned into an available station on his car radio.

19 Although some criticize that the speech rights of minors are not considered sufficiently, cf. e.g. *Calvert*, Sins of Omission and "A Line-Drawing Exercise": A Response to FCC Chairman Kevin Martin's Comments on the "Expansion of Indecency Regulation", 60 Fed. Comm. L.J. F. 1 (2008) at 6 [this and all other quotes from Fed. Comm L.J. and F. available at http://www.law.indiana.edu/fclj/]. In this direction also the very recent decision of the Supreme Court when it struck down a California Law prohibiting the sale of violent video games to minors: *California v. Entertainment Merchants Association, et al.*, Decision of June 27, 2011 (docket No. 08-1448).

> "First, the broadcast media have established a uniquely pervasive presence in the lives of all Americans. Patently offensive, indecent material presented over the airwaves confronts the citizens, not only in public, but also in the privacy of the home, where the individual's right to be left alone plainly outweighs the First Amendment rights of an intruder [...] Second, broadcasting is uniquely accessible to children, even those too young to read [...] The ease with which children may obtain access to broadcast material [...] amply justif[ies] special treatment of indecent broadcasting."[20]

As mentioned above, this approach however does not answer which kind of content is indecent in a way that the restriction of dissemination via broadcast is actually constitutionally valid.

2. Fleeting Indecent Content

a) The case of Fleeting Explicatives

The first category of cases which turned out to be indecent in the understanding of the FCC concerned what one might call inappropriate language and was decided in the Pacifica case. In 1975, in response to the midday broadcast of *George Carlin's "Dirty Words"* monologue, the FCC established that pursuant to its statutory mandate, the agency had the authority to stop "any obscene, indecent, or profane language by means of radio communications"[21] subjecting broadcasts to regulation in situations where print media would not, mainly because of the danger of being confronted with such content without having consented to it (e.g. by "accidentally" tuning in a specific station) as well as the ease for children to listen to such content unsupervised.

This decision was upheld by the U.S. Supreme Court in the above-mentioned *FCC v. Pacifica* accepting the argument of special circumstances when a speaker uses the broadcast medium to deliver his message. The Court further upheld the Commissions definition of "indecent" speech as

> "language that describes, in terms patently offensive as measured by contemporary community standards for the broadcast medium, sexual or excretory activities and organs, at times of the day when there is a reasonable risk that children may be in the audience."[22]

---

20 *FCC v. Pacifica Foundation*, 438 U.S. 726 (1978) at 748 *et seq.*

21 Id., at 729.

22 *Citizen's Complaint Against Pacifica Found. Station WBAI (FM), N.Y, N.Y.*, 56 F.C.C.2d 94 (1975) at para. 11.

The Court used a nuisance analysis, finding that if the broadcast had been aired at a different time, the outcome of the case may have been different. It was a narrow decision and the Court stated so and relied on the FCC's promise to proceed with great discretion and care, meaning a very restrictive use of its authority to enforce the indecency standards.[23] This resulted in a literal application of the *Pacifica*-standard whereby the FCC would only bring enforcement proceedings if one of the seven "dirty words" that were dealt with in *Pacifica* were actually used; in actual fact there were hardly any proceedings initiated even after the clarification in *Pacifica*.

The FCC later took the view that because broadcasters had found ways to make their indecent messages understood without running afoul of *Pacifica* simply by avoiding the use of the prohibited words and therefore changed its policy to a more "contextual" reading of the case using the accepted definition to find indecent content even if it did not display one of the words. Nonetheless, enforcement was not the rule.[24] In the 1990s the FCC further clarified matters by introducing "safe harbour" rules which limited the indecency rule application to before 10 p.m. and after 6 a.m. To provide guidance to the broadcasters on how the Commission applies the rules an extensive policy paper was released in 2001.[25] The enforcement situation changed significantly in 2003 as a response to specific events that occurred in the broadcast media.[26] The controversy began in 2002 when popular music icon *Cher* used the "F-word" as she accepted a lifetime achievement award at the American Music Awards[27]. The following year, at other renowned awards ceremonies broadcast on television singer *Bono* and entertainer *Nicole Richie* each used the "F-word" during the ceremonies.[28] The uses were unscripted and unknown to the broadcaster and additionally their uses

---

23 Cf. *FCC v. Pacifica, supra* n. 20, e.g. the concurring opinion of Powell at 760, but also the comment in the dissent of Brennan at 769.

24 Cf. *In re Application of WGBH Educ. Found*, 69 F.C.C.2d 1250, at para. 10.

25 Industry Guidance on the Commission's Case Law Interpreting 18 U.S.C. § 1464 and Enforcement Policies Regarding Broadcast Indecency, Policy Statement, 16 F.C.C.R. 7999 (2001).

26 Generally on the changed policy of the FCC e.g. *Levi*, Chairman Kevin Martin on Indecency: Enhancing Agency Power, 60 Fed. Comm. L.J. 19 (2008), at 24 *et seq.*

27 The quote found indecent by the FCC was: "critics [...] saying that I was on my way out every year. Right. So fuck 'em".

28 For illustration, these were the quotes: At the 2003 Golden Globe Awards, as he received an award, *Bono* stated "This is really, really fucking brilliant". At the 2003 Billboard Music Awards as she was presenting an award with Paris Hilton Richie stated: "Have you ever tried to get cow shit out of a Prada purse? It's not so fucking simple".

were explicative.[29] While finding a violation of the FCC's indecency policy, the Commission did not originally impose fines concerning the awards ceremonies, but sought to send a message to broadcasters regarding the new rules.[30] The broadcasters appealed the policy change and the cases were consolidated under one appeal in the Second Circuit Court of Appeals in New York City.

In 2007, the Second Circuit Court decided that the FCC's change in rules regarding fleeting expletives was arbitrary and capricious and violated federal administrative law.[31] The court used the argument that one of the reasons for the Supreme Court in reaching its decision in *Pacifica* was the FCC's assurance that it would only use it's authority to regulate indecency to a limited extent.[32] The Second Circuit Court found that notwithstanding the fact that this restrained policy was applicable at the time of the incidents described above, the FCC by taking action in effect overruled all of its prior cases which held that *fleeting* explicatives were not actionable under the FCC indecency policy.[33] Therefore broadcasters would not be able to foresee what was illegal content and what was protected speech.[34] In the view of the court, the whole process and reasoning of the

29 It should be noted that the FCC argued that Cher's use was not explicative, but connoted a sexual meaning. Additionally, the Commission found that Richie's reference to cow shit was, in fact, literal.

30 *Complaints Against Various Broadcast Licensees Regarding Their Airing of the "Golden Globe Awards" Program*, Memorandum Opinion and Order, 19 F.C.C.R. 4975, para. 16 (2004).

31 *Fox TV Stations, Inc. v FCC*, 489 F.3d 444 (2d Cir. 2007).

32 See above fn. 23.

33 Cf. *In re Complaints Against Various Broadcast Licensees Regarding Their Airing of the "Golden Globe Awards" Program*, 18 F.C.C.R. 19859, para. 12 (FCC Enforcement Bureau 2003): "While prior Commission and staff action have indicated that isolated or fleeting broadcasts of the 'F-Word' such as that here are not indecent or would not be acted upon, consistent with our decision today we conclude that any such interpretation is no longer good law". See also *O'Neil*, Indecency, the First Amendment, and the FCC, 60 Fed. Comm. L.J. 12 (2008), who clearly underlines that fleeting explicatives would not have been included under any of the criteria used after *Pacifica* and in the Policy Statement of the FCC, at 13.

34 The Court recounted the decisions that had been handed down within the administrative proceeding process: At first the Commission had held that the fleeting explicatives were not actionable, pursuant to the Commission's long standing policy. Then that decision was overturned by the full Commission. The FCC then held "the 'F-Word' is one of the most vulgar, graphic, and explicit descriptions of sexual activity in the English language" and therefore the use of that word was patently offensive under contemporary community standards". *In re Complaints Against Various Broadcast Licensees Regarding Their Airing of the "Golden Globe Awards" Program*, 18 F.C.C.R. 19859, para. 8.

FCC were arbitrary and capricious. The FCC appealed against this decision to the Supreme Court.

In a fragmented 5-4 decision, the Supreme Court reversed the Second Circuit's decision and remanded the case back to the Court of Appeals.[35] *Justice Scalia* wrote for the majority decision holding that the Second Circuit erred in its analysis. The Court held that the FCC need not explain to a court's satisfaction that the new regulations were better than the existing regime, it was sufficient that the agency followed the administrative procedure statute and its enabling legislation:

> "More fundamentally [...] the agency's decision to consider the patent offensiveness of isolated expletives on a case-by-case basis is not arbitrary or capricious. 'Even a prime-time recitation of Geoffrey Chaucer's Miller's Tale,' we have explained, 'would not be likely to command the attention of many children who are both old enough to understand and young enough to be adversely affected.' [...] The agency's decision to retain some discretion does not render arbitrary or capricious its regulation of the deliberate and shocking uses of offensive language at the award shows under review."[36]

In essence the Court held that the Second Circuit had based its assumptions on an incorrect analysis:

> "If the Commission's action here was not arbitrary or capricious in the ordinary sense, it satisfies the Administrative Procedure Act's 'arbitrary [or] capricious' standard; its lawfulness under the Constitution is a separate question to be addressed in a constitutional challenge."[37]

In other words, the actually interesting question whether the free speech standards of the First Amendment had been violated was not touched by the Supreme Court because the original decision was based on the requirements of administrative law.[38]

---

35 *FCC v. Fox Television Stations, Inc.*, 556 U. S. ___ (2009),129 S. Ct. 1800 (2009).

36 Id., at 1814.

37 Id., at 1812. Both the defendants in *Fox* and *CBS* (see below) had argued that the FCC's policy regarding broadcast media indecency was an unconstitutional infringement of the freedom of speech. Both Circuits (Second and Third), however, declined to reach this subject as is prerogative of any court, to dispose of the case, whenever possible, on grounds other than constitutional grounds. The courts instead opted to rely on an analysis of administrative law. This is not to say that the courts did not address the constitutional issues at all.

38 For an analysis of the administrative law aspects *Hutchinson*, "Fleeting Expletives" Are the Tip of the Iceberg: Fallout from Exposing the Arbitrary and Capricious Nature of Indecency Regulation, 61 Fed. Comm. L.J. 229 (2009).

On remand the Second Circuit Appeals Court re-heard arguments, and in July 2010 the court ruled that the regulations were unconstitutionally vague and had a chilling effect on protected speech.[39] The court took issue with the shifting sands of FCC indecency analysis, pointing out that while specific words were considered indecent in some contexts, the same words would be considered acceptable by the Commission in others. Additionally, similar words, or words that might be expected to draw a similar outcome, were treated differently.[40] The court stated that while context was important, the reasoning of indecency determinations was indiscernible from the reasoning which held that the same material was ruled to be acceptable:

> "The Commission argues that its three-factor 'patently offensive' test gives broadcasters fair notice of what it will find indecent. However, in each of these cases, the Commission's reasoning consisted of repetition of one or more of the factors without any discussion of how it applied them. Thus, the word 'bullshit' is indecent because it is 'vulgar, graphic and explicit' while the words 'dickhead' was not indecent because it was 'not sufficiently vulgar, explicit, or graphic.' This hardly gives broadcasters notice of how the Commission will apply the factors in the future."[41]

The Second Circuit Court found that the vagueness of the policy had the effect of chilling protected speech. Acknowledging the difficult nature of regulating speech of this nature, the court stated:

> "Sex and the magnetic power of sexual attraction are surely among the most predominant themes in the study of humanity since the Trojan War. The digestive system and excretion are also important areas of human attention. By prohibiting all "patently offensive" references to sex, sexual organs, and excretion without giving adequate guidance as to what "patently offensive" means, the FCC effectively chills speech, because broadcasters have no way of knowing what the FCC will find offensive. To place any discussion of these vast topics at the broadcaster's peril has the effect of promoting wide self-censorship of valuable material which should be completely protected under the First Amendment."[42]

To underline its viewpoint, the Court recounted three examples of the chilling effects that had already been created by the policy wherein broadcasters had opted not to air certain material that while important to public dialogue, it was not broadcasted due to the fear that FCC indecency sanctions would follow.[43]

---

39 *Fox Television Stations, Inc. et al. v. FCC*, 613 F.3d 317 (2d Cir. 2010).

40 Id., at 330.

41 Id., at 330.

42 Id., at 334.

43 Id., at 334.

Significantly, in its decision, the Second Circuit invited the Supreme Court to revisit the issue of whether or not *Pacifica* was good law.[44] In August 2010, the FCC announced that rather than appealing directly to the Supreme Court, the agency would seek a rehearing in the Second Circuit[45] which was denied in November 2010.[46] The government requested for the FCC a writ of certiorari in this case which was granted by the Supreme Court in June 2011 (see below).

b) The case of Fleeting Nudity

Almost simultaneously to the recent fleeting expletive controversy a "fleeting nudity"[47] controversy erupted. While there has not been a wealth of case law dealing specifically with the issue of what amount and circumstances of nudity are permitted on broadcast television[48], the issue came to the forefront in the aftermath of the now notoriously famous "wardrobe malfunction case":

During the halftime show for the 2004 Super Bowl game in Dallas, singers *Janet Jackson* and *Justin Timberlake* performed a duet of "Rock Your Body". As the song concluded, *Timberlake* sang the lyric: "I will have you naked by the end of this song." With this, he ripped off part of *Jackson's* bustier, uncovering her left breast for 9/16 of a second.[49] Parent and family value groups were outraged and the FCC was flooded with complaints.[50] The FCC quickly brought

44 Id., at 334 and 327.

45 Under the Federal Rules of Civil Procedure, a party may seek rehearing of a case in the same court if there has been a mistake of fact or law.

46 *Fox Television Stations, Inc. et al. v. FCC*, Decision of November 22, 2010 (docket No. 06-5358-ag), to be found e.g. in the appendix to the petition for a writ of certiorari to the Supreme Court, at 116a (available at http://www.justice.gov/osg/briefs/2010/2pet/7pet/-2010-1293.pet.aa.pdf).

47 Fleeting nudity occurs when a broadcast reveals an unpermitted visual of a part of a body, which may violate the FCC's indecency rules and this happens briefly.

48 Since there was not a specific nudity case akin to *Pacifica* in the explicative realm, the Court analyzed the fleeting nudity regulations under the *Pacifica* rationale.

49 Consider the fact that the nipple of the breast was never actually exposed. Jackson was wearing a metallic covering over her nipple, which might undercut her assertion that she knew nothing about the incident before it occurred and that the incident was in fact unplanned.

50 *In re Complaints Against Various Television Licensees Concerning Their February 1, 2004, Broadcast of the Super Bowl XXXVIII Halftime Show*, FCC 04-209, para. 2; generally on the procedure and response to individual complaints by the FCC *Belmas/Love/Foy*, In the Dark: A Consumer Perspective on FCC Broadcast Indecency Denials, 60 Fed. Comm. L.J. 67 (2008).

forth an administrative procedure against CBS for showing indecent content and fined the network that had broadcast the show \$ 550 000. This fine was based upon the number of CBS affiliates who had carried the Super Bowl, of which each was fined the statutory maximum of \$ 27 500.[51] CBS appealed and the Third Circuit Court of Appeals found, similar to the Second Circuit Court of Appeals in the above mentioned case, that the new FCC policy regarding fleeting indecency was arbitrary and capricious and violated federal administrative law.[52]

In reviewing the FCC's administrative decision, the Third Circuit summarized the Commission's analysis as follows:

> "[T]he Commission concluded the Halftime Show broadcast was indecent because it depicted a sexual organ and violated "contemporary community standards for the broadcast medium." In making this determination, the FCC relied on a contextual analysis to find the broadcast of Jackson's exposed breast was: (1) graphic and explicit, (2) shocking and pandering, and (3) fleeting. It further concluded that the brevity of the image was outweighed by the other two factors. The standard applied by the Commission is derived from its 2001 policy statement setting forth a two-part test for indecency: (1) "the material must describe or depict sexual or excretory organs or activities," and (2) it must be "*patently offensive* as measured by contemporary community standards for the broadcast medium."[53]

The Third Circuit Court of Appeals underlined that in 2001 the FCC had established new criteria with which the offensiveness of material under review would be analyzed:

> "(1) the explicitness or graphic nature of the description or depiction of sexual or excretory organs or activities; (2) whether the material dwells on or repeats at length descriptions of sexual or excretory organs or activities; (3) whether the material appears to pander or is used to titillate, or whether the material appears to have been presented for its shock value."[54]

In sanctioning CBS, the Federal Communications Commission had found that the broadcaster acted "wilfully" within the meaning of FCC regulation under the theory that the broadcaster had not taken appropriate measures to ensure that the indecent material did not end up on the air. In doing so it argued through

---

51 *In re Complaints Against Various Television Licensees Concerning Their February 1, 2004, Broadcast of the Super Bowl XXXVIII Halftime Show*, FCC 04-209, para. 1.

52 *CBS Corp. et al. v. FCC*, 535 F.3d 167, 209 (3d Cir. 2008).

53 Id., at 173.

54 Cf. *In re Industry Guidance on the Commission's Case Law Interpreting 18 U.S.C. § 1464 and Enforcement Policies Regarding Broadcast Indecency*, 16 F.C.C.R. 7999, 8002 (2001).

a theory of *respondeat superior*, whereby the broadcaster would be liable for the actions of its employees, namely singers *Timberlake* and *Jackson.*[55]

In its appeal, CBS had argued that the FCC's new policy was a departure from the policy that had been in effect at the time of the Super Bowl in 2004. There had not to date been enforcement actions regarding accidental or *fleeting nudity*. The broadcaster argued that quite like the change in the policy regarding *fleeting explicatives*, the sanctioning of the "wardrobe malfunction" constituted a new policy: one which was not foreseeable by the broadcasters and not announced by the Commission. The FCC argued that the decision and sanctions were in line with its case law, that the fleeting nudity had always contravened FCC regulations and that the new FCC policy governing fleeting explicatives did not apply to fleeting nudity. Essentially, the Commission argued that the nudity policy stood separate and independent from the Commissions policy on explicatives.[56]

The Third Circuit Court of Appeals followed the arguments of CBS and rejected the Commission's assertions[57] finding that there was no difference between the two policies, especially at the time of the Half Time Show 2004. The Court, as mentioned, therefore concluded that the FCC's new policy was arbitrary and capricious and void under the Administrative Procedure Act. The FCC appealed against this decision as it had down in the proceedings at the Second Circuit.

Shortly after the Supreme Court's reversal and remand of the *FCC v Fox* case, the Supreme Court also reversed and remanded the *FCC v CBS* case without decision, relying on the reasoning of *Fox* and instructing the Third Circuit Court to re-open the file.[58] While the Third Circuit heard re-argument in 2010,

---

55 Originally, the FCC had also found that CBS had acted "willfully" because CBS had intentionally aired the Half Time show whether or not they had intended to broadcast the nudity. The Commission later withdrew this position.

56 This is significant because of the fines involved. The FCC had declined to impose fines against the broadcasters in the Fox case because of the policy change, the Agency now argued that the nudity policy had not been changed by the policy pronouncements of *Golden Globes*.

57 Cf. *CBS Corp. et al. v. FCC*, 535 F.3d 167 (3d Cir. 2008): "The Commission's determination that CBS's broadcast of a nine-sixteenths of one second glimpse of a bare female breast was actionably indecent evidenced the agency's departure from its prior policy. Its orders constituted the announcement of a policy change – that fleeting images would no longer be excluded from the scope of actionable indecency".

58 The Court did so in a one sentence memorandum decision, *FCC v. CBS*, 129 S.Ct. 2176 (2009). The Supreme Court did not delve into the issue of whether the policy amounted

the court has yet to announce its ruling and there is no time-limit set, so it seems likely that a decision of the Supreme Court following the newly decided case at the Second Circuit will arrive first and possibly give a new general guideline which will then also apply in this case. This seems even more likely since the Supreme Court docketed the fleeting explicatives case (*Fox*) for a writ of certiorari by the FCC together with another Second Circuit Court decision that concerns an FCC decision about scripted nudity.[59]

In that case, the FCC fined the network ABC and its affiliates in 2008 for airing in 2003 an episode of *NYPD Blue*, in which the backside – more precisely the buttocks – of an adult woman in the context of having a shower were depicted for around seven seconds.[60] Each station was fined $ 27 500 amounting to a total fine of more than $ 1 200 000. Although on first view there seem to be differences to the decision of the Second Circuit concerning fleeting expletives, the Court in its summary order does not see a significant distinction, because "the same context-based indecency test that *Fox* found 'impermissibly vague'" was used by the FCC to determine the indecency of the nudity scene, as well.[61] Therefore, the panel of the court held itself bound to the previous decision in *Fox*. This illustrates how broad the Second Circuit Court of Appeals rejection of the FCC indecency policy is, and consequently it was right to join the two cases for a final decision by the Supreme Court.

3. Pacifica's Indecency approach in the test of time

In essence, the Supreme Court in its forthcoming judgment will be answering much more than just the validity of the FCC's decisions on fleeting expletives and scripted nudity (or more precisely the rejection of this policy by the Second Circuit Court). It will decide whether the indecency test upheld by *Pacifica* stands the test of time. Interestingly, the writer of the opinion in *Pacifica* and

---

to a violation of due process rights because of the change in policy as eluded to in the Third Circuit's decision.

59 Supreme Court, docket No. 10-1293, cert. granted on June 27, 2011; decision to be expected in the current term.

60 The show was introduced by a warning that it contains "adult language and partial nudity" and advised viewer's discretion.

61 *ABC et al v FCC*, Second Circuit Court of Appeals, Jan. 4th 2011, not yet published in the Federal Reporter but available at 2011 WL 9307 and to be found e.g. in the appendix to the petition for a writ of certiorari to the Supreme Court (see above fn. 46), at 118a.

last still present Supreme Court justice of that decision was a dissenter on the first *Fox* decision by the Supreme Court.[62] Especially due to the recent replacements on the Court it will be interesting to see whether the very narrow decision in *Fox* not treating the First Amendment issues will see a different outcome now and unsurprisingly court watchers since a while are lining up the votes to see which justice will vote where.[63] The main question will not only be whether the policy concerning indecency is foreseeable for the broadcasters, but also whether treating broadcast differently from other methods of dissemination especially via cable and satellite still makes sense, notwithstanding the even more fundamental question whether the omnipresence of Internet content requires a whole new approach.

The first of the arguments, the difficulty for broadcasters to know whether or not they are entering "dangerous" terrain in screening certain content, was one of the major arguments the networks have been bringing forward and the Second Circuit Court's reason for handing down its decisions the way it did. A prominent example used to display this difficulty, was the FCC's decision concerning the airing of the award-winning Steven Spielberg film *Saving Private Ryan* starring Tom Hanks by the ABC network. Although after previous airing it had already been decided by the FCC the film did not fulfill indecency criteria, as a consequence of the CBS proceedings in the Super Bowl Half Time Show case, a number of ABC affiliates restrained from programming the film when it was foreseen by ABC on Veteran's Day 2004. The film contains a graphic depiction of war and in particular the movie opens with a very graphic and violent portrayal of the beginning of the Normandy invasion in 1944. From the complainants' perspective more important, the film also contains very strong language including the words "fuck" and its derivatives, "shit" and "bastard". ABC preceded the broadcast with a commentary by veteran soldiers warning of the graphic nature of the movie but insisting this was necessary to realistically de-

---

62 Cf. on this observation at length *Barron, FCC v. Fox Television Stations* and the FCC's new Fleeting Expletive Policy, 62 Fed. Comm. L.J. 567 (2010) at 579.

63 Take for instance the position of *Corn-Revere*, an attorney for CBS in the *FCC v. CBS* case and author of *FCC v Fox Television Stations, Inc.*, Cato Supreme Court Review 295-319, available at www.cato.org/pubs/scr/2009/FCCvFox-CornRevere.pdf: "[T]he *Fox* decision is far from the end of the story, and is more like an intermission between acts. The case was decided not only by a close vote, but on a narrow rationale"; *Barron, FCC v. Fox Television Stations* and the FCC's new Fleeting Expletive Policy, 62 Fed. Comm. L.J. 567 (2010) at 584; *Campbell, Pacifica* Reconsidered: Implications for the Current Controversy over Broadcast Indecency, 63 Fed. Comm. L.J. 195 (2011) underlines in an extensive analysis that already the original *Pacifica* decision was a close one.

pict the ravages of war. Additionally, ABC warned viewers the content was not appropriate for children and for mature viewers only, pointing out the "intense adult language" and included the voluntary industry code signalling the content of the film.

The FCC was flooded with complaints from parent and family organizations, focussing on the language used. It found that the film was not indecent under *Pacifica* and the resulting regulations even though it used the "F-word" so intensely. Because in the context of the film and its portrayal of war, it was necessary to use harsh and colourful language to maintain the authenticity, according to the FCC the language was not used in a *patently offensive* way. Although the FCC explained the contextual difference to the use of the word in an awards ceremony with the "missing political, scientific or other independent value" in that context[64] and also the qualification of the corresponding television airing as a family programme (other than the movie of which the network had warned viewers repeatedly), the Second Circuit Court of Appeals in its *Fox* decision used this finding by the FCC as an illustration of the unforeseeable nature of the FCC policy regarding expletives and in particular, "fleeting expletives". What the court seemed to say is that if the expletives were intentional, planned and thought-out, the FCC would find them acceptable if they fit into the context of the story.[65] If, however, the expletives were unintentional, off-the-cuff, or accidental they would be somehow more offensive, more indecent and could potentially incur huge fines to the broadcaster. The court found that this dichotomy put broadcasters in an untenable situation.

How important the decision on whether or not to air "risky" content has become, is further illustrated by a legislative change that accompanied the policy change of the FCC and its increase of enforcement proceedings. The Broadcast Decency Enforcement Act of 2005 increased the fines for violating the rules prohibiting the broadcasting of obscene or indecent material tenfold to $ 325 000 for each violation or each day of a continuing violation.[66] This remarkable increase is a potentially sufficient reason to restrain from showing controversial content.

---

64 And thereby categorizing the use as merely "profane".

65 Whereby the Second Circuit Court criticized the FCC's use of context and reliance on that passage in *Pacifica*, because there the "context" argument was actually used to underline the narrow application and exception of this justification to First Amendment limitations, *Fox TV Stations, Inc. v FCC*, 613 F.3d 317 (2d Cir. 2010), at 333.

66 Public law No. 109-235 in June 15, 2006, which amended 47 U.S.C. 503 (b) (2).

The second argument the U.S. Supreme Court should clarify concerns the distinction between (terrestrially disseminated) broadcast on the one hand and cable or satellite on the other. Although this has been an issue previously and the U.S. Supreme Court has rejected attempts to regulate indecency on cable channels in a similar way than in broadcast[67] the issue remains relevant. Not only because irrespective of the Supreme Court holding there are frequent but unsuccessful attempts to introduce such legislation in Congress[68], such as a couple of years ago in the form of obligatory "à la carte"-cable bouquets, which would require the cable provider to allow his customer to pick his own choice of channels instead of having to subscribe to a predefined package[69], but also because more than 80 percent of U.S. households receive their television feed via cable or also direct satellite to home transmission rather than relying on the traditional antenna system.[70] The general assumption that there has been a previous active decision to have these channels remains valid, it limits however the weight of the argument of pervasiveness of the broadcast content in regard to children, since these typically or at least frequently have unlimited access to the cable channels once a household has subscribed to them. It has to be taken into consideration that there are easier blocking mechanisms available to parents in this model beyond e.g. using the so-called V-Chip that blocks certain predefined content.[71] But one can still pose the question whether under these circumstances there might have to be a media-unspecific categorizing of content that is harmful to children and then apply the same restrictions across at least comparable media

67 *United States v. Playboy Entertainment Group, Inc.*, 529 U.S. 803 (2000). In that case the application of the watershed rules or scrambling requirements for cable channels dedicated primarily to sexually-oriented programming was struck down, because with cable technology unwanted channels can be blocked on a household-by-household basis.

68 Cf. *O'Neil*, Indecency, the First Amendment, and the FCC, 60 Fed. Comm. L.J. F. 12 (2008) at 15 *et seq.* on the attempts at introducing enlarged jurisdiction for the FCC.

69 Cf. *Levi*, Chairman Kevin Martin on Indecency: Enhancing Agency Power, 60 Fed. Comm. L.J. F. 19 (2008).

70 Cf. *Quale/Tuesley*, Space, the Final Frontier—Expanding FCC Regulation of Indecent Content onto Direct Broadcast Satellite, 60 Fed. Comm. L.J. 37 (2008), who also discuss intensively the extension of rules to cable at 39 *et seq.* but denying this possibility; *Thierer*, Why Regulate Broadcasting? Toward a Consistent First Amendment Standard for the Information Age, 15 CommLaw Conspectus 431 (2007) at p. 438 (n. 33)

71 Cf. *Thierer*, Why Regulate Broadcasting? Toward a Consistent First Amendment Standard for the Information Age, 15 CommLaw Conspectus 431 (2007) at 471 *et seq.* on the V-Chip and generally critical of distinction due to convergence.

such as television content (irrespective of the way of dissemination).[72] This would create a significant difficulty in view of the First Amendment rules and therefore it is unlikely that existing *Pacifica*-based indecency rules will ever apply to cable or satellite radio and television, but there might be an alley towards a more comparable approach to the issue in question if it is really the protection of minors that is in the centre of attention. In that context the Supreme Court would also be able to answer the overarching question on whether such "indecent" content still needs to be regulated at all and to which extent, applying the usual strict scrutiny standard; in other words, whether or not societal and technological changes since *Pacifica* make a reassessment necessary or possible.[73]

Therefore, the decision in joined cases *FCC v. Fox and FCC v. ABC* has the potential to redesign a major cornerstone of U.S. free speech logic. That alone would give material for new comparative discussions in the coming years, but to underline the already existing differences, the outcomes of the current *Pacifica*-logic shall be observed briefly in the following from a comparative angle across the Atlantic.

---

72 Very critical of the current distinction e.g. *Calvert*, The Two-Step Evidentiary and Causation Quandary for Medium-Specific Laws Targeting Sexual and Violent Content: First Proving Harm and Injury to Silence Speech, then Proving Redress and Rehabilitation Through Censorship, 60 Fed. Comm. L.J. 167 (2008); in response to that including the problem of cross-media-offerings (same content/different media and regulation) *Holohan*, The Decline of Medium-Specific Content and the End of Medium-Specific Content Regulation: A Response to Professor Calvert, 60 Fed. Comm. L.J. F. 48 (2008). The impact of digital video recorders is discussed by *Steele*, Examining the FCC's Indecency Regulations in Light of Today's Technology, 63 Fed. Comm. L.J. 289 (2011) at 304 *et seq.*; *Pilon*, Expansion of Indecency Regulation: Presented by the Federalist Society's Telecommunications Practice Group, 60 Fed. Comm. L.J. 1 (2008) at p. 13 points to the comparability of broadcast and cable/satellite in practice; similarly *Bloom*, Pervasive New Media: Indecency Regulation and the End of the Distinction between Broadcast Technology and Subscription-Based Media, Yale J.L. & Tech. 2006-2007, p. 109, esp. p. 116 *et seq.*

73 *Kohler*, Sex and Violence in the Media: Some Thoughts on the Importance of Underinclusion as a Barrier to Medium Specific Regulation, 60 Fed. Comm. L.J. F. 38 (2008), esp. 46 *et seq.* argues for a stronger focus on self-help approaches strengthening the abilities of the parents to control without having statutory restrictions. An interesting discussion held after the new FCC decisions can be found here: *Martin/Ciongoli/Peters/Pilon/Sentelle*, Expansion of Indecency Regulation: Presented by the Federalist Society's Telecommunications Practice Group, 60 Fed. Comm. L.J. 1 (2008).

III. Some comparative views from the European angle

1. Some basic rules from the European Union

"Indecency" on television is not restrained to the U.S., regulation of such indecency not unknown to Europe. As a starting point it needs to be underlined that although they remain as 27 sovereign individual Member States in the European Union (EU), these states have decided to transfer a certain amount of competencies to the supranational organization so as to reach a level of harmonized law that allows full benefit of a common market without (trade and other) barriers.[74] According to this approach, the basic rules for television were harmonized in the so-called Television without Frontiers-Directive in 1989 based on the idea that television is a service that profits from one of the fundamental freedoms (that of providing and receiving services cross-border) of the common market.[75] After a revision in 1997 and another in 2007 that adapted the set of rules to technological developments the now so-called Audiovisual Media Services Directive (AVMSD)[76] includes in its scope not only traditional television distributed by any technical means, but also video-on-demand-offers including those offered via the internet and potentially also services with audiovisual content such as "Youtube" if an editorial responsibility can be construed.[77]

Some of the basic rules in that directive concern the protection of minors as an objective of general interest.[78] With this aim in focus there is a differentiation

---

74 *Cole*, Überblick zum Europarecht und zu den Medien, in: Fink/Cole/Keber, Europäisches und Internationales Medienrecht, Heidelberg 2008, paras. 1 *et seq.* and Medien im Primärrecht der EG, paras. 10 *et seq.*

75 Id., Medienrechtliches Sekundärrecht der EG, Fernsehen als zentrale Regelungsmaterie, paras. 60-81.

76 Directive 2007/65/EC of the European Parliament and of the Council of 11 December 2007 amending Council Directive 89/552/EEC on the coordination of certain provisions laid down by law, regulation or administrative action in Member States concerning the pursuit of television broadcasting activities, OJ L 332, 18.12.2007, p. 27 as codified by Directive 2010/13/EU of the European Parliament and of the Council of 10 March 2010, OJ L 95, 15.4.2010, p. 1.

77 On the scope cf. *Cole,* The European Legal Framework for On-demand Services, What Directive for Which Services?, in: Whose boots are made for walking? On-demand services - a case for passing regulation, entrusting self-/co-regulation or leaving it to general legislation?, European Audiovisual Observatory (ed.), IRIS Special 2011, forthcoming autumn 2011.

78 *Cole,* Medienrechtliches Sekundärrecht der EG, Fernsehen als zentrale Regelungsmaterie , in: Fink/Cole/Keber, Europäisches und Internationales Medienrecht, paras. 77 *et*

made between the ways content is disseminated. In traditional television programmes all content that "might seriously impair the physical, mental or moral development of minors" (Art. 27 para. 1 AVMSD) is prohibited and specifically "pornography or gratuitous violence" are mentioned as examples for such content. In on-demand services where the individual recipient decides on when and what to consume more directly, there is no general prohibition but an obligation to make this content available in a way that ensures that minors will not normally hear or see these services (Art. 12 AVMSD). Such measures are typically technical access blocking measures that require e.g. a de-scrambling by entering a specific identification number or similar. In television there is an additional requirement that programmes which are only "likely to impair" (and not "might seriously") the development of minors, are shown at times during which minors do not usually see or hear them or by limiting access with technical measures (again e.g. the above-mentioned scrambling). If the programme is shown during the watershed times – which can be defined by the Member States individually, but are typically starting between 9, 10 and 11 p.m. and lasting until 5, 6 or exceptionally 7 a.m. – programme providers have to additionally pre-advise the consumers by an acoustic warning concerning the content, or label the content with a visual symbol throughout the duration of the programme.

As with all EU directives, Member States are obliged to transpose these rules into national law whereby the aim of the directive is binding but the exact method and wording with which the inclusion in national law happens is subject to Member State's discretion as long as an efficient enforcement of the European law is guaranteed. Therefore, one can observe differences and variations in the Member States of the EU, although key provisions of the AVMSD tend to have very similar transpositions everywhere.[79]

---

seq.; *Füg*, Save the Children: The Protection of Minors in the Information Society and the Audiovisual Media Services Directive, Journal of Consumer Policy 2008, 31, 1, p. 45 *et seq.*; *Lentzen,* Protection des mineurs et de la dignité humaine, in: Regulating the new media landscape, A Directive for Audiovisual Media Services without Frontiers, EMR Schriftenreihe, Baden-Baden 2008, vol. 36, p. 39 *et seq.*

79 For English language versions of all the national AVMSD transposition acts cf. www.medialaw.lu.

2. The German example: Pornography and Nudity

In order to exemplify the national application of the AVMSD and be able to contrast the reality of broadcast with the U.S. situation (and for obvious reasons in the context of this collection), the German example is being used here.

At first, there is a provision in criminal law prohibiting the dissemination of pornography if accessible to minors. This, however, acknowledges the possibility of using technical or other measures that block this access and therefore exempt the disseminating person from liability (sec. 184/184d Criminal Code, Strafgesetzbuch, StGB[80]). The prohibition is also included in the so-called Interstate Treaty on the Protection of Minors in the Media (Jugendmedienschutzstaatsvertrag, JMStV)[81] concluded between the German Laender, but for both – as well as with the provision in the EU AVMSD – the actual definition of pornography is not included. Similar to US case law regarding obscenity, according to jurisprudence of German courts a determination of illegality is made if the depiction of sexual interaction mainly appeals to the prurient interest and focuses alone on lust and the sexual and thereby degrades human beings to objects of lust.[82] One of the criteria indicating (but not deciding) such a situation is the graphic depiction of and focusing on genitals. However, this does not mean that any depiction of naked bodies is a violation of indecency standards, on the contrary it is quite normal to see semi-exposed female bodies also during daytime free-TV and certainly before the watershed at 10 p.m.

Nudity occurs not only in documentation series / reality TV shows accompanying parents during pregnancy and birth, it is also seen in episodes of series shown in the evening and even in advertisements, a famous example being spots for margarine. A brief image of the backside of a female body such as in the *NYPD Blue* episode mentioned above would not be regarded as inappropriate content by German standards. And most certainly, fleeting and unscripted nudity would neither be a problem. In actual fact there have been "boob incidents" on German television shows, most recently in June 2011 on one of the still most popular family shows aired live on free TV during which accidentally singer *Jennifer Lopez's* breast was exposed due to the wind lifting the loosely fit dress and showing the breast completely without the cover of underwear or any other

80 Available in English at http://www.gesetze-im-internet.de/englisch_stgb/index.html.

81 Available in English at http://www.kjm-online.de/files/pdf1/_JMStV_Stand_13_RStV-mit_Titel_english.pdf.

82 Cf. with further sources *Cole*, Medienstrafrecht, in: Dörr/Kreile/Cole (eds.), Handbuch Medienrecht, Heidelberg 2011, paras. G 21 *et seq*.

attire.[83] This as little as earlier incidences in which transparent clothing was displayed by female guests in similar shows has resulted in action by media authorities nor would there be a legal basis for it.

To return to the question of prohibited pornography: This prohibition only extends to television, but then irrespective of the way it is disseminated. Because in so-called telemedia – basically internet and comparable content that is not television – it is technically possible to block access to content in a reliable manner, certain exceptions to the ban of pornography apply. If a closed user group exists to which access is only granted if the person requesting access has been pre-identified (verifying the age of the person by personal contact e.g. via the post) and then it needs to authenticate each time access to the group is requested, such content can be made available. Therefore not only online video-on-demand services can profit from this exception. Also digitally broadcast television that needs a decoder and a personal identification number for access falls under the category of merely a telemedium, if certain channels are blocked and only accessible via the above mentioned two-step approach.[84] In that way similar content as is presumably available via the respective U.S. cable channels can also be available on the German "TV set" although legally spoken it is then not television content and only if the descrambling or decoding has taken place in order to avoid accidental confrontation.

The reason for this prohibition is that such – as well as other comparable content – is evidently able to seriously impair the development of minors. In addition to this absolute prohibition (with the mentioned exception for telemedia) there is a general obligation not to transmit or make accessible content that is (if you want: in principle and not evidently) able to impair (and not seriously impair) the development of minors in a way other than in which it is usually not accessible to these. The access limitation can – for all kinds of television or telemedia – either be reached by technical measures or by respecting certain time schedules. For the second possibility a differentiation is made according to which the watershed is between 10 p.m. and 6 a.m. if the content is unsuitable for individuals under 16 years old, but not before 11 p.m. if unsuitable for all

---

83 Any combination of the artist's name and the TV show "Wetten Dass" will produce results in a web search, so an official source need not be mentioned here.

84 More details in *Cole*, Jugendmedienschutz, in: Dörr/Kreile/Cole (eds.), Handbuch Medienrecht, paras. H 16 *et seq*.

minors (and there are certain further obligations to be respected e.g. if the content is only suitable for children over 12[85]).

The general rule about not being allowed to show potentially inappropriate content when it is freely accessible also determines how to deal with the second category analyzed here, although it more frequently concerns violence than the use of specific language as in the U.S.

3. The German Example: Inappropriate Content and Expletives

The requirement to either block access by technical measures or schedule it during night time requires a prognosis of the content provider on the potential danger of the material offered. In order to support the provider, be it a television channel or a web content provider, a complex system of so-called co-regulation or regulated self-regulation has been established by the German legislator. According to this system providers can use existing age classifications for (movie theater and other) films to decide about the adequate scheduling, they can have the films assessed by self-regulatory bodies which can be certified by a supervising authority introduced by the Laender, the Commission for the Protection of Minors in the Media[86] (Kommission für Jugendmedienschutz, KJM). In case of certification which basically confirms the ability both in procedural and substantial terms of the self-monitoring organization to offer providers efficient guidelines in view of rules on the protection of minors, the providers are exempt from direct enforcement action by the authority even in case of a wrongful assumption in a concrete case. This privilege does not apply to providers that do not use such an organization; in case of violation of the rules against harmful content these are subject to administrative offence/misdemeanour proceedings initiated by the KJM.

Unsurprisingly, the assessment of material presented to the self-regulating bodies differs from time to time compared with the KJM's view, although with extensive criteria catalogues that have been established a majority of cases are evaluated in a similar fashion.[87] The high-profile cases in which differences ap-

85 Such content should not be shown during daytime, but closer to the watershed without having to wait right until that time, so e.g. 8 p.m. is regarded as appropriate timing.

86 Cf. overview of activity in English on http://www.kjm-online.de/en/pub/the_kjm/remit.-cfm.

87 On the discretion of the self-regulatory bodies cf. *Cole*, Der Dualismus von Selbstkontrolle und Aufsicht im Jugendmedienschutz – Zum Verhältnis von FSF und KJM im

pear are usually the ones that have received largest attention or were discussed intensively in public. And there are a lot of parallel instances to the examples mentioned in the U.S., although often with a different outcome.

The airing of *Saving Private Ryan* (*Der Soldat James Ryan*) on a commercial free TV channel in 2003 sparked a controversy in advance of the screening. According to its movie theater rating a scheduling on television before 10 p.m. was not possible but the channel Pro7 applied for an exception wanting to show it at 8 p.m. The accompanying court case mainly dealt with the question of the (then different) relationship between self-regulatory bodies and the supervising authority[88], but the substantive question was whether the opening scenes (depicting as mentioned above in a very realistic way the casualties and injuries involved in the landing) were so violent that they had a disturbing nature potentially frightening or disorienting minors of a certain age.[89] The isolated question of the intensive use of explicit language as in the U.S. was not an issue at all and could not have served as a reason for requiring late airing. Expletives or vulgar language – at least the counterpart to "shit" – are quite commonly seen and heard in talkshows (also in the afternoons, although those typically bleep stronger swearwords or very vulgar language), reality TV, afternoon films and series.[90]

System der "regulierten Selbstregulierung" – Eine Untersuchung aus Anlass des Konflikts um Schönheitsoperationen im Fernsehprogramm, Zeitschrift für Urheber- und Medienrecht 2005, p. 462 *et seq.* (concerning a controversy around the reality TV show *I want a famous face*); cf. also *id.*, Zum Beurteilungsspielraum der KJM bei der Bewertung von Jugendmedienschutzfragen, Zeitschrift für Urheber- und Medienrecht 2010, p. 929 *et seq.*

88 *VG Berlin*, Zeitschrift für Urheber- und Medienrecht 2002, 758; cf. on this decision *Ladeur*, 'Regulierte Selbstregulierung' im Jugendmedienschutz, Zeitschrift für Urheber- und Medienrecht 2002, p. 859 *et seq.*; *Bornemann*, Der Soldat James Ryan und der Jugendschutz, Kommunikation & Recht 2002, p. 474 *et seq.*

89 The courts did not decide the case on this issue but remanded it back to the supervisory authority under the assumption that the assessment of the self-regulatory body (supporting an earlier screening) had not sufficiently been taken into account. However, without a new decision having been handed down, the channel once aired the film at an earlier time risking a fine, see http://www.tagesspiegel.de/medien/jugendschutz-ausgehebelt-pro-7-sendet-soldat-james-ryan-zu-frueh-medienanstalt-reagiert/378490.html. Ever since, the film has not been shown before 10 p.m. on free TV.

90 It needs to be pointed out, however, that there were intensive activities of the media authorities against changing the way the afternoon talkshows were designed on TV in the late 1990s, cf. *Dörr/Cole*, „Big Brother" – oder: Menschenwürde als Grenze der Programmfreiheit„ Kommunikation & Recht 2000, p. 369 *et seq.*; *Di Fabio*, Der Schutz der Menschenwürde durch Allgemeine Programmgrundsätze, München 2000, p. 54 *et seq.*

Even less problematic from a legal point of view are such words if they occur as a "fleeting" expletive: it hardly raises an eyebrow, let alone initiate enforcement proceedings if a football player after a lost match of his team declares "it was a shite performance tonight" or – to make the comparison even clearer – if during an awards ceremony such a word would be used, although evidently many viewers would disagree with the quality of language used by that individual.

On the other hand, content can be regarded as inappropriate even without using explicit language but by portraying a behaviour which can be regarded as antisocial and insulting. Such display can have a disorienting effect especially on children. For this very reason the most popular television casting show in recent years – *Deutschland sucht den Superstar* modeled after the U.K. show *Pop Idol* (in the U.S. known as *American Idol*) – was fined 100 000 Euro in 2008 because both the presenter ridiculed the candidates and these were presented in a way that made them look silly, also during daytime airing. In the most recent season the KJM came to a similar conclusion but because the television channel RTL had now first presented the shows to a self-regulatory body that had cleared them for earlier screening, it was exempt from any enforcement proceedings.[91] Some shows even wander on the borderline to a violation of human dignity.

Human dignity is a value not only absolutely protected by the German Constitution in its Art. 1[92], but is also part of the JMStV and the provisions the KJM has to monitor. Any infringement of human dignity standards is automatically a violation which is why – although it is often closely connected to standards protecting minors – it hardly ever is used as an argument in enforcement proceedings since it is meant to only rule out as a last resort the "worst" possible content in which human beings are being degraded to objects.[93] Examples have been the repeated showing of secretly filmed scenes in a news format showing an old age person in a home being mistreated by the staff or in the reality TV show "Super

---

91 Cf. the two press releases http://www.kjm-online.de/de/pub/aktuelles/-pressemitteilungen/pressemitteilungen_2010/pm_032010.cfm and http://www.kjm-online.de/de/pub/aktuelles/pressemitteilungen/pressemitteilungen_2008/pm_132008.-cfm.

92 On the significance cf. also in this collection the contribution of *Dörr* and the comments from U.S. perspective in the contribution of *Stenger*.

93 Cf. in detail *Dörr*, „Big Brother" und die Menschenwürde, Die Menschenwürde und die Programmfreiheit am Beispiel eines neuen Sendeformats, Frankfurt a. M. 2000; *Dörr/Cole*, „Big Brother" – oder: Menschenwürde als Grenze der Programmfreiheit, Kommunikation & Recht 2000, p. 369 *et seq*.

Nanny" in which a mother was shown actually hitting her child.[94] The television channel in the first case had tried to argue that it wanted to show the serious deficits in the professional care of elderly persons. The courts rejected this as an insufficient argument and actually saw a repetition of the violation of the person's dignity by showing the scenes over and over for dramatic purposes.[95]

Although not explicitly based on the violation of human dignity standards a close connection could be seen in the case of MTV's *Freak Show* series, a variation of the U.S. *Jackass* format. The then responsible media authority had prohibited a future airing of some episodes, especially one in which a human being received a "branding", because this was not only inappropriate for minors but seriously endangering. Without explicitly mentioning the human dignity standard the court followed the position by underlining the "branding" limited the individual to being a "cattle".[96]

The examples show that the media authorities and in cases of disputes the courts (although there is limited jurisprudence) are much more concerned about violent content than about the use of explicit language.

IV. A brief concluding note

This contribution has shown in very brief terms that there is not only a divide between Pacifica-defenders and opponents in the First Amendment discussion in the U.S., but that there are also significant and principal differences in approaching the question of indecency regulation on both sides of the Atlantic. The analysis was limited mainly to fleeting expletives and fleeting nudity and connected issues. Beyond the substantive differences in evaluating the situations and on how to deal with them, there remain further interesting questions: the question of enforcement and supervisory authorities – on the one hand the FCC that only takes action on consumer complaints, on the other models of regulated self-

94 An extensive recent study gives an overview of relevant situations and cases *Klass*, Unteeerhaltung ohne Grenzen?, Berlin 2011; esp. p. 52 et seq.; cf. also *Hartstein/Ring/Kreile/Dörr/Stettner*, Rundfunkstaatsvertrag – Kommentar, Heidelberg, Looseleaf commentary, 48th suppl. 2011, § 3 at 10 *et seq*.

95 *OVG Lueneburg*, Multimedia & Recht 2009, p. 203 *et seq*. with comment by Hopf/Braml, p. 209 *et seq*.; *VG Hannover*, Zeitschrift für Urheber- und Medienrecht Rechtsprechungsdienst 2007, p. 332 *et seq*.

96 *VG Muenchen*, Zeitschrift für Urheber- und Medienrecht 2005, p. 252 *et seq*. with comment by *Liesching*, p. 224 *et seq*.

regulation that include public authorities but include self-regulation by the industry beyond agreeing on voluntary standards; the category of obscenity and how to deal with efficient blocking of unwanted content without being in contradiction to censorship prohibition; and many more issues in concrete cases of enforcement such as in the context of news versus entertainment programmes etc.

In all of this it is self-evident how helpful an exchange on the different viewpoints is which is why interaction with scholars from – in this case – the other side of the Atlantic is so helpful. Taking a comparative approach to important legal issues and not only relying on the way it has been done under one's own framework is valuable and worthwhile the effort even if it includes stepping over divides. The value of comparative work is one of the reasons why teaching and researching at the University of Luxembourg is so fascinating where this approach is embodied in the law faculty due to the magnitude of different legal backgrounds of the staff. Personally, I first learnt more about the value of such exchange and especially the personal discussions in the Mainz-Louisville exchange programme that has been inspiring in the Brandeis/Gutenberg-approach as described in this collection and has been accompanying me also in recent years. For this reason I am especially indebted to Russ Weaver who was the driving force behind the exchange from the U.S. side while I was participating.

Public international law rules concerning the extension of national jurisdiction on the internet

*by Udo Fink**

I. Introduction

Public international law does not yet allow states to exercise their jurisdiction through courts or authorities over internet content which has not been uploaded in the respective country. Even though such content through the global reach of the internet has a local effect in every state, it is questionable whether mere accessibility from within the state is enough to submit the content to the jurisdiction of that State.

The territorial principle as a universally recognized principle of public international law concerning state jurisdiction suggests in such cases that the competence to exercise jurisdiction lies with the state in which the contentious act has been committed. That is the state on whose territory the contentious content has been uploaded onto the internet. If, however, a state exercises its jurisdiction over acts which have taken place outside its territory, the state needs to show a certain connection to the act in question, a genuine link. Otherwise the extension of state jurisdiction over extraterritorial activities contravenes the principle of non-intervention, which protects the sovereignty of those states which either are directly territorially affected or can show another genuine link to the activity. This question has been first dealt with in the Lotus case.[1]

---

* Chair for Public Law, European and International Law, International Trade Law, Johannes Gutenberg-University Mainz.

1 Permanent Court of International Justice (StIGH), *The Case of the S.S. "Lotus"*, Series A.-No. 10, pp. 18 et seq.; See also *V. Bruns*, Völkerrecht als Rechtsordnung, ZaöRV I (1929), pp. 1 et seq.

There the Permanent Court of International Justice had to decide whether Turkey had violated international law by bringing criminal proceedings against the commanding officer of the French ship "S.S. Lotus", which collided with the Turkish ship "Boz-Court" on the High Seas. Eight Turkish seamen had died as a result of the collision. In its judgment the PCIJ established that the effect of the contentious act has materialised on a ship flying the Turkish flag. Due to the jurisdiction of the flag state derived from the law of the sea the act had a close connection to Turkey. One can derive from the decision of the PCIJ in the Lotus case that international law as it stood in the year 1927 gave the states a certain discretion when applying their laws to persons and acts outside their territory.

Next to the territorial principle, a state can base its jurisdiction on the nationality of a person committing a certain act. In contrast to that, the nationality of the victim of a crime is not universally accepted as sufficient to establish jurisdiction of the state whose nationality the victim had. This follows from the fact that in such a case the acting state wants to extend its penal power to foreign nationals.

II. The Yahoo! Case

If neither the perpetrator nor the victim of a crime possess the nationality of the state wanting to exercise jurisdiction, it appears *prima facie* to be an illegal intervention in the affairs of such states that possess a recognised connection to the contentious act on grounds of the territorial link or nationality of the actors. Nevertheless, courts have asserted jurisdiction in such extraterritorial internet cases several times.

In the year 2000 the Union des Etudiants Juifs de France and the Ligue contre le Racisme et L'Antisémitisme initiated proceedings before the Tribunal de Grande Instance of Paris against Yahoo! with the aim to order Yahoo! to deny French users access to auctions of Nazi-memorabilia and objects having a relation to the Holocaust. The motion was directed not only against the French subsidiary Yahoo! France SAS, who immediately deleted the content from its website. It was also directed against the parent company Yahoo! Inc., having its seat in Sunnyvale, California. Because the French users were still able to access the auctions by switching to Yahoo! Inc.'s American website, proceedings only against Yahoo! France SAS were absolutely insufficient to block access to Nazi objects.

Yahoo! Inc. had argued that the French court is not territorially competent over the matter, because the alleged fault is committed on the territory of the

United States. But the Court decided that the exposition for the purpose of sale of Nazi objects constitutes a violation of French law (Article R.645-2 of the Criminal Code) as well as an offence against the "collective memory of a country profoundly wounded by the atrocities committed by and in the name of a the Nazi". So in the view of the court the harm was suffered in France and therefore French jurisdiction was competent over this matter pursuant to article 46 of the New Code of Civil Procedure.[2] The Court ordered Yahoo! Inc. to take such measures as will dissuade and render impossible any and all consultation on Yahoo.com of the auction service for Nazi objects as well as any other site or service which makes apologies of Nazism or questions of the existence of Nazi crimes.

However, the District Court for the Northern District of California, San Jose Division, decided upon application by Yahoo! Inc. that the decision of the French Tribunal de Grande Instance cannot be enforced in the United States. The Court decided: „The Paris Courts May 22nd and November 20th Orders are not recognizable or enforceable because they violate U.S. and California public policy of protecting free speech. Moreover, because the Orders direct Yahoo! to implement filtering mechanisms and to individually monitor, a priori, all postings to all of its sites and services -- in the U.S. and elsewhere -- they constitute an unconstitutional prior restraint on speech that is protected by the First Amendment to the Constitution of the United States and by Article I of the Constitution of California."

The French parties challenged this decision before the United States Court of Appeal for the Ninth Circuit[3]. By a majority of 6 to 5 votes the Court reversed the District Court's decision and remanded with instructions to dismiss the action without prejudice. The majority relied in its decision partly on the lack of personal jurisdiction over the French parties and partly on the lack of ripeness of the case. The Court of Appeal stressed the importance of the First Amendment issues highlighted by this case. However, it refrained from deciding on these issues as it already dismissed the case for other reasons.

---

2 Tribunal de Grande Instance de Paris, decision of 20.11.2000, MMR 2001, 309 – *LICRA v. Yahoo! Inc.*

3 *Yahoo! Inc. v. La Ligue contre le Racisme et L'Antisemitisme*, No. 01-17424.

III. The Töben case

The most-discussed German case is the Töben case. Frederick Töben is an Australian citizen of German descent. In 1994 he founded together with several like-minded people the Adelaide Institute and was made its director. The Institute concentrates in particular on the Holocaust. Between 1997 and 1999 Töben published on the website of the Institute three articles written in English, in which he asserted that the number of Jews killed in Auschwitz was significantly lower than the 4 million assumed so far. He denied the existence of gas chambers and declared that Germans could therefore live without the "guilt complex" which was forced upon them. The website on which the articles were published was saved on an Australian server.

The Bundesgerichtshof[4], the German Federal High Court of Justice, accepted German penal jurisdiction with the following reasoning (own translation): "In cases such as the case at hand there exists a jurisdictional basis for the application of German criminal law legitimized by international law. The act affects an important domestic concern, which moreover shows an important connection with the territory of the Federal Republic of Germany. The incitement to hatred offence of Section 130 paragraph 1 of the German Criminal Code protects parts of the domestic population already in the forefront of immediate violations of human dignity and – due to the special history of Germany – aims at preventing a development which history showed to be dangerous from gaining momentum. The denial offence of Section 130 paragraph 3 of the Criminal Code shows a special connection with the Federal Republic of Germany due to the uniqueness of the crimes against the Jews committed under Nazi rule."

The Töben case had an epilogue which demonstrates the problems with the competition between different jurisdictions in extraterritorial cases. In the year 2008 German authorities issued an European Arrest Warrant against Mr. Töben on grounds of further offences committed by him. On October 1st 2008 Mr. Töben was arrested by British authorities during a stop-over at Heathrow airport and brought before Westminster Magistrates' Court. However, the German request for extradition has been refused due to deficiencies in the documentation and because the publication of anti-Semitic content is not penalized in the UK.

The Töben case has not remained singular in Germany. Ernst Zündel, a German citizen who emigrated to and lived for 19 years in Canada, published Nazi propaganda and anti-Semitic hate speech in Canada. Furthermore, he

---

4 BGHSt 46, 212.

founded in the seventies the world's biggest publishing house for the publication of right-wing extremist content (Samisdat Publishers). Mr. Zündel also ran a website with such content. In 2001 Mr. Zündel, pressured by Canadian authorities to do so, emigrated to the USA, but was deported back to Canada in 2005. He was arrested at Toronto airport and extradited to Germany upon German request. On grounds of his publications on the internet Mr. Zündel was tried and sentenced to 5 years imprisonment by the district court (Landgericht) of Mannheim. His attorney has been convicted to 3,5 years imprisonment because of utterances made by her in her written pleadings.

IV. Minimum Contact and Effects Doctrine

To assess whether the extension of a state's jurisdiction to extraterritorial events fulfills international law standards Europeans often refer to US-American doctrine. Based on Supreme Court jurisprudence in the *International Shoe* case[5], US courts demand in cases where the contentious events have taken place outside the territory of a state that the respondent has a sufficient **Minimum Contact** to the forum state, that the claim is based on this Minimum Contact and that the exercise of jurisdiction is reasonable.[6]

In matters pertaining to the internet US courts have developed the so-called **Zippo Test.**[7] Following the Zippo Test, websites can be divided into three categories, depending on their Minimum Contact:

- Passive websites that only offer information are not sufficient to create a minimum contact, unless they themselves amount to libel or an otherwise tortious act

- Interactive websites which allow the exchange of information between the website and its users can create a minimum contact, depending on the level of interactivity. This is in particular the case if enough users participate in the exchange of information within the forum state.

- Commercial websites which give their users the ability to form a business contact with the website provider always create a minimum contact.

---

5 *International Shoe Co. v. Washington*, 326 U.S. 310, 90 L.

6 *Burger King Corp. v. Rudzewicz*, 471, U.S. 462, 475, 85 L.

7 *Zippo Manufacturing Co. v. Zippo Dot Com, Inc*, District Court for the Western District of Pennsylvania, 952 F. Supp. 1119, 1997.

To submit totally passive websites, which do not create a minimum contact, to national jurisdiction, courts inside and outside the USA have applied to internet-related activities the Effects Doctrine, which in this respect modified the Minimum Contact Doctrine. According to this doctrine, which can also be found in section 402 of the Restatement 3rd of Foreign Relations Law of the United States, jurisdiction is given to a court of the act of a defendant creates a substantial effect, usually some sort of injury or harm, in the forum state. However, the injury must manifest itself in the forum state in a special way, which exceeds potential interests of other states to submit the event to their own jurisdiction. This is the case if a website is specifically directed at (or against) a private person or a company having its seat in the forum or if the website is directed against specific interests of a state.

Insofar the legal assets of natives or of the state are affected, the jurisdictional basis is given by the passive personality principle or the protection of state sovereignty. Insofar one can also speak of the protective principle.[8] If, however, no targeted connection to a certain state or its citizens can be found, as is often the case with websites, the protective principle fails. In such a case one has to look for another objective domestic jurisdictional basis. Such a domestic link can be created by the language the website uses, the offered content or the market which is being targeted by the content. The mere accessibility of a website in a forum state is, however, generally considered not to be sufficient.[9] A similar conclusion has been reached by the *Bundesgerichtshof*, the Federal High Court of Justice, in the Töben case. There the *Bundesgerichtshof* states (own translation): "It can remain undecided whether the defendant could have acted within the state (Sec. 9 para 1, 1st alternative Criminal Code), if a domestic internet user had accessed the website on the Australian server and downloaded the file into German territory. However, the Senate would have doubts to see an action having its effects in the territory of the state in the defendant using the computer, proxy-servers, data cables and internet transmission software as a tool to physically "transport" the files into German territory. A transfer of the definition of an act (or action), developed in conjunction with the sending of a letter, onto acts of data transfer over the internet is rather not possible."

---

8 See *United States v. Yousef*, 327 F2d 56 , 2d Cir. 2003.

9 See Landgericht Düsseldorf (Beschl. v. 09.01.2008 - 12 O 393/02).

Online Surveillance within the framework of German Data Protection Law - License to infiltrate?

*by Tobias O. Keber**

I. Introduction

> "That the individual shall have full protection in person and in property is a principle as old as the common law; but it has been found necessary from time to time to define anew the exact nature and extent of such protection. Political, social, and economic changes entail the recognition of new rights, and the common law, in its eternal youth, grows to meet the demands of society.[1]

In their famous article published 1890 in the Harvard Law Review, Samuel D. Warren and Louis D. Brandeis gave birth to "The Right to Privacy". Written 120 years ago, the name patron of Johannes Gutenberg-University's partner law school and his law firm partner are still right. The second sentence of the initial quotation maybe just needs a little "updating" supplement: *technical* changes entail the recognition of new rights.

In spring 2008, the German Federal Constitutional Court (FCC) delivered a judgment regarding the online search of computers.[2] With that decision, the Court gave birth to a "new fundamental right".[3] The right to "the guarantee of the confidentiality and integrity of information technology systems" protects "IT systems which alone or in their technical networking may contain personal data of the person concerned to such a degree and in such diversity that access to the system facilitates insight into significant parts of that person's life[4] and arguably builds a fourth pillar of German constitutional Data Protection Law. The deci-

---

* Dr. iur. Tobias Keber is writing his second doctoral dissertation (Habilitation) at the Chair of Professor Udo Fink, Johannes Gutenberg-University Mainz. Dr. Keber visited the Louis Brandeis Law School in Louisville in 2007, 2009, 2010.

1 *Warren and Brandeis*, The Right To Privacy, Harvard Law Review, 4, 1890, 193.

2 FCC (BVerfG), 1 BvR 370/07, February 27th 2008, German text online available at: http://www.bverfg.de/entscheidungen/rs20080227_1bvr037007.html. Unofficial translation into English available at: http://legislationline.org/documents/action/popup/id/16133 (last visited August 2011).

3 More precisely, it is not a new fundamental right, but a new aspect of the general personality right. See *Hoffmann-Riem*, Der grundrechtliche Schutz der Vertraulichkeit und Integrität eigengenutzter informationstechnischer Systeme, JZ 2008, 1009 (1018).

4 FCC, (Fn. 2), recital 137 in the translated text (203 within the original German text).

sion gained positive and critical comments within the German scientific community[5] and international attention as well.[6]

II. Privacy and Data Protection Law in Germany

In order to understand the reasoning of the Court, a short introduction in German Data Protection Law is necessary. The legal framework consists of constitutional law, decisions of the FCC and statutory law.

1. Data Protection on the constitutional level

In the Basic Law (Grundgesetz, the German Constitution), Privacy and Data Protection as such are not specifically designated fundamental rights.[7] However,

5 For the discussion in Germany see: *Bär*, Verfassungsmäßigkeit der Online-Durchsuchung und anderer verdeckter Ermittlungsmaßnahmen in Datennetzen, MMR 2008, 315; *Böckenförde*, Auf dem Weg zur elektronischen Privatsphäre, JZ 2008, 925; *Buermeyer*, Die "Online-Durchsuchung". Technischer Hintergrund des verdeckten hoheitlichen Zugriffs auf Computersysteme, HRRS, 4/2007, 154; *Hirsch*, Das Grundrecht auf Gewährleistung der Vertraulichkeit und Integrität informationstechnischer Systeme, NJOZ 2008, 1907; *Hoeren*, Was ist das „Grundrecht auf Integrität und Vertraulichkeit informationstechnischer Systeme“?, MMR 2008, 365; *Hoffmann-Riem*, Der grundrechtliche Schutz der Vertraulichkeit und Integrität eigengenutzter informationstechnischer Systeme, JZ 2008, 1009. *Roßnagel/Schnabel*, Das Grundrecht auf Gewährleistung der Vertraulichkeit und Integrität informationstechnischer Systeme und sein Einfluss auf das Privatrecht, NJW 2008, 3534. *Sachs/Krings*, Das neue „Grundrecht auf Gewährleistung der Vertraulichkeit und Integrität informationstechnischer Systeme, JuS 2008, 481. For comments on the decision in English language, see *Hornung / Schnabel*, Data Protection in Germany II: Recent Decisions on Online-Searching of Computers, Automatic Number Plate Recognition and Data Retention, Computer Law & Security Review, Volume 25, Issue 2, 2009, 115; *Rösler*, The Secret Intrusion into IT Systems (“Online-Durchsuchung”), Osaka University Law Review, No 56 (2009), 55.

6 *Abel/Schafer*, The German Constitutional Court on the Right in Confidentiality and Integrity of Information Technology Systems, SCRIPTed 106, available at: http://www.law.ed.ac.uk/ahrc/script-ed/vol6-1/abel.asp ; De Hert /de Vries/Gutwirth, La limitation des “perquisitions en ligne” par un renouvellement des droit fondamentaux, Note d’observations sur Cour constitutionelle fédérale allemande, 27 février 2008 (Online Durchsuchung), Revue du droit des Technologies de l’Information, Jurisprudence, 2009, 89.

7 In that context, the Constitution of the Federal Republic of Germany differs from the constitutions of some Federal States. For example, the Constitution of Berlin (Art. 33),

certain aspects of these rights are protected by Article 10[8] and 13[9] of the Constitution.

According to the FCC, Article 10.1 guarantees "the free development of personality through the private exchange of messages, thoughts and opinions that are not addressed to the public. Article 10 thus preserves the dignity of thinking and liberally acting people".[10] Article 10 of the Basic law is not limited to the protection of the messages content but also applies to the circumstances of a telecommunication process that means data recording the beginning and the end of the process.[11] Restrictions in the sense of Article 10.2 are for example the G-10 Law[12] and certain provisions of the criminal procedure act.[13]

---

the Constitution of Bremen (Art. 12 para 3), Constitution of North Rhine-Westphalia (Art. 4 para 2), the Constitution for Rhineland-Palatinate (Article 4a) and the Constitution Saarland (Article 2) explicitly mention data protection. For an overview see *Gola/Schomerus*, in: Gola/Schomerus, BDSG Commentary, Introduction, No. 3.

8 Article 10 of the German Constitution states:
(1) The privacy of correspondence, posts and telecommunications shall be inviolable.
(2) Restrictions may be ordered only pursuant to a law. If the restriction serves to protect the free democratic basic order or the existence or security of the Federation or of a Land, the law may provide that the person affected shall not be informed of the restriction and that recourse to the courts shall be replaced by a review of the case by agencies and auxiliary agencies appointed by the legislature.

9 Article 13 reads (in excerpts):
(1) The home is inviolable.
(2) Searches may be authorized only by a judge or, when time is of the essence, by other authorities designated by the laws, and may be carried out only in the manner therein prescribed.
(3) If particular facts justify the suspicion that any person has committed an especially serious crime specifically defined by a law, technical means of acoustical surveillance of any home in which the suspect is supposedly staying may be employed pursuant to judicial order for the purpose of prosecuting the offence, provided that alternative methods of investigating the matter would be disproportionately difficult or unproductive. The authorisation shall be for a limited time. The order shall be issued by a panel composed of three judges. When time is of the essence, it may also be issued by a single judge.
(4) To avert acute dangers to public safety, especially dangers to life or to the public, technical means of surveillance of the home may be employed only pursuant to judicial order. When time is of the essence, such measures may also be ordered by other authorities designated by a law; a judicial decision shall subsequently be obtained without delay.

10 BVerfGE 67, 157 (171); 106, 28 (35); 110, 33 (53).

11 See the FCC decision of February, 3rd 2010 on data retention. BVerfG 1 BvR 256/08, 1 BvR 263/08, 1 BvR 586/08, MMR 2010, 356. The FCC made clear that certain provi-

Article 13, the second pillar of German Privacy and Data Protection Law, was substantiated by the FCC in a decision of 2004.[14] The legal background of this ruling was the implementation of electronic eavesdropping measures by the amendment of Article 13 of the German Constitution in 1998 and the ensuing modifications of the German Code of Criminal Procedure. The Court substantiated the relationship between the inviolability of the home and the admissibility of acoustic surveillance arguing that certain communications are protected by an absolute area of intimacy wherein citizens can communicate privately without fear of government surveillance.[15]

The third traditional constitutional basis for privacy and data protection is less explicit. However, it is the central cornerstone and was elaborated in the so-called census-judgment of the FCC in 1983.[16] The Court derived a fundamental "right to informational self-determination" (Recht auf informationelle Selbstbestimmung) from the more general right to personality (Allgemeines Persönlichkeitsrecht), enshrined in Article 2.1 and Article 1.1 of the Constitution.[17] The Court argued inter alia:

---

sions of the telecommunications act (rules implementing the European Data Retention Directive) did not meet the principle of proportionality. For a detailed discussion see *Hornung/Schnabel*, Data Protection in Germany II: Recent decisions on onlinesearching of computers, automatic number plate recognition and data retention, Computer Law & Security Review 2009, 115 (119).

12 The Article 10 Act (Artikel 10 Gesetz) allows warrantless automated wiretaps of international communications by the Intelligence Service (BND) for purposes of preventing terrorism and illegal trade in drugs and weapons.

13 For example, section 99 German Criminal Procedure Code (Strafprozessordnung) legitimizes the seizure of postal items and telegrams. Section 100a German Criminal Procedure Code sets out the conditions regarding the interception of telecommunications.

14 BVerfG 1 BvR 2378/98; 1 BvR 1084/99; English Text available at: http://www.utexas.edu/law/academics/centers/transnational/work_new/german/case.php?id=658.

15 For details see *Cohen*, Germany: The Electronic Eavesdropping Case, Int J Constitutional Law, October 2005, 3 (4), 680.

16 BVerfG 1 BvR 209, 269, 362, 420, 440, 484/83 = BVerfGE 65, 1 ff. = NJW 1984, 419. Instructive: *Simitis, Spiros*: Die informationelle Selbstbestimmung – Grundbedingungen einer verfassungskonformen Informationsordnung, NJW 1984, 394.

17 The Federal Constitutional Court had recognized such a general right of personality long before the population census decision. See BVerfGE 54, 148, 153; BVerfGE 27, 1, 6; 27, 344, 350; 32, 373, 379; 35, 202, 220; 44, 353, 372. The Federal Constitutional Court argued that the legal basis for this right is a combination of the protection of general personal liberty (Article 2.1) and the protection of human dignity (Article 1.1). According to the court, the general right of personality has several implementations, e.g.

> "Who cannot overlook which information related to him or her is known to certain segments of his social environment, and who is not able to assess to a certain degree the knowledge of his potential communication partners, can be essentially hindered in his capability to plan and to decide. The right of informational self-determination stands against a societal order and its underlying legal order in which citizens could not know any longer who what and when in what situations knows about them."[18]

The FCC in its decision also made clear that informational self-determination is not guaranteed without limits. Restrictions are permissible under certain, narrowly defined conditions. They must serve an overwhelming public interest and must comply with the requirement of norm-clarity.[19] The FCC applied these principles for Article 10 as well.[20]

2. Data Protection in Statutory Law

At the level of statutory law, the Federal Data Protection Act (Bundesdatenschutzgesetz, BDSG) regulates the general admissibility of data processing and the use of data. The Act covers the collection, processing and use of personal data by public federal authorities and state administrations (as long as there is no state regulation and insofar as they apply federal laws), and by private bodies, if they rely on data-processing systems or non-automated filing systems for commercial or professional use. The sixteen German States have their own specific data protection regulations that cover the public sector of the States administrations. Both at the level of Federal as well as State law, there is a vast number[21] of sector-specific data protection provisions taking precedence over the general rules.[22] Telecommunications-,[23] Telemedia-,[24] as well as unfair

---

the right to one's own image and word or the right to counterstatement. For details see *Jarass*, Das allgemeine Persönlichkeitsrecht im Grundgesetz, NJW 1989, 857.

18 BVerfGE 65, 1 ff. = NJW 1984, 419. For a discussion see *Hornung/Schnabel*, Data Protection in Germany I: The population census decision and the right to informational self-determination, Computer Law & Security Report, Vol. 25, Issue 1, 2009, 84.

19 BVerfGE 65, 1 ff. = NJW 1984, 419.

20 BVerfGE 100, 313 (359).

21 For an overview see *Weichert*, in: *Kilian/Heussen*, Computerrechts-Handbuch, Teil 13, recital 11.

22 See Section 1.3 of the Federal Data Protection Act. English Text of the Act available at: http://www.bfdi.bund.de/cln_111/EN/DataProtectionActs/DataProtectionActs_node.html

23 Sections 91 – 107 of the Telecommunications Act (TCA) refer to data protection. The scope of the telecommunication specific safeguards is described in section 91 TCA.

competition law[25] provides for special data protection. There is also a self-contained social security data protection law.[26]

III. FCC decision regarding "online searches"

In its landmark decision of February 27th 2008, the FCC recognized a fourth pillar of constitutionally-based data protection. The Court gave birth to the "constitutional right in the confidentiality and integrity of information technology systems".[27] The judges in Karlsruhe argued that for several reasons the existing rights canon was not sufficient to protect the constitutional rights of citizens from the potential loss of liberty that the secret remote searching of computers could cause.

1. Facts and presented arguments

On December 20th 2006, the Act on the Protection of the Constitution in North Rhine-Westphalia (Verfassungsschutzgesetz NRW) was amended.[28] Article 5.2

Section 95 TCA refers to the collection and use of inventory data. The collection and use of traffic data is set out in section 96 TCA and section 98 TCA addresses location data. Sections 101-107 TCA finally provide for special rules regarding subscriber protection.

24 The Telemedia Act (TMA) applies to all electronic information and communication services that neither are telecommunications services in the sense of the telecommunications act nor broadcasting in the sense of the Interstate Agreement on Broadcasting and Telemedia (sec. 1.1 TMA). English text of the TMA available at: http://www.cgerli.org/index.php?id=74&tx_vmdocumentsearch_pi2%5bdocID%5d=1438. The obligations of service providers and the legality of the collection and processing of certain data are laid down in Sections 11-15a TMA.

25 Section 7 of the German Unfair Competition Act (UCA) addresses certain direct marketing issues. Section 7.1 UCA states that a commercial practice unconscionably pestering a market participant shall be illegal. Section 7.2, no. 3 provides that such pestering shall always be assumed in the case if someone uses an automated calling machine, a fax machine or electronic mail without the addressee's prior express consent.

26 Sections 67–85a German Social Code (SGB) X; section 35 German Social Code (SGB) I.

27 BVerfG, 1 BvR 370/07, (Fn. 2).

28 Law and Oridinance Gazette of North Rhine-Westphalia, GVBl. NRW 2006, 620.

of this Act[29] defines permissible actions to acquire information and private data from suspects. The amendment in question (Article 5.2 No. 11) empowered the Constitution Protection Agency to carry out two types of investigative measures: the secret monitoring and the reconnaissance of the internet (alternative 1) and the secret access to information technology systems (alternative 2).

Secret access to an information technology system means a technical infiltration either through already existing security loopholes of the target system or through the secret installation of a specifically designed computer program (remote forensic software, RFS). Such a program shares crucial features with well-known malware, in particular viruses and Trojans.[30] The infiltration of the target system makes it possible to monitor its use, to view the storage media or to remotely control the target system.[31] In comparison to traditional investigation methods, the infiltration offers significant advantages. The access is secret, so the person concerned is not forewarned for the future.[32] If the user stores data in encrypted form, an "online search" enables investigators to access this data in unencrypted form.[33] The fact that encrypted data may be accessed is also very important in the case of internet based speech telephony.[34] A further advantage of the infiltration is that volatile data such as passwords and other information on the usage pattern of the person concerned can be collected.[35]

Against this background, a journalist predominantly publishing online, an active member of the political party "DIE LINKE"[36] and two attorneys[37] filed a constitutional complaint (Verfassungsbeschwerde) arguing that legitimizing investigators to secretly capture data from information-technology systems was a

29 The Act is the legal basis for operations by the Constitution Protection Agency, North Rhine-Westphalia's secret service for internal affairs.

30 *U. Buermeyer*, "Die 'Online-Durchsuchung' – Technischer Hintergrund des verdeckten hoheitlichen Zugriffsauf Computersysteme", Höchstrichterliche Rechtsprechung im Strafrecht 4, 2007, 154.

31 BVerfG, 1 BvR 370/07, recital no. 5 (translation and original text).

32 A traditional house search would have to be carried out openly.

33 BVerfG, 1 BvR 370/07, recital no. 11 (translation and original text).

34 For example Skype, a software application that allows users to make voice and video calls and chats over the Internet, encrypts every user initiated communication process. It therefore can only be monitored at the terminal (target system).

35 BVerfG, 1 BvR 370/07, recital no. 11 (translation and original text).

36 DIE LINKE is being observed by the North Rhine-Westphalian constitution protection authority.

37 The attorneys assisted asylum-seekers potentially under observation by the North Rhine-Westphalian constitution protection authority.

violation of Article 2.1 in conjunction with Article 1.1, Article 10.1 and Article 13.1 of the Basic Law.

The Government of North Rhine-Westphalia as the Respondent accepted that strict constitutional scrutiny of the new measure was necessary. The Land identified primarily the constitutional right guaranteeing the privacy of telecommunications in Article 10.1 Basic Law as the applicable law.[38] The Federal Government (not involved directly in the case but anticipating a similar issue arising in the future for the federal agencies) argued that such investigative measures would be covered by the fundamental guarantee to the inviolability of the home (Article 13 Basic Law), seeing the online search as the equivalent to the physical search of a suspect's home.[39] After all, the Land and the Federal Government both conceded that the remote online search affected certain fundamental rights but also agreed that the measure may be justified.

2. FCC′s line of reasoning

The Court declared § 5.2 no. 11, second alternative of the North Rhine-Westphalia Constitution Protection Act as unconstitutional and therefore null and void.[40] The judges argued that the mentioned provision violated the general right of personality (Article 2.1 in conjunction with Article 1.1 of the Basic Law) in its particular manifestation as a fundamental right to the confidentiality and integrity of information technology systems.[41] The Court further made clear that this new manifestation of the general right of personality had a loophole closing function and hence was subsidiary to the guarantees of Article 10, 13 and the right to informational self-determination.[42]

38 BVerfG, 1 BvR 370/07, recital no. 68 in the translated text (134 within the original German text).

39 BVerfG, 1 BvR 370/07, recital no. 65 in the translated text (131 within the original German text).

40 BVerfG, 1 BvR 370/07, recital no. 99 in the translated text (165 within the original German text).

41 BVerfG, 1 BvR 370/07, recital no. 100 in the translated text (166 within the original German text).

42 BVerfG, 1 BvR 370/07, recital no. 101 in the translated text (167 within the original German text).

a) Article 10.1 Basic Law – The Secrecy of Telecommunications

Analyzing Article 10.1 Basic Law, the Court recited established case law and reiterated that the guarantee of the secrecy of telecommunication protects the non-physical transmission of information to individual recipients with the aid of telecommunications devices[43] regardless of the method of transmission and the form of expression[44] and therefore also covers communication services of the internet. Accordingly, state measures by means of which the contents and circumstances of the ongoing telecommunication are collected in the computer network, or the data related thereto is evaluated have to be measured against Article 10.1 Basic Law the Court argued.[45]

The Court also made clear that Article 10.1 does not apply if a state agency monitors the use of an information technology system as such or if telecommunication data stored on such devices is collected after the communication process is completed.[46] Analyzing the problem of "source telecommunication surveillance",[47] the Court first conceded that the secret infiltration of a complex information technology system – even if this is done in order to "just" perform telecommunication surveillance - offers the opportunity to spy on the system as a whole.[48] The Court underlined that in contradiction to what is usually the case with traditional network-based telecommunication surveillance – there is always a risk for the person concerned that further personal information (over and above the contents and circumstances of telecommunication) is collected.[49]

Having established these premises, the Court then argued that Article 10.1 is the sole fundamental right-related standard for the source telecommunication surveillance if the surveillance is restricted exclusively to data emanating from

---

43 See e.g. BVerfGE 67, 157 (172); 106, 28 (35).

44 Regarding e-mail, the court recited BVerfGE 113, 348 (383).

45 BVerfG, 1 BvR 370/07, recital no. 118 in the translated text (184 within the original German text).

46 BVerfG, 1 BvR 370/07, recital nos. 119, 120 in the translated text (185, 186 within the original German text).

47 See Fn. 34.

48 BVerfG, 1 BvR 370/07, recital no. 122 in the translated text (188 within the original German text): "The endangerment thereby brought about goes far beyond what is entailed by the mere surveillance of ongoing telecommunication. In particular, the data stored on personal computers which does not relate to the use of the system for telecommunication can also be obtained."

49 BVerfG, 1 BvR 370/07, recital no. 123 in the translated text (189 within the original German text).

an ongoing process. This must be ensured by technical precautions and legal instructions, the Court pointed out.[50]

b) Article 13.1 Basic Law – The Inviolability of the Home

Regarding Article 13.1, the Court reaffirmed that this fundamental right protects the spatial sphere in which private life takes place.[51] The fundamental right protects this space from physical intrusion, as well as from the use of technical measures. Such measures are the acoustic and optical surveillance of a living space[52] or the measurement of electromagnetic radiation to monitor the use of information technology systems inside the dwelling. The Court made clear that Article 13.1 can provide protection of the private living space against the secret intrusion by police or secret service to physically manipulate information technology systems, and against the infiltration of such systems to monitor the events in a flat using peripherals connected to the system. Hence, Article 13.1 is applicable if system immanent microphones are used for eavesdropping.[53]

But the Court also stated that Article 13 is insufficient to protect the user against the general infiltration of information technology systems using remote forensic software, e.g. a Trojan. According to the court, one specific problem created by RFS searches is that infiltration and monitoring can be performed regardless of where the information technology system is located. A location-dependent protection fails if the system is located outside the private space or on the move between "protected" areas. Especially small information technology devices like personal digital assistants (PDAs), mobile (smart-) phones and laptops, are designed to be carried around.[54]

50 BVerfG, 1 BvR 370/07, recital no. 124 in the translated text (190 within the original German text). However, this is technically still impossible to ensure. For this problem see Keber, Jüngste Änderungen des Hessischen Gesetzes über die Öffentliche Sicherheit und Ordnung im Lichte verfassungsgerichtlicher Entscheidungen, Die Polizei, 2006 (6), 167 (170).

51 BVerfG, 1 BvR 370/07, recital no. 126 in the translated text (192 within the original German text).The private living space is not limited to the private flat or house of the rights holder, but also includes business and office space, BVerfGE 32, 54 (69); 44, 353 (371); 76, 83 (88); 96, 44 (51).

52 BVerfGE 109, 279 (309, 327).

53 BVerfG, 1 BvR 370/07, recital no. 127 in the translated text (193 within the original German text).

54 BVerfG, 1 BvR 370/07, recital no. 128 in the translated text (194 within the original German text).

c) Article 2.1 in Conjunction with article 1.1 Basic Law – The Right to Informational Self-Determination

Having rejected as insufficient both Article 10 and Article 13, the Court further stated that neither of the two manifestations of the general right of personality enshrined in Article 2.1 in conjunction with 1.1 German Constitution (protection of privacy and the right to informational self-determination) do comply sufficiently with the special need for protection of the user of information technology systems.[55]

According to the Court´s reasoning, especially the right to informational self-determination (that goes beyond the protection of privacy) does not fully consider elements of personality endangerments which emerge from the mere fact that the individual relies on the use of information technology systems for his or her personality development. In its severity for the personality of the person concerned, the access to a whole information technology system with a huge amount of personal data goes far beyond individual data collections against which the right to informational self-determination provides protection.[56]

3. The Right in the Confidentiality and Integrity of Information Technology Systems

Having concluded that existing rights are not sufficient to protect citizens from the threat against their personality rights, the Court established a new facet of the general right of personality to close the gap. The right in the confidentiality and integrity of information technology systems protects, so the Court, the personal and private life of rights holders from the state accessing information technology devices, and in particular against access by the state of the information technology system as a whole.[57]

---

55 BVerfG, 1 BvR 370/07, recital no. 130 in the translated text (196 within the original German text).

56 BVerfG, 1 BvR 370/07, recital no. 133, 134 in the translated text (199, 200 within the original German text).

57 BVerfG, 1 BvR 370/07, recital no. 135 in the translated text (201 within the original German text).

a) Protective Scope - Information Technology System

Systems which alone, or in their technical interconnectedness, can contain personal data of the person concerned are potentially protected. The crucial question is whether access to the system facilitates insight into significant parts of the life of a person or indeed provides a revealing picture of their personality.[58] As the Court makes clear, this would not be the case for intelligent housing technology systems (only data with a partial connection to a certain area of life) but would for personal computers and smartphones.[59] The degree of difficulty in accessing the system is irrelevant. However, a protection only exists if the person concerned considers the system his own, and thus may presume that he alone or others authorized by him, use it in a self-determined manner.[60]

b) Restrictions

The court finally stated that the right in the confidentiality and integrity of information technology systems is not absolute. It can be restricted for both preventive purposes and to prosecute crimes. Infiltration measures must be based on a statutory foundation that is constitutional. Inter alia, that means that the relevant norms must meet the principle of clarity and determinedness of provisions.[61] Regarding the measure mentioned in § 5.2 no. 11 sentence 1 alternative 2 North Rhine-Westphalia Constitution Protection Act, the Court argued that neither the principle of determinedness nor the principle of clarity were met.[62]

The Court also found that the provision did not comply with the principle of proportionality. Even if the norm did serve a legitimate purpose (to ensure an effective fight against terrorism),[63] the secret access to information technology

58 BVerfG, 1 BvR 370/07, recital no. 136 in the translated text (202 within the original German text).

59 BVerfG, 1 BvR 370/07, recital no. 136, 137. In that context, the Court also points out that the mere ability of the system to store personal data is sufficient. It does not matter if the system does not actually contain sensitive personal data.

60 BVerfG, 1 BvR 370/07, recital no. 140 in the translated text (206 within the original German text).

61 BVerfG, 1 BvR 370/07, recital no. 141 in the translated text (207 within the original German text).

62 Essentially that was because of the complex legislative referrals technique used in the provisions. BVerfG, 1 BvR 370/07, recital no. 146 in the translated text (212 within the original German text).

63 BVerfG, 1 BvR 370/07, recital no. 153 in the translated text (214 within the original German text).

systems appeared as suitable to serve this purpose[64] and did not violate the principle of necessity,[65] § 5.2 no. 11 sentence 1 alternative 2 did not comply with the principle of appropriateness in the narrower sense.[66]

Because of the intensity[67] of encroachments through one-off, partial access[68] and a fortiori through longer-term surveillance,[69] a measure restricting the right would only be proportionate where there is sufficient evidence for a concrete danger for significant higher-ranking fundamental values. Higher-ranking fundamental values are the life and integrity of other citizens, the foundations of the state, and essential values of humanity.[70]

Furthermore, effective procedural safeguard regulations would be essential. Any such measure had to be scrutinized and confirmed by a judge on a case-by-case basis to guarantee an objective and independent control prior to the execution.[71] According to the judges in Karlsruhe, a final requirement (not met by § 5.2 no. 11 sentence 1 alternative 2) is the need for statutory precautions to avoid encroachments on the absolutely protected core area of private life. This core area emerges from Article 1.1 of the Basic Law (human dignity). In that context, the Court elaborated a "two-tier protection concept".[72] The statutory provision must endeavor to ensure that collection of data that is relevant to the core area is avoided as far as possible (tier 1). Since it will often be very difficult to differentiate between core area and non-core area data during the investigation process, adequate procedures regarding the examination stage of the data are essential. If

64 BVerfG, 1 BvR 370/07, recital no. 155 in the translated text (216 within the original German text).

65 BVerfG, 1 BvR 370/07, recital no. 158 in the translated text (219 within the original German text).

66 BVerfG, 1 BvR 370/07, recital no. 160 in the translated text (221 within the original German text).

67 High intensity follows from the fact that access is secret, accessible data are comprehensive, threat for the integrity of the target system and potential involvement of third parties.

68 BVerfG, 1 BvR 370/07, recital no. 164 in the translated text (230 within the original German text).

69 BVerfG, 1 BvR 370/07, recital no. 168 in the translated text (234 within the original German text).

70 BVerfG, 1 BvR 370/07, recital no. 176 in the translated text (242 within the original German text).

71 BVerfG, 1 BvR 370/07, recital no. 192 in the translated text (258 within the original German text).

72 BVerfG, 1 BvR 370/07, recital no. 214 in the translated text (280 within the original German text).

core area data is detected, this data has to be deleted immediately and the use of this data by the state is prohibited (tier 2).[73]

III. Further developments – the Federal Police Act

Shortly after the Decision of the Federal Constitutional Court, the German Federal Police Act (Bundeskriminalamtgesetz) was revised.[74] According to section 20k of the amended Act, the remote search of personal hard drives is possible, if concrete facts support the supposition that there is a threat to life, physical integrity or freedom of a person or a threat to the basis or the existence of states or people. The amended law that (according to the reasons given for the law) was drafted in line with the reasoning of the FCC[75] further states that such online searches are inadmissible if it is suspected that only data relevant to someone's personal life would be collected in such a "cyber patrol". As this is a rather unlikely scenario, the new law has again been challenged with a constitutional complaint. The plaintiffs argue that the new law mixes up principle and exception. A further criticism is that the technical side of such searches or the placing of Trojan horses is not defined at all in the law, leaving a high risk of nonsuspects being affected by this extraordinary invasion of privacy. The case before the FCC is still pending.[76]

IV. Conclusion

In the online search decision, the FCC established that remote online search of computers is not generally unconstitutional. But the Court made also very clear that legislation allowing this will have to be in strict compliance with the right in the confidentiality and integrity of information technology system. The Court has established very high procedural hurdles for the use of this technology. In the light of these narrow guidelines it is questionable whether this investigation

73 BVerfG, 1 BvR 370/07, recital no. 216 in the translated text (282 within the original German text).

74 Gesetz zur Abwehr von Gefahren des internationalen Terrorismus durch das Bundeskriminalamt, Law of December, 25th 2008, Federal Law Gazette (BGBl.) I, 3083.

75 Parliamentary printing matter (BT-Drucks.) 16/9588, 26.

76 1 BvR 966/09, 1 BvR 1140/09. „Verfassungsbeschwerden gegen Bestimmungen des Bundeskriminal-amtgesetzes (BKAG) in der Fassung vom 31. Dezember 2008 (BGBl I S. 3083), mit denen dem Bundeskriminalamt Befugnisse zur Abwehr von Gefahren des internationalen Terrorismus eingeräumt werden“.

instrument will have any practical significance in the future.[77] Section 20k Federal Police Act is under constitutional review and it is doubtful whether the FCC will consider it constitutional especially as the law does not give any guidelines concerning the infiltration process.

The FCC decision regarding online searches is very important as far as it underlines the fact that the German constitution (and the FCC as the authentic interpreter) is generally capable to handle the challenge of the Digital Age.[78] In that sense and in the words of Brandeis, the Basic law is blessed with "eternal youth" as well. On the other hand, the decision raises numerous questions which have to be addressed in the future. The Court did not conclusively clarify the question of what exactly is an information technology system. Is it also the individual presence on Facebook? What are the implications of the Right in the Confidentiality and Integrity of Information Technology Systems for cloud computing? What does it mean that the person concerned has to consider the system his own – is it ownership and / or possession as defined in civil law or something completely different? Finally, the two-tier protection concept is subject to the dilemma that the requirement to delete the collected core area data cannot undo the violation of the absolute right to human dignity.

Against this background, one may safely argue that the fourth pillar of German constitutionally-based data protection law is still under construction.

---

77 According to an official statement of the interior ministry, there were no online searches in 2009. Recently, there was an inquiry of some members of the Bundestag addressed to the Federal Government asking if there were cases in 2010 and 2011. The answer was denied due to secrecy reasons. BT-Drucksache 17/6079, available at http://dip.bundestag.de/btd/17/060/1706079.pdf.

78 In this regard see *Baer*, Braucht das Grundgesetz ein Update? Demokratie im Internetzeitalter, Blätter für deutsche und internationale Politik 1 (2011), 90.

Federal States and International Law

*by Walter Rudolf**

I. Introduction

The exchange of visiting professors between the Law School of the University of Louisville and the Law Faculty of the University of Mainz started 20 years ago with lectures of Prof. Eckart Klein. I was the second professor coming to Louisville. There I was cordially welcomed above all by Prof. Russell Weaver who put me up in his house and by the dean and other members of the faculty. The dean asked me to attend the next session of the faculty. My impression was that there were no significant differences between a faculty's meeting in Louisville or in Mainz. It took only a short time until I felt an integer part of the faculty. Moreover, I had the opportunity to discuss with the vice-chancellor of the UoL and municipal authorities. My idea to give lessons on the adoption of international law in federal States, especially the United States and the Federal Republic of Germany, was quite adequate because the students were interested in a comparison of the different systems of the two States. Even some colleagues and the dean occasionally attended the lectures.

II. Manifestations of Federal States

Comparison in the field of federations is programmatic because any of the existing nineteen federal States is unique.[1] There are multifarious manifestations of federal States. The first modern federation was established by the US constitution in 1787, followed by Switzerland in 1848, Canada and the North German federation in 1867 and the German Reich in 1871. Since then several new federal States were built in South America, Australia, Europe, Asia, Africa and the Pacific.

In a unitary State all State power, of course, emanates from the unitary State, for example, all the constitutions of France since 1791 had referred to the State

---

* Professor Emeritus. Walter Rudolf held the chair for Public Law, European and International Law at the Johannes Gutenberg-University from 1971-1999.

1 This script is mainly based on my article "Federal States" in the Encyclopedia of Public International Law, 10/29/2008, epil/entries/law-97800199231690.

as being "one and indivisible". Nevertheless, for some decades there has been a tendency towards regionalization in several unitary States in Western Europe, the purpose of which has not only been to devolve functions from central to regional and local authorities but also to de-concentrate competences from the State to self-governing bodies. This tendency is no special modern modification of federalism: Self-government of regional or local authorities is a matter of de-concentration, not of federalization. The crucial issue is the legal qualification of the member units as States. Unlike a federal State, a regionalized State is not composed of territories possessing the quality of States. The units remain dependent on the unitary State. The statute of autonomy of autonomous regions is issued and modified by the unitary State, while member States of a federal State possess the power to enact and amend their own constitution, of course, in the framework of the federal constitution. In respect of the application of international treaties to the municipal legal order, problems analogous to the case with federations may occur in States which have delegated powers to autonomous territories. Therefore, it is more helpful to look at the actual distribution of powers than to overemphasize the mere classification of a State as federal, regional or unitary with autonomous territories.

III. Crucial Elements of a State

The crucial elements of a State are territory, people and territorial sovereignty. In a federation these elements are divided between the federal State and the member States. The territory of a federal State is composed of the territories of the member States and, in some federations, of federal territory not belonging to a member State. Examples of federal States solely composed of the member States' territories are, eg Austria, the Federal Republic of Germany and Switzerland. In some federal States, parts of a country, especially the federation's capital, possess the status of federal territories not constituting a territorial entity with the same competences of a member State, as eg Washington D.C. is not represented in the US senate. Federal territories with a minor legal position are Puerto Rico and the Northern Mariana Islands and the US Virgin Islands, American Samoa and Guam. Such legal status normally, but not necessarily, applies only to the territory's competences and not to the civil status of its citizens and their rights regarding their legal position in the federation.

Sovereignty over the internal waters and the territorial Sea is divided between the federation and the affected member States. According to *United States v California* (United States Supreme Court [23 June1947] 332 US 19), a marginal belt had been created purely as an attribute of federal sovereignty. But the United States Submerged Lands Act 1953 granted States title and ownership of all lands underlying navigable waters within their boundaries, which in no event extended beyond three nautical miles from the coastline. Sovereign rights for the purpose of exploring the continental shelf and exploiting its natural resources as well as rights, jurisdiction and duties of the coastal State in the exclusive economic zone may be divided between the federation and the member States. In the Federal Republic of Germany the legislative power on the offshore maritime zones beyond the basis line is federal, while administration mainly is with the States. The US claims exclusive sovereign rights over the continental shelf and the exclusive economic zone while the member States being excluded from these maritime areas.

In most federations the member States are the fixed result of a historical development and cannot be abolished by the federation without the consent of the member States. Likewise, the formation of new member States and the alteration of areas and boundaries of existing member States are generally not possible without the consent of the affected States. However, in some federal States the reorganization of territory can be introduced merely by federal laws without the decisive participation of the States concerned. The German Constitution provides for the decision as to the preservation of each member State and establishment of new States to be reserved to the legislative branch of the federation. Moreover, Art. 29 of the Constitution stipulates that confirmation by referendum in the States thus affected is necessary, while the States themselves are only to be consulted. Such a provision manifests a dynamic federal State which does not render permanent the present territorial division but leaves room for further developments. Several adjourning States modified their frontiers by treaty with the neighbouring States. In Germany we had only one unification of three member States in 1951, while the establishment of new member States formed by separation from existing member States did not happen at all. We had this situation in the US when Vermont separated from New York, Kentucky from Virginia, Tennessee from North Carolina, Maine from Massachusetts, West Virginia from Virginia.

Citizens of a federal State hold the citizenship of the federation. In the German Reich of 1871 federal citizenship based on the member States' citizenship. In the Federal Republic no rules on member States' citizenship exist except Art. 6-8 of the Bavarian Constitution. But no legal consequences emerged from it. With regard to international law the point of reference is, without exception, the individual's federal citizenship. Consequently, German and US citizens enjoy diplomatic protection and assistance by the consuls and diplomats of the respective federation when abroad.

IV. Allocation of Competences

The allocation of competences to the federation and to the member States varies considerably in the US and Germany. Generally, the legislative competences are separated between the federation and the member States. In the United States each side is strictly limited to its own sphere of legislation, administration and adjudication without any institutionalized co-operation. When the federation is legislatively competent in a public function it is necessarily also competent for the execution and jurisdiction in this field with the consequence that federal administrative agencies and courts must also be established on a lower level. In Germany the competences of the federation and of the member States gear into each other. In areas of exclusive legislation only the federation has legislative jurisdiction. Areas of concurrent legislation are under the competence of the Member States as long as and to the extent that the federation has not exercised its legislative powers. In all other areas the legislative power is incumbent on the member States. The powers of both sides are harmonized in such a way that the member States become primarily responsible for administering not only their own but also the federal laws and collect both their own taxes and those of the federation. The federal administration is confined to matters of national importance, eg foreign service, border control, customs administration. As for jurisdiction, federal courts are competent only as supreme courts of last resort. For the majority of law suits under federal and member States' law the courts of the member States are competent also as appellate courts and in most cases courts of last resort. In the legislative process and administration of the federation and in matters concerning the European Union the States participate through the Bundesrat (Federal Council). The Bundesrat consists of members of the States' governments which appoint and recalls them. Each State shall have at least three votes. States with more than two million inhabitants have four, States with more than six million inhabitants five and States with more than seven million inhabitants six votes. The votes of each State may be cast only as a block vote and only by members present. Apart from this, member States' participation instruments of co-operative federalism have been developed. The co-operation between member States on the one hand, and between the federation and member States on the other, is not only indispensable for negotiating treaties between them but seems to be necessary also for preparing decisions to be taken by either an organ of the federation or a member State. In reality, the federation and the member States are dependent on each other.

The functioning of federalism is dependent above all on a well-balanced and continually updated distribution of financial resources. Generally, a federation with a flexible financial and fiscal policy is more stable than a federal State with an unalterable system of tax allocation or with a financial structure to the disadvantage of one side.

V. Conduct of Foreign Relations

The conduct of foreign relations is a proper function of the federation and a necessary concomitant of nationality *(United States v. Curtiss-Wright Export Corporation),* 299 U.S. 304. (1936)). From the point of view of international law there is generally no difference between a federal and a unitary State because both are subjects of international law with equal rights and duties under such law. Consequently, in most federal States the units have no competence at all regarding foreign affairs and thus no power to conclude treaties with foreign countries, to exchange diplomats and consuls or to join international organizations. In these cases international relations are exclusively reserved for the federation to the total exclusion of all member States.

Notwithstanding the usual assignment of competence for foreign relations to the federation the constitutions of the US (Art. 1(c)(3)) and the Federal Republic of Germany (Art. 32 (3)) provide for the right of their respective member States to enter into relations with foreign States. The German member States of the federation insofar as they have power to legislate they may, with the consent of the federal Government, conclude treaties with other countries. However, their recognition as subjects of international law is solely a question of the international legal order, which can only be answered by the international community. Because of the heterogeneity of the presently existing federal States and the variety in the allocation of powers to their member States, a general rule of international law on treaty-making competences of member States does not exist. Attempts by the International Law Commission and by the International Law Association codifying a general norm have failed. However, in accordance with the prevailing opinion there is no doubt that, as far as the federal Constitution permits, member States of a federation can enter into international relations with foreign powers. As soon as a foreign State enters into such relations with a member State the latter is, at least partially, recognized as a subject of international law. However, a foreign State may only enter international relations with the member State if the federation's constitution so allows or special approval is provided. Obligations and rights governed by international law can only be established for member States with the consent of the federation. If there is no federal consent, a foreign State's relations with member States constitute an unauthorized intervention in the affairs of the federation. Recognition of the member State of a federation as an international treaty partner is a special case in which international law defers to the municipal laws of a State.

If an organ or an authority of a member State violates international law the federation as subject of international law is liable, except in the cases where a treaty contains a federal clause stipulating that member States shall be exempted from the application of the treaty. Therefore, the federation is liable for all wrongful acts according to international law committed by member States' authorities *(La-Grand Case (Germany v. U.S.A.,27.6.2001, I.C.J. Reports 2001, p. 466)*. It normally makes no difference as to whether the violation has been caused by an authority of the federation. Only when an obligation based on a member State's treaty with a foreign power is violated does the member State become responsible.

According to the German constitution the competence of the member States to conclude treaties is linked to the power to legislate. The States may conclude treaties in the field in which legislation is exclusively reserved to them and also in such matters of concurrent legislation which have as yet not been settled by the federation, though in this field the room for action is rather limited, since the federation has almost exhausted its concurrent competences. The question as to whether States may also conclude agreements on matters falling not under federal legislative competence but under State executive competence is disputed. Since the States execute federal laws essentially as affairs of their own (Art. 83 German constitution) it has been argued that the States are authorized to conclude agreements on all subjects falling under their administration. This view, however, is not endorsed in the texts of the constitution. On matters which concern federal legislation, the States are not entitled to conclude any administrative agreements with foreign countries, nor are they authorized to do so in the case of concurrent competence, if the federation has made use of its legislative competence. The administrative practice, too, seems exclusively to follow legislative but not the administrative competence in these cases.

VI. International Treaties

The parties to international treaties with member States of federal States are, first of all, foreign States or member States of other federal States. They may also be other entities recognized as subjects of international law. In respect of treaties it is irrelevant whether these foreign partners are full subjects of international law or mere entities which are authorized to conclude treaties under their federal constitutions. The prerequisite for the right of the member States to conclude treaties with foreign partners, however, is the recognition as subjects of international law by the federation. It would be contrary to the principle of political homogeneity inherent in the federal State, if a member State were to recognize a foreign country as a subject of international law whilst the federation itself refuses this recognition. In addition to concluding treaties with foreign States the member States of the German Federal Republic should be permitted to join non-political international organizations. The States can, within their legal competence, become parties to treaties providing for the establishment of international commissions, such as, for instance, the International Commission for the Environmental Protection of Lake Constance. In addition, objections are not likely to be raised when a member State participates in international arbitration aimed at the settlement of the dispute resulting from a treaty of which it is a party.

Since member States of federations have no foreign service at their disposal, they may either appoint ad hoc delegates or make use of the federal diplomatic service when negotiating international treaties. During negotiations, such representatives possess diplomatic immunity abroad. If the foreign partner makes use of his diplomatic representatives at the federal level, the latter will require specific authority with regard to concluding treaties with a member State. The competent organ for the conclusion of treaties between member States and foreign partners is either the head of government or a minister, the government plenary of the member State or an organ of the federation, usually the Head of State, or the competent authority according to the federal Constitution. The rights of the member States to conclude international treaties is subject to federal consent, which in the Federal Republic of Germany must be given by the federal government. In its decision whether or not to consent, the government exercises preventive federal supervision in order to avoid a conflict between a member State's treaty and federal interests. Federal consent thus always means *nihil obstat* with regard to federal interests and is a prerequisite for the internal effectiveness of a treaty. Such consent must be obtained before the conclusion of a treaty, invariably requires a cabinet decision, and must be addressed to the member State and not to the foreign power. Moreover, federal consent is a prerequisite for legal effectiveness in international law because the Member States of a federation are given the opportunity to conclude treaties only through and within the framework of the federal Constitution.

VII. Treaty-making Competence of the States in Germany

In Germany there is disagreement as to whether the member States are solely competent to conclude treaties in fields where legislative competences are exclusively reserved for them or whether the federation also possesses treaty-making powers in these areas. From the federal point of view, the treaty-making power of the States does not limit that of the federation. This is exemplified by the German Constitution, according to which relations with foreign States shall be conducted by the federation (Art. 32 (1)), thus the treaty-making competence of the States (Art. 32 (3)) is only an exception to this general principle and does not confine the federation only to treaties on matters over which it has power to legislate. The Constitution provides that a member State must be consulted in sufficient time before the conclusion of a treaty 'affecting the special circumstances of a State' (Art. 32 (2)). Practice largely follows the opinion which favours the federation since, in many cases regulated by treaty, the legislative competences of the federation and the States are more or less indissolubly mixed. It is mainly for practical reasons that the idea of an exclusive allocation of treaty-making power to the member States in matters affecting State legislation has been rejected. Therefore some of the member States have shared this opinion although the majority have refused to accept it. From the latter point of view, there is no reason to deviate from the internal allocation of competences regarding the conclusion of treaties with foreign States. Under the Constitution, the federation cannot be placed in the position of executing treaty obligations on matters within the legislative competence of the member States which would result in creating ineffective treaties.

In order to overcome the difficulties arising from the conflicting opinions of the federation and the majority of the States, both sides have agreed on a feasible *modus vivendi* while retaining their diverging legal points of view. In the Lindauer Abkommen ('Lindau Agreement') of 14 November 1957 (ZaöRV [1959–60] 116 note 102) the Federal Foreign Office and the heads of the State chancelleries agreed that the States would make some concessions under certain clauses of the German Constitution so as to cede to the federation full competence for consular treaties, trade and navigation agreements, treaties of settlement and residence, trade and payments agreements, and treaties providing for the accession to or the establishment of international organizations. The federation was authorized to conclude treaties on matters under the exclusive legislative competence of the States, especially cultural agreements, provided it previously obtained the consent of all member States. Regarding treaties affecting essential interests of the States, whether they concern State legislative power or not, the federation was obliged to inform the States in advance in order to enable them to express their demands in time.

In accordance with the Lindau Agreement, a Permanent Treaty Commission of the States has been established as the Foreign Office's interlocutor. Every member State is represented in this Permanent Treaty Commission by the head or an officer of its permanent mission at Berlin. The Permanent Treaty Commission seeks to co-ordinate the States' policies and to reach accordance with the federation through discussion with the Foreign Office. Cultural agreements are also treated in the Permanent Conference of the State Ministers for Education and Cultural Matters in the Federal Republic. Though in political practice this procedure of participation of the States is fairly time-consuming, it grants the State governments the right to participate in the performance of treaties as far as the legislative competence of the States or their essential interests are concerned. The competence of the State governments in the Federal Council concerning the legislative procedure for federal laws governing the conclusion of treaties, are not thereby affected.

This method of reaching an agreement at governmental level is not entirely unobjectionable from a constitutional point of view. An interpretation agreement may, perhaps, be of some help for the executive, but it cannot bridge the lack of treaty competence of the federation. There is no doubt that the member States were not authorized to delegate to the federation their competences in some areas within their legislative power. Therefore there is a consensus that the Lindau Agreement does not legally obligate the federation and the States but is only a *gentlemen's agreement* which sufficiently solves the questions which arise in practice.

VIII. Transformation of Treaty Obligations into National Law

The adoption or transformation of treaty obligations into national law on matters under the legislative competence of the member States does not seem to cause serious problems in most of the current federal States. In the United States the decision of the US Supreme Court in *Missouri v. Holland* (252 U.S. 416 (1920)) established that treaties made by the federation, irrespective of whether they affect matters of federal or State legislation, can in any case be implemented internally by US federal authorities. Nevertheless, the problem as to whether the States are bound by treaties and the treaty implementing laws of the federation or whether they may legislate contrary to existing federal norms has not been satisfactorily solved. It may happen that, for instance, regulations of a State on environmental protection are issued contrary to rules of a treaty concluded by the union. In the Federal Republic according to the German Federal Constitutional Court (BVerfGE 6, 309, 353-54), there is no enforceable right of the federation towards the States with regard to their passing the necessary implementing legislation. The federation cannot order the States to provide for necessary legal norms in the States' own sphere of competence. Federal treaty-making power on matters under the legislative competence of the States is virtually a meaningless right unless the States co-operate with the federation. Even non-self-executing treaties made by the federation affecting matters within State legislative competence may remain unimplemented if the federation does not have special organs or agencies for this purpose at its disposal and the States do not co-operate in the execution of such treaties. Thus, the federation is not able to infringe upon the constitutional division of competences by way of a treaty with a foreign power. On the other hand, it is unobjectionable for the federation to enter into an obligation within its competence, to seek to influence the States or to suggest that they adopt certain legislative measures by way of implementation. The federation is also authorized to conclude treaties containing a federal clause, such as Art. 18 (7) of the Constitution of the International Labour Organization (ILO) or Art. 34 UNESCO Convention for the Protection of the World Cultural and Natural Heritage 1972, since no obligations which might be impossible to fulfil are entered into in this respect.

In actual State practice in the Federal Republic the legal difficulties are overcome by the Lindau Agreement. Under its provisions the States do not only agree that the federation may negotiate and sign a treaty in areas of their legislative competence, but also give their consent to ratification, partly in advance. In accordance with the federation, the States accept the tacit obligation, if necessary, to take all measures for the treaty's internal implementation. As early as the 1960s three south German States adopted the practice of obtaining parliamentary consent by law or resolution (*Beschluss*) in their States for federal treaties affecting matters within their sphere of legislative competence. The other States have followed this practice since the 1970s.

Treaties concluded by the States relating to matters within their legislative competence require the consent of the State parliament in accordance with the respective State's constitution, either in the form of a law or by resolution, as internally required. If there is any change in the allocation of competences the treaties concluded by the States remain valid. When the federation makes use of its concurrent legislative authority with regard to a matter on which a State has previously concluded a treaty with a foreign State, the continued validity of the treaty is limited to the territory of the affected member State. The federation's succession to the State's treaty obligations is justified by its consent to the State's treaty, by which it has accepted certain co-responsibility for the implementation of the treaty.

IX. Exchange of Diplomats and Partnership Relations

No member State of a federation exchanges representatives with diplomatic status. The German Constitution of 1871 conceded to its member States the right to exchange diplomats, but not consuls. The major member States initially made use of this right. In the end, only Bavaria maintained diplomatic missions in a few foreign countries. The Weimar Constitution of 1919 no longer conceded this privilege to the States. Bavaria, nevertheless, still had a French and a Vatican mission in Munich until 1934. Visits of heads of States, heads of government and other official representatives of foreign States to the member States of a federation are in no way different from visits of these persons to territorial subdivisions of unitary States. As member States have no foreign relations competence except within the limits of their treaty-making power, they are not authorized in respect of State visits to act as equal partners of a foreign State but only as territorial entities of the federation.

Irrespective of the competence of the Member States of some federations to conclude treaties governed by international law, member States may maintain partnership relations with foreign States or subdivisions of foreign States. There are many examples of international co-operation and exchange activities by member States of federations as well as by territorial and functional entities of unitary States, such as regions, counties, municipalities, universities or chambers of commerce, handicrafts, advocates or notaries which are not governed by international law. The transboundary co-operation between local or regional authorities is generally covered by treaty provisions of the respective federal or unitary States. They are subject to private law, or fall outside the legal sphere entirely. Moreover, for the promotion of trade, exchange or tourism some member States of the Federal Republic maintain agents in several countries, though not necessarily in their capitals, on a *iure gestionis* level and are not recognized as diplomatic or consular agencies by the foreign State. Partnership relations of this kind are only permitted within the limits set by the respective federal State or member State. Therefore it would offend against the Constitution and also against international law's reference to municipal law, if a member State tried to evade the constitutional allocation of competences by making an agreement with a foreign State on the level of a gentlemen's agreement or by exchanging agents on a quasi-diplomatic level.

X. European Union and the Committee of the Regions

Regarding the European Communities, which now constitute the European Union, the establishing treaties did not originally provide either for the participation of the federal units of the EU's member States in the law-making process or for their representation in the organs. From the EU's point of view, federal units are nothing but administrative units of the EU's member States, a view which fails to take into account that the EU has taken over some of the competences of the member States which, for example, in the case of the Federal Republic of Germany, have been distributed between the federation and the member States in accordance with the German Constitution. Members of the EU are solely the signatory States of the EU treaties and not the member States of the three federations Austria, Belgium and Germany in the EU. This situation changed only negligibly after the establishment of the Committee of the Regions according to the Treaty of Maastricht 1993. The members of the Committee of the Regions are appointed by qualified majority by the Council of the European Union on the proposal of the EU's Member States. According to the Treaty of Nice 2001 they must have a mandate in a regional or local territorial entity. The member States of Austria, Germany and the Belgian entities are represented in the Committee. The influence on the law-making process is modest because the Committee of the regions only has consultative functions. But it can make commitments and has to be involved in several cases either obligatorily or optionally. If the hearing is obligatory but did not take place, the decision of the EU Council or the European Commission is void and the EU Council has no right of action. According to the European Court of Justice a member State of the federal State can file an action for annulment. As a result, according to European law the federal units of the member States lack the right of substantial participation.

But the participation of the member States is possible on the national federal level according to federal law in Austria and Germany. In Germany, the member States participate through the Federal Council in matters concerning the EU. The procedure is provided in detail by the Federal Constitution (Art. 23) and a special federal act. The Federal Government shall inform the Federal Council comprehensively and as quickly as possible in all matters concerning the EU. The Federal Council shall be involved in the decision-making process of the federation insofar as it is involved in a corresponding internal measure or insofar as the member States are internally responsible. The Federal Government shall take into account the opinion of the Federal Council. Even in areas in which the federation has exclusive legislative jurisdiction but which affect the interests of member States, the Federal Government shall take into account the opinion of the Federal Council. Its opinion shall prevail in the decision-making process of the federation where essentially the legislative powers of the member States, the establishment of their authorities or their administrative procedures are affected. On matters touching the exclusive legislative competence of the States, the States have the opportunity to express their ideas extensively and in detail. The federation expects the States to contribute to the objectives and necessities of the federation's foreign and integrating policy. The federation is obliged to take steps to arrive at a mutually agreed standpoint which it will try to realize in the European Union as far as possible and from which it shall deviate only for reasons of foreign or integration policy. Where the exclusive legislative jurisdiction of the member States in the areas of education and culture or broadcasting is affected, the exercise of the rights of the Federal Republic as a member State of the EU shall be transferred by the federation to a representative of the States designated by the Federal Council. Those rights shall be exercised with the participation of and in agreement with the Federal Government; in this connection the responsibility of the federation for the country as a whole shall be. Moreover, the constitutions of several member States of the Federal Republic contain provisions concerning the federal principles of European unity and the principle of subsidiarity. They promote the participation of autonomous regions in the legislation of the European Union.

German Copyright Contract Law since 2002 and the Effects on Publishing

*by Jessica Sänger**

In 2002, German copyright law was reformed, and a number of provisions regulating copyright contract law were introduced into the Copyright Act[1]. Until this time, the German Copyright Act had not dealt in detail with contractual obligations in the field of copyright, but had left it largely to the contracting parties to shape their relations as they saw fit[2]. An ancillary Act comprehensively codifying copyright contract law was considered from time to time, but never came into being[3]. It was therefore the reform of 2002 that first created provisions specifically introducing copyright contract law into German legislation. They deal mainly with enforcing the author's claim to "adequate" or "appropriate"[4] remuneration.

This paper gives a brief summary of these new provisions of copyright contract law (part I), and takes a closer look at these rules in the context of book publishing, where it becomes clear that the reform causes serious difficulties for publishers (part II). This analysis is followed by a demonstration of the effects of the legislation on the market for literary translations (part III).

---

* RAin B. Jessica Sänger is Legal Counsel and Deputy Head of the Legal Dept. at Börsenverein des Deutschen Buchhandels e.V. She is currently working on her Ph.D thesis at Prof. Dr. Dieter Dörr's Chair, Johannes Gutenberg-Universität, Mainz. She visited the Louis Brandeis Law School in Louisville in 2006.

1 The reform came into force on July 1st, 2002. The reform Act was passed on March 22nd, 2002. This Act altered the provisions of the existing Copyright Act (UrhG) of 1965.

2 Only a few provisions, such as §§ 31 et seq, §§ 88, 89 et seq of the old UrhG, were designed to influence contractual relationships in the field.

3 The statute applying to publishing contracts for literary and musical works ("Verlagsgesetz") only covers a small part of the contracts which are regularly concluded on the basis of copyright. Besides, none of the provisions of this statute are binding upon the parties, who remain free to contract as they see fit.

4 In the following, I will use the term "adequate" remuneration to refer to this concept.

I. The Provisions

The German Copyright Act (UrhG[5]) grants the author or translator[6] the right to an agreement affording him or her "adequate" remuneration for the commercial exploitation of his or her work (§ 32 I 1 UrhG). This claim applies at the time of conclusion of the contract. Though contrasting with the basic civil law principle of freedom of contract, the concept of fair remuneration has long been a basic principle of German copyright law, as developed by the courts. It is based on the fundamental Constitutional rights of the creative originator[7]. Newly introduced § 36 UrhG permits organisations representing authors/creators and creative industries to negotiate collective agreements defining the adequate level of remuneration for various types of works.

One of the new provisions now gives the author a cause of action in order to enforce this principle. Even after concluding a contract concerning rights to his work, the author is not necessarily bound by the agreement. If a contract has been concluded that does not grant "adequate" remuneration (at the time of conclusion), the author of the work has a claim against the rightsholder for alteration of the contract in such a way as to guarantee "adequate" remuneration owed from the time of contracting (§ 32 I 3 UrhG).

But besides influencing the initial publishing agreement, the reformed Copyright Act now also grants the author the right to request alteration of the existing deal at a later time, if circumstances have changed so that remuneration may be considered inadequate in retrospect (§ 32a UrhG). This is another remarkable deviation from the fundamental principle of *pacta sunt servanda.*

Finally, the author has a further claim to "additional adequate remuneration" if the publisher makes use of the work in a way which is covered by the publishing contract, but which was not a known form of use at the time of conclusion of the contract (§ 32c UrhG)[8].

---

5 Urheberrechtsgesetz, commonly abbreviated as UrhG.

6 The provision applies to all originators of creative works, but because this article focuses on the book sector, I speak only of authors and/or translators here.

7 *Hilty/Peukert*, GRUR Int. 2002, 643 (645). This aspect demonstrates the fundamental difference between the "Copyright" tradition and the "Droit d'Auteur" tradition of copyright law. German copyright law is based firmly on moral rights and the Continental European Droit d'Auteur model.

8 This provision is less relevant to publishing today, as it is geared to cater for the future. Therefore, I will not analyse this rule separately in part II.

These rights cannot be waived by the author (§§ 32a III 1, 32b UrhG). The rules in their current form apply without restriction to all German contracts concluded on and after July 1st, 2002. The author's claim under § 32 I 3 UrhG applies to all contracts concluded on or after June 1st, 2001, if uses continue beyond March 28th, 2002. The claim for subsequent alteration of the contract (§ 32a UrhG) applies to all existing contracts, though the relevant change in circumstances must have taken place after March 28th, 2002[9].

II. Analysis

This set of rules in copyright contract law is unique to Germany. They were conceived with the explicit goal of improving the economic situation of authors, artists, and other creative individuals, as they were perceived to be at a disadvantage in comparison to the rightsholders who engaged in commercial exploitation of their works. Their apparent weakness vis-à-vis rightsholders was seen as a structural imbalance which required a legislative remedy[10]. This view at the very least ignored the tremendous diversity within the creative sector, which consists of a huge variety of artists, art forms, rightsholders and business models[11]. But nevertheless, it gained sufficient support, leading to the unusual result we now see in the UrhG. In no other country has the attempt at protecting the economic interests of creative originators gone thus far[12]. One observer has referred to the legislation as "Pandora's Box"[13]. Some observers have termed the reform a misguided attempt at affording authors "total justice" in contractual relationships, which is by definition unattainable[14]. At the same time, at closer scrutiny, it becomes clear that these rules were hastily drafted and are ill-

---

9 OLG Munich, decision of June 17th, 2010, case 29 U 3312/09 – *Das Boot*, GRUR-RR 2010, 416; LG Munich I, decision of May 7th, 2009, case 7 O 17694/08, ZUM 2009, 794; LG Hamburg, decision of April 18, 2008, case 308 O 450/07, ZUM 2008, 608.

10 See *Schack*, ZUM 2001, 453 (454) for an analysis of the political impetus of the government which proposed the reform. Cf .also *Flechsig*, ZUM 2000, 484 (485).

11 *Schack*, ZUM 2001, 453 (454). See also *Flechsig*, who points to the many different creative vocations which are covered by collective agreements in employment law (*Flechsig*, ZUM 2000, 484 [485 f.]).

12 *Thüsing*, GRUR 2002, 203 (208); *Georgios Gounalakis/Meinhard Heinze/Dieter Dörr*: Urhebervertragsrecht – Verfassungs- und europarechtliche Bewertung des Entwurfs der Bundesregierung vom 30. Mai 2001, p. 141.

13 *Jacobs*, GRUR 2011, 306.

14 *Castendyk/Kirchherr*, ZUM 2003, 751 (760, Fn. 65).

conceived. When applied to the book publishing sector, the problems become evident: Not only do the current rules entirely ignore legitimate needs of publishers, but in practice, they also fail to fulfil their promise to authors and translators[15].

1. § 32 UrhG

The concept of "adequate" or fair remuneration for authors of creative works is not new[16]. It reflects the general objective of the copyright regime to respect the value of creative achievement. But the 2002 reform has elevated the principle of "adequate" remuneration and given it a status equal to that of the moral rights of the author[17]. This is a most remarkable development indeed, and with a view to the principle of freedom of contract, it seems highly questionable[18]. A contract law provision which calls into question the validity of a contract as soon as it is concluded to the disadvantage of one party seems strange and highly biased[19].

Furthermore, adequate remuneration, which was formerly a general requirement on the basis of the UrhG and good faith, is now enforceable against the author's contracting partner. At the same time, there is no clear definition of what "adequate" remuneration actually means. § 32 II UrhG offers only a vague indication, insufficient for determining the actual level of fees or royalties or other forms of remuneration envisaged here. Essentially, the provision tells us that "adequate" remuneration is what may be considered fair remuneration under the circumstances (§ 32 II 2 UrhG). The circumstances to be taken into account here are type and extent of agreed uses of the work, timing of such uses, and accepted business practice.

Clearly, in combination with a cause of action for alteration of a publishing contract, these general criteria amount to tremendous uncertainty for any publisher entering into a contract with an author. They also leave a huge margin of discretion for the court, in effect forcing a court to set remuneration rates without much guidance. For these reasons, the reform met with firm opposition from

---

15 *Sprang*, ZUM 2010, 116 (118); Schack, ZUM 2001, 453 (455, 464).

16 See e.g. two decisions from 1930 and 1931: RGZ 128, 102 (113) – *Schlager-Liederbücher*; RGZ 134, 198 (201) – *Schallplattenrechte*.

17 *Hilty/Peukert*, GRUR Int. 2002, 643 (645).

18 *Schack*, ZUM 2001, 453 (458).

19 *Flechsig*, ZUM 2000, 484 (491).

the outset[20]. Though some modifications were made along the way, i.a. the addition of a clarification that collective agreements reached under § 36 UrhG could determine adequate remuneration levels, the provision remains unclear to the extent that it essentially denies publishers the legal certainty they need in order to run a reliable business[21]. The courts themselves have criticised the lack in clarity in unusually clear terms[22]. In fact, given the incredible variety of creative works in terms of type, volume, and quality, as well as the many different scenarios of their commercial exploitation, it seems simply impossible for the courts to define a fair price for them[23].

2. § 23a UrhG

a) Effects on the Publishing Contract

This provision, which gives authors and translators a claim for "adequate remuneration" over and above what was adequate at the time of conclusion of the publishing contract, at first glance seems beneficial to creativity. At the same time, it is quite obviously extremely onerous for publishers. For them, the provision results in constant legal uncertainty. Contracts affording the writer fully adequate and fair remuneration at the outset may be overturned at a later point in time in order to raise remuneration to a higher level, irrespective of whether a change in circumstances was foreseeable for the parties, or not. The only requirement is, that remuneration seems "strikingly disproportionate" at some point – no matter how many years or decades after conclusion of the contract. Again, we are dealing with terminology which lacks essential clarity, requires extensive interpretation – possibly by the courts – and leaves a broad margin for interpretation and argument[24].

---

20 See e.g. *Gounalakis/Heinze/Dörr* who evaluated the government draft for legislation (of May 30th, 2001) and came to the conclusion that the provision on adequate remuneration was vague to the extent of being impracticable and possibly unconstitutional (pp. 62 et seq, 136 et seq).

21 *Jacobs*, NJW 2002, 1905 (1907).

22 OLG Munich, judgment of February 8th, 2007 – 6 U 5785/05, ZUM 2007, 317 (325). Cf. also Süddeutsche Zeitung of June 23rd, 2009, p.14, where *Prof. Bornkamm*, a senior judge from the German Federal Court of Justice describes the lack of clarity of the statute as "a real imposition".

23 *Czychowski*, GRUR 2010, 793; Schack, ZUM 2001, 453 (459).

24 For a detailed analysis of the various unclear elements in the requirements of § 32a UrhG, see Poll, ZUM 2009, 611 (614 et seq).

This permanent situation of uncertainty has been denounced by one observer as an insufferable burden on rightsholders[25]. In fact, publishers who have properly calculated their risks and offered the writer a fair deal face losing out if a particular title turns out to be a success – a result which will no doubt be owed to a certain extent to the publisher's efforts in i.a. editing, design, marketing, and distribution. In this case, the author may claim additional remuneration, the level of which is unpredictable, as it must be determined by a court. So far, there is no case law that can offer even the slightest indication of what courts might consider "adequate" in terms of subsequent remuneration of authors or translators for best-selling books. For this reason, publishers are increasingly unable to risk giving emerging or unknown authors a chance, as they can no longer rely on successful best-selling titles for secure revenues to subsidise titles generating smaller print runs. Inevitably, catering to specialised readers or niche markets becomes extremely difficult.

On the whole, the uncertainty and insecurity that this provision brings to the publishing sector, is a most unusual feature in German civil law. Unfortunately, it does not give publishers – or any other creative industry – any way of concluding contracts which deserve to be described as binding – at least on their counterparts.

b) Effects on Licensing

But besides causing problems with the initial publishing contract, § 32a UrhG also affects the licensing business. The author's claim for adjustment of the contract is not limited to his contracting partner (§ 32a II UrhG). In fact, the author – besides asking his publisher for more money later – may also claim "subsequent adequate remuneration" from licensees of the publisher's with whom the author has no contractual relationship at all. It is very strange that the author has a claim for alteration of the contract against a third party with whom he has not dealt[26]. But for the time being, this seems to be what the UrhG indeed provides[27]. Of course, this situation makes matters far worse for the publisher. Because successful titles are frequently licensed to partners all over the world, this puts

25 *Schack*, ZUM 2001, 453 (458).

26 *Schulze* in: *Thomas Dreier/Gernot Schulze*: Urheberrechtsgesetz, Urheberrechtswahrnehmungsgesetz, Kunsturhebergesetz – Kommentar, 3. Aufl., § 32a, Rn. 44.

27 Various other questions are left unanswered by the provision, see e.g. *Schack*, ZUM 2001, 453 (458). For a detailed analysis, see *Poll*, ZUM 2009, 611 (618 f.); *Reinhard/Distelkötter*, ZUM 2003, 269; *Brauner*, ZUM 2004, 96.

German publishers offering licenses to third parties in an extremely difficult situation. They have no way of protecting licensees from unforeseeable future claims from authors if the work is indeed successful and the purpose of the licensing deal is achieved.

If under these circumstances doing serious business seems hardly feasible in the publishing world, where usually only a small number of contracting parties are involved, the effects in other sectors are potentially chaotic[28]. In cases where numerous authors, artists, and/or other creative originators are involved in the creation of a work (e.g. a film) each of them may sue any licensee or sub-licensee of his or her contracting partner subsequently for additional remuneration. The rightsholder may therefore be ordered to pay a large number of different individual claimants additional "adequate" remuneration as the result of any number of separate lawsuits[29]. This also means that the cumulative burden on the rightsholder of remunerating different claimants will not be taken into account by any of the – possibly numerous – courts when determining the "adequate" level of fees or royalties[30]. There is no mechanism which could limit overall liability concerning one work to a certain level, so that the risk for rightsholders becomes literally incalculable[31].

But even from the point of view of authors, who are clearly meant to benefit from this arrangement, the lack of co-ordination between different claims against a single rightsholder can pose a risk. In practice, where a number of authors or artists are claiming against their publisher or a licensee of their publisher's for additional remuneration, they will find themselves in a first-come-first-served situation. By the time the last contributor to e.g. a successful anthology or textbook has come forward, the economic evaluation of the gain on the part of the licensee by the court may have changed considerably, due to the suc-

---

28 For an analysis of how the reform affects the film sector, see *Poll*, ZUM 2009, 611; *Brauner*, ZUM 2004, 96.

29 OLG Munich, decision of June 17th, 2010, case 29 U 3312/09 – *Das Boot*, GRUR-RR 2010, 416; LG Munich I, decision of May 7th, 2009, case 7 O 17694/08, ZUM 2009, 794.

30 *Sprang*, ZUM 2010, 116 (117).

31 Again, the situation is even more difficult in the film sector, where far more parties are involved, cf. *Poll*, ZUM 2009, 611 (618, 620); *Brauner*, ZUM 2004, 96 (101 f.). Though in a recent case, the Higher Regional Court in Munich has indicated that contributors whose contributions to the overall work are relatively insignificant may not claim under § 32a UrhG, see OLG Munich, decision of Feb. 10th, 2011, case 29 U 2749/10, ZUM 2011, 422.

cessful claims of other co-authors, translators, or artists[32], leaving the last in line at an unfair disadvantage, irrespective of the value of their contribution. The UrhG provides no mechanism for preventing such an outcome, which would clearly run counter to the central aim of the reform, which is ensuring fair remuneration for authors.

These problems lead us to another difficulty with the current system, which has already been mentioned in the context of § 32 UrhG. The reform puts courts in a position which requires them to determine the exact level of what is adequate in terms of remuneration for each creative work. It is difficult to conceive how judges will be able to do this in practice without conducting major investigations into the economics and customs of the sectors involved. In situations where cross-border licensing deals have been struck, this seems particularly impracticable. In fact, as some observers have aptly put it, the courts are virtually required to perform magic[33], or indeed square the circle[34].

c) Enforcement outside Germany?

Another open question is whether it will be possible to enforce these rules in foreign courts according to the relevant rules of conflict of laws. The German statute indeed seems to assume that §§ 32, 32a UrhG will be enforced against foreign licensees. Nevertheless, because these rules are so unusual, and because they run counter to the fundamental principles of freedom of contract and *pacta sunt servanda*, it seems unlikely that foreign courts will be willing to apply them without modification[35]. Besides the more fundamental question of whether these rules contravene basic civil law principles, there is the practical difficulty mentioned above: foreign courts would be even less in a position – and most probably even less willing – to determine the "adequate" level of remuneration applicable to a German publishing contract. All aspects considered, it seems at best uncertain whether a German author or translator would succeed with a claim based on §§ 32, 32a UrhG against a foreign rightsholder. In this respect, the reformed UrhG could lead to erratic and unreliable results on the part of those it is meant to benefit.

---

32 *Poll*, ZUM 2009, 611 (620).
33 *Poll*, ZUM 2009, 611 (614).
34 *Jacobs*, GRUR 2011, 306.
35 *Sprang*, ZUM 2010, 116 (117); *Hilty/Peukert*, GRUR Int. 2002, 643 (658).

On the other hand, if a foreign court, according to the requirements of rules concerning conflict of laws, felt obliged to apply the German rules and uphold the author's claim[36], the foreign licensee would be highly likely to sue the German licensor (i.e. the publisher) for damages. Any court order against the German publisher granting such damages would in turn most probably be enforceable in Germany[37]. This puts German publishers in a precarious position in their licensing business: in effect, they risk being held liable (indirectly by the author) for revenues (generated by their licensee) from which they did not necessarily benefit.

Finally, the question of enforcement of German judgments on the basis of §§ 32, 32a UrhG against rightsholders outside Germany, remains open. It seems unlikely that other Member States of the European Union would deny enforcement of a German court's enforcement order. This is due to the fact that such denial would require a serious contravention of the ordre public of that state, on the scale of a breach of Human Rights[38]. But where the United States are concerned, it is difficult to predict whether the successful plaintiff, brandishing a German enforcement order awarded him on the grounds of §§ 32 or 32a UrhG, would be able to recover funds in the U.S. It does not seem equally unlikely that the enforcement order would be deemed to run counter to U.S. civil law principles to the extent that enforcement would be denied[39].

3. § 32b UrhG

§ 32b UrhG creates further difficulties by making the application of this set of rules (§§ 32 and 32a UrhG) to their contracts mandatory for German rightsholders. Even if the contracting parties have actively chosen a foreign copyright regime to govern their relations, § 32b UrhG stipulates that §§ 32 and 32a UrhG shall nevertheless apply to that contract, provided that the contract would have been governed by German law without the explicit choice of foreign law by the parties (§ 32b lit.1 UrhG). Wherever uses take place within Germany, § 32b lit. 2 UrhG determines that the author may not waive his rights under §§ 32 and 32a UrhG. In effect, § 32b UrhG is a case of discrimination against nationals by the legislator – permitted within the European Common Market – which puts Ger-

36 For an investigation of the requirements for such application in the United States, see *Hilty/Peukert*, GRUR Int. 2002, 643 (658).

37 *Schulze* in: Dreier/Schulze, UrhG, 3. Aufl. 2008, § 32a, Rn. 55.

38 *Hilty/Peukert*, GRUR Int. 2002, 643 (659).

39 *Hilty/Peukert*, GRUR Int. 2002, 643 (659).

man publishers at a disadvantage in relation to the publishing industries of other countries[40].

4. § 36 UrhG

Along with the abovementioned provisions which grant authors and translators claims against rightsholders, an attempt was made by the legislator to offer a mechanism for determining what is "adequate" in terms of remuneration. But in practice, § 36 UrhG, which provides for collective agreements to be negotiated in order to determine adequate remuneration levels, does not offer a viable solution to the problem of defining what is adequate[41]. The provision is modelled on collective agreements in employment law. Some observers doubt whether it is constitutional in its effect on the fundamental freedom of coalition[42] of artists and rightsholders[43]. Essentially, the provision aims at vocation-based regulated remuneration comparable to that of medical doctors, architects, or legal professionals[44]. But whilst collective agreements are manifold in the field of labour law, only one single such agreement has been concluded under § 36 UrhG in the space of eight years. This fact alone is an indication that the provision is not having the desired effect.

The reason for the lack of agreements on adequate remuneration is quite simply, that collective agreements are not a helpful instrument in the book sector. A huge effort went into the negotiation of the single existing agreement – which governs remuneration of authors for works of fiction – but the result in essence simply re-iterates basic principles of the publishing business, neither putting authors in a better position nor giving publishers sufficient legal certainty.

All the operative clauses of the agreement which stipulate the various adequate levels of remuneration require extensive interpretation in order to be applied to a concrete case, thereby again leaving a significant margin for negotiation between the parties. In practice, the parties applying the agreement will still be starting from more or less the same initial negotiating positions as before the

40 *Sprang*, ZUM 2010, 116 (118).

41 For an in-depth analysis, see *Thüsing*, GRUR 2002, 203.

42 „Freedom of coalition" in Germany describes the right of each individual or company to join or form bodies representing their interests in the realm of employment or industry, such as trade unions or industry associations, respectively.

43 See *Thüsing*, GRUR 2002, 203 (204).

44 *Flechsig*, ZUM 2000, 484 (494).

agreement came into existence. The reasons for leaving such a relatively broad margin for negotiation in the agreement are at the heart of the publishing business itself. Put simply, it is extremely difficult to compare creative works of different authors with each other, even within the segment of e.g. fictional books. Experience has shown that even individual publishing houses find it impossible to establish uniform remuneration rates for their authors[45]. Different authors write different types of books, in different styles, of varying literary quality, for different audiences. Different book projects require different calculation models in order for them to be economically viable. It is obvious that there is a huge difference in economic potential between a début by an unknown author, and a sequel to a best-selling title by an author of renown. Remuneration also differs on the basis that some authors write to make a living from their royalties, whilst others only write on the side, perhaps in order to build a reputation in a more specialised area.

In practice, Negotiations between writers and publishers in Germany have shown that authors expect remuneration levels which would render more than 90% of non-fiction titles unprofitable[46]. Authors realise that attaining the remuneration levels they consider necessary would cause a dramatic decline in the number of books published. In other words, the "cake" would shrink, offering a much smaller number of authors a – perhaps larger – piece of the cake. At the same time, under the current market conditions[47], publishers are not in a position to raise book prices, and most have already reduced internal costs to a minimum, so that the chances of generating more overall income from each individual work are slim.

Finally, another mechanism, already mentioned above in the context of § 32a UrhG, plays a role here. From the point of view of the publisher, successful books, such as best-selling novels by established authors, are essential as the source of a relatively secure revenue stream. Only if a publishing house has managed to establish such titles will it be in a position to give emerging writers their chance at publication, or to cater to special interests – and hence small audiences. Publishing in Germany is largely based on this model of mixed calculation which allows the publishing house to minimise its overall risk whilst offering a diverse range of books to readers. Because of this, publishers will always have to calculate royalties according to what is economically viable within their business framework. Uniform tariffs cannot ensure the survival of this business.

45 *Sprang*, ZUM 2010, 116 (118).
46 *Sprang*, ZUM 2010, 116 (118).
47 For an analysis, see *Homburg/Klarmann*, ZUM 2004, 704 (705).

As we will see in the next section, negotiations have proven that authors' and publishers' positions are still very far apart on questions of adequate remuneration. It is sufficient to say in short, that the relevant associations are not likely to conclude further agreements on "adequate" remuneration any time soon.

These circumstances show why blanket collective agreements fixing authors' remuneration to uniform rates are not well suited to publishing as an industry[48]. Whereas in other sectors, it seems entirely feasible to establish fixed tariffs for certain types of work, as indeed we have seen in many areas, the creative process is not as easily evaluated in economic terms. Neither the value of the effort invested nor the economic potential of the work itself are easy to gauge and quantify in terms of money. This is why the system of collective agreements has not helped to define what "adequate" remuneration means in practice. Finally, the idea of having uniform remuneration rates for artists and authors is an entirely different kettle of fish in comparison to the norms which apply to architects, doctors or lawyers. These groups are homogeneous in terms of education. Their qualifications are comparable, and their work to a large extent standardised. At the same time, they each have important responsibilities towards society as a whole. This is the basis upon which they are paid standardised fees[49]. The same cannot be said in either respect of artists, authors, or other creative individuals, the definition of whose qualification is by nature elusive, and whose responsibility could be said to be to art alone.

III. The Effects of the 2002 Reform on the Situation of Literary Translators in Germany

Eight years after the introduction of the concept of "adequate" remuneration to German copyright contract law of 2002, it is worth taking a closer look at the practical effects of the reform. These effects are best demonstrated on the basis of the situation concerning translations. One of the consequences of the new legislation, perhaps inevitably, has been litigation.

---

48 Furthermore, there are indications that § 36 UrhG might in fact be unconstitutional, cf. e.g. Thüsing, GRUR 2002, 203.

49 *Schack*, ZUM 2001, 453 (465).

1. Court Decisions

In 2004 and 2005, number of translators brought a total of 14 suits against their publishers claiming for "adequate" remuneration according to § 32 UrhG. The claims were directed at adjusting the existing contracts. The initial decisions of three different regional courts (Hamburg, Berlin and Munich) were very varied in what they defined as adequate in terms of remuneration. Five of the Munich cases went on through the courts and were decided in final instance by the Federal Court of Justice[50] in October 2009 in the so-called *Talking to Addison* case[51]. The judgment is the first of its kind and will therefore have major influence on future decisions in the field.

During the proceedings at the Federal Court of Justice, the court repeatedly made it clear that it was not happy with the role accorded it by the reformed UrhG[52]. It criticised the legislation as unclear, because it gives next to no guidance on remuneration levels. Nevertheless, the court was forced to specify acceptable fee and royalty levels for literary translations. The end result is very close to the so-called "Berlin Model" of remuneration[53], a compromise which publishers had offered translators in 2008, but which they had refused at the time. In essence, with respect to additional remuneration for best-sellers, the Federal Court of Justice held that such remuneration is owed if more than 5,000 copies of the relevant title are sold. It set the usual royalties for these cases at 0.8% of the net retail price for hard cover copies, and at 0.4% for paperbacks. As a general rule, translators are due remuneration equalling 20% of author remuneration.

In the *Talking to Addison* decision of 2009, the court did not make a clear statement the translator's share in licensing revenues[54], but this question was decided by the Federal Court of Justice in a "second round" of a further five cases affecting four publishing houses. In January 2011, in the *Destructive Emotions* case[55], the court applied one of the principles developed in *Talking to Addison*

---

50 Bundesgerichtshof, the highest court and final instance in civil and criminal cases.

51 BGH, decision of October 7th, 2009, case I ZR 38/07 – "Talking to Addison", GRUR 2009, 1148. For a short analysis, see Jacobs, GRUR 2011, 306.

52 During a hearing on September 9th, 2010, the presiding judge *Prof. Bornkamm* once again repeated his criticism voiced earlier in the year, see footnote 21, above.

53 *Dresen*, GRUR-Prax 2009, 4.

54 *Dresen*, GRUR Prax 2009, 4. For an analysis of all questions left open by Talking to Addison, see *Czychowski*, GRUR 2010, 793.

55 The leading judgment in the „second round" was BGH, decision of January 20th, 2011, case I ZR 19/09 – *"Destructive Emotions"*, BeckRS 2011, 03965.

and held that the 20% rule applies to licensing revenues also: the adequate share of licensing revenues for a translator amounts to 20% of the author's share. At the same time, the translator's share may not exceed the publisher's share of licensing revenues. At first glance, this seems to make sense. Nevertheless, the court unfortunately did not take into account the practical effect of this ruling on publishing. In effect, this ruling means that publishers who engage only in hard cover publishing are at a serious disadvantage in comparison to publishers who also publish paperbacks.

The difficulty with the *Destructive Emotions* ruling becomes evident when we take a look at how the licensing business works in practice. Traditionally, in Germany – as in many countries – many titles are first published in hard cover editions. After a certain period, a paperback edition is usually put on the market. Wherever the publisher of the hardback edition does not produce the paperback itself, the paperback edition is licensed to another publisher. At this point, the 20% rule, if applied to licensing revenues, kicks in. The licensing (hard cover) publisher must give the translator 20% of the author share of licensing revenues. Within the framework of the customary licensing deals, this is a lot more than a publisher who publishes its own paperback edition would have to pay.

The facts of the *Destructive Emotions* case illustrate this problem clearly: The net retail price of the relevant book was 11.68 €. According the rules laid down by the court in *Talking to Addison*, a publisher putting its own paperback edition on the market would have to pay the translator a share in sales of 0.04672 € for all sales over and above 5,000 copies. But the defendant publisher in *Destructive Emotions* does not engage in paperback publishing. Therefore, the defendant licensed the paperback edition to another publisher, at a customary license fee of 6% of the net retail price (for 1 to 25,000 copies sold). According to the decision of the Federal Court of Justice, the defendant has ended up having to pay the translator more than double the 0.04672 € it would have had to pay for its own paperback edition. This is because the licensing model, which is entirely customary within the German book sector, foresees an author share of 70% in the licensing revenue. This share comes to 0.49 € per copy. If the translator receives remuneration calculated as 20% of this share, the translator's royalties amount to 0.098 € (instead of 0.04672 €) per copy sold – simply because the title was licensed for paperback publication rather than published as paperback in house.

Quite clearly, this result is unjust, as it imposes a drastically different result on one publisher than on another for reasons that have nothing to do with remuneration issues. It shows that the Federal Court of Justice in *Destructive Emotions* did not sufficiently take into account the practical application of its decision. This is surprising, given that the parties to the dispute explained the mechanics of the licensing business to the court in detail.

Because of this unfair competitive disadvantage that the latest decision on adequate remuneration means for hard cover (only) publishers, the defendant has in March 2011 lodged a complaint with the Constitutional Court[56] in order to obtain redress. This is an unusual step to take for any litigant, as the Federal Court of Justice is the highest court in civil cases in Germany, and thus normally the last resort. But this shows the importance of this case for the sector as well as the shortcomings of the decision. The Constitutional Court hears complaints only on the grounds that the Constitution has been violated, usually by an unconstitutional piece of legislation or an administrative act. Nevertheless, if a judgment of final instance infringes fundamental (or basic) rights[57], which are at the heart of the German Constitution[58], a complaint may also be lodged with the Constitutional Court. The court will only accept the matter for hearing if the case of violation of fundamental rights is argued forcefully from the outset.

In this case, the complaining publisher will be arguing that the Federal Court of Justice's decision in *Destructive Emotions* violates the fundamental right of equal treatment (Art. 3 GG) by arbitrarily putting a certain type of publishers at a serious disadvantage in relation to publishers with a different business model. An important argument will be that the viability of the legitimate business model of hard cover publishers is in serious danger for no good reason. At the same time, these publishers have a distinctive function within the German book sector, and for a number of good reasons cannot simply start publishing paperback titles themselves. Also, the number of translated titles available from fiction publishers in Germany is particularly high at around 30%.

The chances for a re-opening of the case of adequate remuneration either at the Federal Court of Justice (after the obligatory appeal on grounds of violation of the right to be heard) or through acceptance for hearing of the Constitutional Complaint seem slim. Judging by statistics, chances for the case being accepted for hearing at the Constitutional Court (after about 12 months) are at 3%. Should the case in fact be heard, another three years are likely to pass before a decision is handed down. Nevertheless, it is to be hoped that the Constitutional Court will recognise the need for adjustment of *Destructive Emotions*. It seems that – entirely without intending to interfere with publishing business models – the Federal Court of Justice has, in its desire to find a solution for adequate remunera-

---

56 Bundesverfassungsgericht in German.

57 The equivalent of Human Rights in German constitutional law.

58 The Grundgesetz (GG), often referred to as the „Basic Law".

tion for translators, caused significant "collateral damage" to the book publishing sector. This presumably accidental, but no less serious, result must be addressed as soon as possible if the question of adequate remuneration is not to become the nemesis of book publishing in Germany.

Besides the most serious problem caused by the *Destructive Emotions* judgment, the decision is interesting in two further points. Firstly, it does not tell us exactly what is meant by the author's share (on the basis of which the translator's share is to be calculated). It is not clear whether the term refers to the net amount that the author actually receives (as *Destructive Emotions* seems to indicate), or whether it comprises fees for a foreign publisher and/or agent which are deducted from the publisher's "gross" payment to the author (*Talking to Addison* seems to favour this interpretation). If the creative value of the translator's work is to be reflected by the remuneration, as the court claims in laying down the 20% rule, it seems that the amount the author actually receives should be used as the basis for calculation[59]. Nevertheless, the two decisions do not satisfactorily answer this question which is important for the practical application of the rulings.

The second interesting point is that the defendant publisher in *Destructive Emotions* had in fact paid the translator a significantly higher rate per standard page than average. The court determined that the average rate for the type of translation in question was between 15.40 € and 17.90 € per standard page. The defendant had paid 19 € per page. Interestingly, this generous basic translation fee had no effect whatsoever on the determination by the court of what was considered adequate in terms of participation in sales or licensing fees. This shows that adequacy of remuneration is not determined by an objective assessment of the overall deal that has been struck, but rather on the basis of inflexible rules laid down by courts which have no experience of the book sector. The effect of this decision is extremely likely to be that publishers will feel less inclined to agree to generous page rates for their translators. In this respect, the decision may backfire on translators, reversing the intended effect of adequacy of remuneration[60].

Further litigation is to be expected in the wake of these decisions, as translators and possibly other creative originators pursue claims for adequate remuneration on the basis of § 32 or even § 32a UrhG. Whatever the details of the remuneration models that the courts develop in the future, the problem of constant legal uncertainty of publishing contracts remains. This kind of situation is

59 See also *v. Becker*, GRUR-Prax 2011, 96, at V.3.

60 *Jacobs*, GRUR 2011, 306 (309) shares this fear.

bound to influence the economic decisions of publishers, who need to evaluate their risks in order to run a business. In fact, figures from the sector show that the reform of 2002 is taking its toll on the market for translations.

2. Remuneration Models

While litigation goes on in the courts, publishers and translators have been negotiating for years to come to an agreement setting standards for adequate remuneration, as foreseen by § 36 UrhG. So far, these negotiations have proven extremely difficult. In this context, it is interesting to take a closer look at the mechanisms of translator remuneration.

We know that in 2002, before the reform came into force, translators of fiction titles were paid an average fee of 16.60 € per standard page for hardcover, and 12.80 € per standard page for paperback editions. Only in less than 10% of cases did translators receive royalties calculated on the basis of the number of copies sold. There are no figures concerning translators' participation in licensing revenues. But there are indications that such participation was seldom part of the agreement[61].

By 2005, we have evidence of widespread use of a different type of remuneration model. Besides a fee per standard page, which was insignificantly lower than before, publishers were paying translators additional royalties based on sales. In some cases, this is a percentage of the net retail price, e.g. for hard cover titles 0.5% per copy starting at 30,000 copies sold (Random House). In other cases, translators were paid royalties calculated as percentages of the initial fees, e.g. 50% of total standard page fee for every 50,000 copies sold, to a maximum of double total standard page fee (Rowohlt). This shows that publishers had begun to give translators a share in the success of a title in order to allow for the new model of copyright contract law.

This tendency was reinforced after January 2007, when publishers had developed the so-called "Munich Model" for remuneration. The model was adopted by a large number of publishing houses. The Munich Model foresees initial standard page fees which are paid as a non-reimbursable advance on royalties. This way, royalties based on sales became the main element of translator remuneration. In this model, royalties begin at 3% of gross retail price per copy sold for the first 999 hardcover copies; then they drop to 2% per copy between 1,000 and 9,999 copies sold; and further to 1% (from 10,000 copies); and finally

61 *Sprang*, ZUM 2010, 116 (119).

0.25% (from 50,000 copies). For paperback sales, royalty rates are half the rate for hardcover copies. According to this model royalties from sales over and above 50,000 copies are to be paid into a special fund to support translators of particularly demanding works, selling fewer copies. The Munich Model was geared to benefit translators of works which did not turn into best-sellers, i.e. the translators of the vast majority of works on the market.

However, the principle of fixing royalties on a declining scale in relation to the number of copies sold was criticised by translators. The result of a further round of negotiations with the support of the German Justice Ministry as mediator finally led to the proposal of the "Berlin Model" (mentioned above) in June 2008. In this model, standard page fees are paid as a gross fee. On top of this fee, translators receive royalties depending on sales. The main difference in comparison to the Munich Model is a shift in the scale of royalties in relation to number of copies sold. The example of hard cover royalties shows how progressive and declining scales are combined: The translator receives 0.5% of the net retail price starting at 5,001 copies sold. From 10,000 copies, he receives 0.75% each, and a full 1% for each copy from 15,000 copies. For sales over and above 75,000 copies, royalties drop back to 0.5%. This Berlin Model benefits translators whose titles sell particularly well – arguably a much smaller group. Despite the intensive negotiations which led to this compromise, and despite mediation by the Ministry of Justice, the German union of translators finally declined to accept this model in March 2009. Therefore, it has only been applied in very few cases in practise.

The impasse in negotiations left it to the courts to come up with a solution. As described above, the Federal Court of Justice has established a system which is close to the Berlin Model. On the whole, we can safely estimate that translator remuneration per book has grown by about 20-25% during the last ten years on average. This rise is mainly due to higher royalties for best-selling titles, because these have been primarily affected by the 2002 legislative reform. At first glance, this might look like good news for translators. But a closer look at the actual market situation will show why this is not the case.

3. Effects on the Market for Literary Translations

As described above, the concept of adequate remuneration means a considerable risk for publishers. Also, we have seen that litigation has resulted in judgments which will make publishers extremely cautious when negotiating translation fees. But besides these effects, data shows that the market situation for translators is deteriorating. A study[62] conducted at the University of Mannheim for the German publishing industry has given us some reliable figures concerning the impact of the 2002 reform. An adequate sample of publishing houses engaging in fiction and non-fiction trade publishing formed the basis of the analysis. In the context of the ongoing litigation between translators and publishers, the figures give us an indication of what the realities of that market look like.

The increase in translator remuneration is particularly significant in comparison to the remuneration of the author of the work. The suits filed against publishers showed that those translators, who evidently felt they were being under-paid, were receiving on average 85% of what the actual author of the work was being paid. This amounts to an average of 15% of the gross turnover generated with each book. At the same time, the Federal Court of Justice has ruled that on principle, translators should be receiving about 20% in relation to the author.

If we take a look at the economic situation in the publishing houses, we see that most titles marketed by trade publishers are generating losses. Among these titles, translated books are particularly unprofitable. As described above, offering these books is only viable on the basis of a mixed calculation relying on a few best-selling books to support variety. The Homburg study revealed that 52% of translated fiction titles were unprofitable. 9% of trade publishers were incurring overall losses in 2002. A further 30% were operating at a profit margin of less than 3%[63]. Overall, the study shows the general economic situation for publishing in Germany is not improving.

Against this background, it becomes clear why the publishing sector is extremely sensitive to increases in cost. Model calculations show that an average German-language hard cover fiction title leaves the publisher with a profit of 3%. Translated titles usually mean an extra 4% translation costs, and only a slightly reduced royalty rate for the foreign author. This frequently leaves the publisher without a profit. The Homburg study shows how sensitive the publishing business model is to increases in fees. For example, if fees went up by 5% from 10% to 10.5% of the net retail price of the book, 21.1% of publishing houses would suffer overall losses. If the increase was 10%, 26.6% of publishers

62 Study by *Professor Dr. Christian Homburg* (Chair: Economics and Marketing) of the University of Mannheim "Gutachten Betriebswirtschaftliche Auswirkungen möglicher Veränderungen der Honorarsituation in Verlagen als Folge der Urheberrechtsnovellierung", October 2003. A summary was published by *Homburg/Klarmann*, ZUM 2004, 704.

63 *Homburg/Klarmann*, ZUM 2004, 704 (705).

would be in trouble, and a raise of 20% would put 38.6% of publishers in the red.

All this goes to show how dependent publishers are on reliable figures in order to run viable businesses. Legal uncertainty and unforeseeable increases in translation costs are bound to create serious difficulties in this economic environment. Indeed, statistics show that between the start of the negotiations with translators in 2001, and 2005, the proportion of translated titles among new publications dropped by a dramatic two thirds. Since 2005, we have seen a slight recovery, but in 2008, the percentage of translated books among new titles was still about a third below what it had been in 2001[64]. During the same period, the overall numbers of new publications per year grew by over 25%[65]. This is clear evidence that the market for literary translations has shrunk dramatically and disproportionately since the introduction of copyright contract law. The ensuing negotiations for collective agreements, and not least the litigation the reform has prompted, have had a tremendous negative effect on the size of the "cake" representing translation fees.

From the point of view of translators, this means that their market has suffered severely. Whereas a few translators have benefited from the reform in the shape of increased royalties, the majority is suffering from a decline in business. At the same time, the fact that publishers are no longer able to invest as much in translations means a sad decline in variety for readers in Germany. Whereas the German book market has long been unusually rich in translated books from all manner of different cultures and literary traditions, the future looks less appealing. Overall, fewer individuals will be able to make a living from their valuable translation work, and at the same time, readers will find fewer and fewer books from all over the world available in the German language. The attempt of the legislator at improving the lot of creative originators has backfired – at least in the context of the book world. It is time that at least the most destructive of these provisions are defused, and the principles of freedom of contract and *pacta sunt servanda* are once again respected in the realm of copyright.

64 *Sprang*, ZUM 2010, 116 (123).
65 *Sprang*, ZUM 2010, 116 (122).

The Inter-American System of Human Rights and the United States

*by Ines Gillich**

I. Introduction

The Inter-American System, i.e. the regional system of the Organization of American States (OAS)[1], including the American Convention of Human Rights, is one of the three major regional human rights systems in the world.[2] Amongst them, the Inter-American System is the world's oldest one. The notion of closer hemispheric union in the Americas was first put forward by Simón Bolívar (also known as „El Libertador" to many South American States) who, at the Congress of Panama in 1826, proposed creating a league of American republics within a system of regional solidarity and cooperation. The roots of the Inter-American System date back to the First International Conference of American States, held in Washington, D.C., in 1889.[3] That meeting established the International Union of American Republics served by a permanent secretariat (the so-called Commercial Bureau of the American Republics) with the participation of 18 States from the Western Hemisphere. In 1910, the name of this organization was changed into the "Union of American Republics" and ist Commercial Bureau was renamed in "Pan American Union". Both bodies are the point of inception to which the OAS of today and its General Secretariat trace their origins.

Even though the early Pan American Union was created as a mere economic and trade union with a high emphasis on the respect of national souvereignty, the protection of human rights has also been a matter of concern in the Americas. The American Declaration of the Rights and Duties of Man of 1948 is the world's first modern human rights instrument of a general nature. It predates the

---

* The author is a Research Assistant to Prof. Dr. Udo Fink, Johannes-Gutenberg University of Mainz, Germany and was a visiting scholar at the University of Louisville, Brandeis School of Law, from August 20 – 27, 2011.

1 The Organization of American States is a regional organization within the meaning of Chapter VIII of the UN-Charter.

2 The three major regional human rights treaties are: European Convention of Human Rights, African Charter of Human Rights and American Convention of Human Rights.

3 The International Conferences of American States were first introduced by James G. Blain of Maine with the aim of establishing closer ties between the United States and its southern neighbors in order to open Latin American markets to U.S. trade.

Universal Declaration of Human Rights by more than six months. The American Declaration marked the beginning of an evolving human rights system in the Inter-American region. It was followed by the creation of the American Convention of Human Rights in 1969 (the first human rights treaty in the Inter-American System, binding upon the States who ratify it), two Protocols to it[4] as well as other, more specific, Inter-American human rights treaties.[5] The two major human rights supervisory organs are the Inter-American Commission on Human Rights and the Inter-American Court of Human Rights.

The following article will give a brief overview about the development of Inter-American System until today and remark on the implications for the United States as Member State of the OAS in the area of human rights.

II. Background: The Inter-American System of Human Rights in its modern form

The Inter-American System in its modern form came into being at the Ninth International Conference of American States held in Bogotá, Columbia, in 1948. This conference was attended by several Latin American States and the United States. The participating states founded the OAS by signing and later ratifying the Charter of the OAS, which entered into force in 1951.[6] Article 1 of the Charter states: „The American States establish by this Charter the international or-

4 The Protocol to the ACHR on the Protection on Economic, Social and Cultural Rights „San Salvador Protocol“ (entered into force: 1999) and the Protocol to the ACHR on the Abolishment of the Death Penalty (entered into force: 1991).

5 These treaties dealing with specific human rights are i.a.: the Inter-American Convention to Prevent and Punish Torture (entered into force: 1987), the Inter-American Convention on the Forced Disappearances of Persons (entered into force: 1996), the Inter-American Convention on the Prevention, Punishment and Eradication of Violence Against Women (entered into force: 1995) and the Inter-American Convention on the Elimination of All Forms of Discrimination Against Persons with Disabilities (entered into force: 1999).

6 The 21 original member states who signed the OAS Charter on April 30, 1948, are: Argentina, Bolivia, Brazil, Chile, Colombia, Costa Rica, Cuba, the Dominican Republic, Ecuador, El Salvador, Guatemala, Haiti, Honduras, Mexico, Nicaragua, Panama, Paraguay, Peru, the United States, Uruguay and Venezuela. The following states have joined the OAS since then: Barbados (1967), Trinidad and Tobago (1967), Jamaica (1969), Grenada (1975), Suriname (1977), Dominica (1979), Saint Lucia (1979), Antigua and Barbuda (1981), Saint Vincent and the Grenadines (1981), The Bahamas (1982) St. Kitts and Nevis (1984) Canada (1990) Belize (1991) and Guyana (1991).

ganization that they have developed to achieve an order of peace and justice, to promote their solidarity, to strengthen their collaboration, and to defend their sovereignty, their territorial integrity, and their independence.“ The OAS Charter provides for a regional collective security system to deal with threats to the peace and security of the Americas, including mechanisms to prevent disputes among member states, to ensure the peaceful settlement of disputes that did arise and provisions allowing common actions by the American states in the event of aggression. Also, the Charter makes a very general reference to human rights in Articles 3 lit. l and 17. Article 3 lit. l titled „principles“ states: „the American States proclaim the fundamental rights of the individual without distinction as to race, nationality, creed or sex." Article 17 states: "Each State has the right to develop its cultural, political and economic life freely and naturally. In this free development, the State shall respect the rights of the individual and the principles of universal morality."

In addition to the signing of the OAS-Charter, the participating states also adopted the American Declaration of the Rights and Duties of Man in 1948.[7] Despite the effort of some South American States to create a binding human rights treaty, in the end, the American Declaration was adopted as a mere non-binding declaration of principles, a statement of political goals the American States wanted to progressively achieve in the future. Furthermore, any relationship between the OAS-Charter's human rights provisions and the Declaration was excluded by the OAS-States.[8] The Declaration contains in Chapter I (Articles 1 to 28) both classical civil and political rights (such as the right to life, the freedom expression, the right to a fair trial, the right to property, the right of protection from arbitrary arrest etc.) as well as economic, social and cultural rights. Also, the Declaration includes a "general limitation clause", stating that the rights of each person are necessarily limited by the rights of others, by the security of all, and by the just demands of the general welfare and the advancement of democracy" (Article XXVIII). Chapter II of the Declaration lists duties of the human beings towards the state or society, such as the duty to vote, the duty to pay taxes, the duty to serve the community and the nation.

In 1959, the States created the Inter-American Commission on Human Rights as the first international body for the promotion of the observance of

7 Res. XXX, Final Act of the Ninth International Conference of American States, Bogotá, Colombia, March 30-May 2, 1948, at 38 (PAU 1948).

8 Dept. of State, Report of the Delegation of the United States of America to the Ninth International Conference of American States, Bogotá, Colombia, March 30-May 2, 1948, (Publ. No. 3263, 1948), at 35-36.

Human Rights in the Americas. Article 1 of the Commission's original Statute states: „ The Inter-American Commission on Human Rights, created by the Fifth Meeting of Consultation of Ministers of Foreign Affairs, is an autonomous entity of the Organization of American States, the function of which is to promote respect for human rights."

Today, the Commission is a part-time body that meets in sessions for 8 weeks a year, held in Washington D.C at the Headquarters of the OAS. It is composed of seven independent experts who do not necessarily have to be jurists and who are elected to a four-year term by the OAS General Assembly.

Initially, the Commission was only empowered to generate so-called "country reports" on the general human rights situation in the Americas. But the States soon expanded the powers of the Commission to make specific country reports about a specific State and, moreover, added the competence to receive and examine individual petitions against a Member State of the OAS claiming a human right abuse of at least one of the rights listed in the American Declaration.[9] Article 2 of the Comission's original Statute states: „For the purpose of this Statute, human rights are understood to be those set forth in the American Declaration of the Rights and Duties of Man." So the American Declaration became the working instrument for the Commission. To put it in other words: the American Declaration defines for the Commission its subject-matter jurisdiction. The Commission is empowered to measure the actions of the States by the standards set in the American Declaration.

When finding a breach of the Declaration, the Commission can make "recommendations" to the state. As the term "recommendation" already implies, these findings are legally non-binding and can only be regarded as political or moral guidelines for the states. Nevertheless, the Commission is empowered to publish these recommendations if the state fails to comply with it. Publication of a negative human rights record of a particular OAS-Member State can cast a bad

9 Res. XXII "Expanded Functions of the Inter-American Commission on Human Rights", Second Special Inter-American Conference, Rio de Janeiro, Brazil, November 17-30, 1965, Final Act, OAS Off. Rec., OEA/Ser.C/I.13 at 32-34 (1965), in: Human Rights, Vol. 6 (1982), pp. 163 ff. The new function was implemented in Article 9 bis lit. b): "to examine communications submitted to it and any other available information; to address the government of any American state for information deemed pertinent by the Commission; and to make recommendations, when it deems this appropriate, with the objecive of bringing about more effective observance of fundamental human rights". This provision corresponds to Article 20 of the Commission's actual statute.

light on that state and therefore can have political impacts and at least moral force.

In 1969, the so-called Protocol of Buenos Aires amended the OAS-Charter and brought major structural changes to the OAS-System. These major changes include i.a. the creation of the OAS General Assembly as the the supreme decision-making body of the OAS, empowered to set the OAS's general course and policies by means of resolutions and declarations. Furthermore, the Inter-American Commission on Human Rights (originally an "autonomous entity" outside the OAS-Charter) was now integrated into the OAS-System as an organ of the OAS. Articles 106 and 145 of the Charter were included and delineate the Commission's mandate "to promote the observance and protection of human rights and to serve as a consultative organ of the Organization in these matters" (Article 106) and – respectively - "to keep vigilance over the observance of human rights" (Article 145).

In 1969, the American Convention on Human Rights was adopted and entered into force in 1978. Since the American Declaration was only created as a non-binding instrument, the American Convention (being an international treaty) constitutes the first binding human rights instrument in the Inter-American System. The Convention contains a catalogue of classical civil and political rights similar, but not identical, to those of the European Convention on Human Rights, which served – together with the International Covenant on Civil and Political Rights - as a model for the American Convention. The Convention also established two supervisory bodies: The already existing Inter-American Commission on Human Rights and the newly created Inter-American Court of Human Rights, who holds advisory and contentious jurisdiction. Individual and inter-states complaints under the American Convention must first be addressed to the Commission, who – after considering the admissibility and the merits – forwards the case to the Court.[10] In contrast to the Commission's "recommendations", the Court's judgements in contentious cases (individual complaints as well as inter-state complaints) are final and binding upon the Parties.[11] The jurisdiction of the Court in contentious cases must be accepted by the Parties (additionally to the ratification of the Convention). This can be done either generally or individually for a specific case. The Convention is open to all OAS member states, but there is no obligation for them to ratify it. To date, it has not been

10 Individuals cannot bring a claim directly to the Inter-American Court.

11 Pursuant to Articles 67 and 68 of the American Convention.

ratified by Canada and some English-speaking Caribbean states.[12] The United States signed the Convention in 1977 but has not proceeded with ratification since that time.[13]

Ever since the entry-into force of the Convention, the Inter-American Commission obtains a double role in the Inter-American System, both as a main OAS-organ that is competent for individual complaints against any OAS-Member States alleging a breach of the Declaration and as a Convention organ competent for receiving individual complaints alleging a violation of the rights listed in the Convention. However, because not all OAS Member States are parties to the Convention, the Declaration remains for them the only applicable human rights instrument within the Inter-American System.

II. The role of the United States within the Inter-American Human Rights System

As shown above, the Inter-American Human Rights System is based on two pillars: First, the OAS-Charter-based system (encompassing human rights provisions of the OAS-Charter and the American Declaration, with the Inter-American Commission on Human Rights as the principal supervisory institution) and second, the Convention-based system (encompassing the American Convention on Human Rights and other, more specific human rights treaties).

The United States is not formally involved in Convention-based system as it neither is a party to the American Convention of Human Rights nor a party to any other specific the Inter-American human rights treaty. This is seems to be surprising since the US played a major role in the negotiating and drafting process of the American Convention in 1969.[14] Even though some provisions of

12 Antigua and Barbuda, the Bahamas, San Kitts and Nevis, Santa Lucia and San Vicente and the Grenadines.

13 Until today, 24 of the 35 OAS's member states have ratified the Convention. These States are: Argentina. Barbados, Bolivia, Brazil, Chile, Colombia, Costa Rica, Dominica, Dominican Republic, Ecuador, El Salvador, Grenada, Guatemala, Haiti, Honduras, Jamaica, Mexico, Nicaragua, Panama, Paraguay, Peru, Suriname, Uruguay and Venezuela.

14 At a meeting of the Ministers of Foreign Affairs in 1959, the US voted for a resolution asking for the creation of a human rights convention, but excluding US participation in any institutions or organs that were to be established by such a convention. See: *Fox*, The American Convention on Human Rights and Prospects for United States Ratification, 3 Hum. Rts. (1973), 243-282, at 245.

the American Convention were actively framed by US Delegates[15], it took another 10 years until the US (under the Carter administration) finally signed the Convention. Yet to date, the US has not proceeded with ratifying it.[16] Reasons for this positions were fears about the effect the Convention may have on US law.[17] Moreover, potential impediments to the US ratification of the American Convention are seen in Article 4 (the right to life).[18] Controversal aspects con-

---

15 The so-called Federal Clause of Article 28 ACHR states:
" (1) Where a State Party is constituted as a federal state, the national government of such State Party shall implement all the provisions of the Convention over whose subject matter it exercises legislative and judicial jurisdiction.
(2) With respect to the provisions over whose subject matter the constituent units of the federal state have jurisdiction, the national government shall immediately take suitable measures, in accordance with its constitution and its laws, to the end that the competent authorities of the constituent units may adopt appropriate provisions for the fulfillment of this Convention. (...)". The other major addition to the Draft made by the US is expressed in Article 2 ACHR, which reads: „Where the exercise of any of the rights or freedoms referred to in Article 1 is not already ensured by legislative or other provisions, the States Parties undertake to adopt, in accordance with their constitutional processes and the provisions of this Convention, such legislative or other measures as may be necessary to give effect to those rights or freedoms." According to the US interpretion, this Article permits state parties to treat the substantive provisions of the ACHR as being non-self-executing.

16 The US State Department and the Senate Foreign Relations Bureau has categorized the American Convention as being "under review", but it is not on the top list of conventions the US is willing to ratify in the near future.

17 International Human Rights Treaties, Hearings Before the Committee on Foreign Relations, United States Senate, 96th Cong., 1st Session 29 (1979).

18 Article 4 ACHR states:
(1) Every person has the right to have his life respected. This right shall be protected by law and, in general, from the moment of conception. No one shall be arbitrarily deprived of his life.
(2) In countries that have not abolished the death penalty, it may be imposed only for the most serious crimes and pursuant to a final judgment rendered by a competent court and in accordance with a law establishing such punishment, enacted prior to the commission of the crime. The application of such punishment shall not be extended to crimes to which it does not presently apply.
(3) The death penalty shall not be reestablished in states that have abolished it.
(4) In no case shall capital punishment be inflicted for political offenses or related common crimes.
(5) Capital punishment shall not be imposed upon persons who, at the time the crime was committed, were under 18 years of age or over 70 years of age; nor shall it be applied to pregnant women.

cerning Article 4 are whether legal abortions are allowed, the concrete scope of the term arbitrary deprivation of life in para. 1 and the restrictions to the death penalty according to paragraphs 2-5, especially in regard to persons under the age of 18.[19] Legal experts have already shown that these worries are not justified.[20]

Furthermore, it has to be taken into account that many of American Convention's human rights guarantees are similar to those of the ICCPR, a treaty which has been ratified by the US and, therefore, already imposes international human rights obligations upon the US (independently from the fact that the US has not adhered to the ICCPR's Optional Protocol I establishing the jurisdiction of the Human Rights Comittee).[21]

Since there are no legal impediments to the ratification of the American Convention, the reason for the US position may be spotted in the political area.[22]

---

(6) Every person condemned to death shall have the right to apply for amnesty, pardon, or commutation of sentence, which may be granted in all cases. Capital punishment shall not be imposed while such a petition is pending decision by the competent authority.

19 Another issue is Article 13 (Freedom of Thought and Expression). For a legal discussion see: Fox, The American Convention on Human Rights and Prospects for United States Ratification, 3 Hum. Rts. (1973), 243-282, at 263.

20 See for example: *Kirk*, Should the United States ratify the American Convention on Human Rights?, Revista IIDH Vol. 14 (1991), 65-89; *Fox*, The American Convention on Human Rights and Prospects for United States Ratification, 3 Hum. Rts. (1973), 243-282, at 263.

21 The former practice in some US States to impose the death penalty to persons under 18 years, the US' reservation to Article 6 ICCPR (right to life), allowing the sentencing of a person regardless of his age to death was declared incompatible with the objects and purposes of the ICCPR by several ICCPR Parties. Furthermore, the Human Rights Committee in its General Comment No. 24 of 04.11.1994 (CCPR/C/21/Rev.1/Add.6) stated: "(…) provisions in the Covenant that represent customary international law (and a fortiori when they have the character of peremptory norms) may not be the subject of reservations. Accordingly, a State may not reserve the right to (…) to execute pregnant women or children." This issue has also been dealt with by the Inter-American Commission in the cases *Roach and Pinkerton vs. USA*, Case 9647, Inter-Am. C.H.R., Report No. 3/87 (1987), and *Michael Domingues vs. USA*, Case 12.285, Inter-Am. C.H.R, Report No 62/02 (2002).

22 A Member of the US Senate once has expressed the fear that „international human rights treaties require a surrender of the United States' exclusive juisdiction over ist own internal order" and „human rights treaties might enhance federal powers at the expense of the States", for further references see: *Fox*, The American Convention on Human

Certainly, ratification of the American Convention would increase the political pressure to also accept the binding jurisdiction of the Inter-American Court, which the US always has rejected to do.

Leaving behind the discussion about joining the American Convention, it has to be recalled that the US (as a Member State of the OAS) is legally bound by its obligations arising from the OAS-Charter. As mentioned earlier, Articles 3 lit. l and 17 OAS-Charter impose upon the OAS Member States - at least in a very general way - legally binding obligations concerning the protection of human rights.[23] Most importantly, the US stands under the jurisdiction of the Inter-American Commission on Human Rights, which is competent to act on individual complaints against all OAS Member States, alleging a violation of the human rights listed in the American Declaration. In exercising this function, the Inter-American Commission has decided on many cases against the US over the last decades and, consequently, has issued "recommendations", in which it asked the US to stop violating certain rights of the American Declaration.

The first individual petition the US was confronted with was the Case Baby Boy vs. USA of 1981.[24] In this case an individual complaint launched by an NGO alleged a breach of Art. I Declaration (right to life) in light of US law allowing abortion of a fetus undertaken by a doctor. While, in the end, the Commission did not find a violation of the Declaration, it made some remarks on the nature of the Declaration:

> "The international obligation of the United States of America, as a member of the Organization of American States (OAS), under the jurisdiction of the Inter-American Commission on Human Rights (IACHR) is governed by the Charter of OAS (Bogotá, 1948) as amended by the Protocol of Buenos Aires on February 27, 1967, ratified by United States on April 23, 1968.

Rights and Prospects for United States Ratification, 3 Hum. Rts. (1973), 243-282, at 245.

23 The concrete scope of these Charter obligations can be a matter of dispute and this issue still needs be analysed in detail. There are good reasons to hold that the OAS-Charter (by means of interpretation – imposes on the States an obligation to refrain from serious and grave human rights violations similar to the obligation under Articles 55, 56 UN-Charter.

24 *Baby Boy vs. USA*, Case 2141, Inter-Am. C.H.R., Report No. 23/81, OEA/Ser.L./V/II.54, doc.9 rev.1 (1981).

> As a consequence of articles 3 i, 16, 51 e, 112 and 150 of this Treaty[25], the provisions of other instruments and resolutions of the OAS on human rights, **acquired binding force**. Those instruments and resolutions approved with the vote of U.S. Government, are the following:
>
> - American Declaration of the Rights and Duties of Man (Bogotá, 1948)
> - Statute and Regulations of the IACHR 1960, as amended by resolution XXII of the Second Special Inter-American Conference (Rio de Janeiro, 1965)
> - Statute and Regulations of IACHR of 1979-1980."[26]
>
> (highlighted by the author)

The Commission repeated and specified its argumentation in other cases, all of which were brought against the US.[27] In the Case Mary and Carrie Dann vs. USA (1999) the Commission explained:

> „The State's observations fail to consider, however, the well-established and long-standing jurisprudence and practice of the inter-American system according to which the American Declaration is recognized as constituting a source of legal obligation for OAS members states, including in particular those states that are not parties to the American Convention on Human Rights. These obligations are considered to flow from the human rights obligations of member states under the OAS Charter, which member states have agreed are contained in and defined by the American Declaration (...). As a source of legal obligation, therefore, it is appropriate for the Commission to consider and, where substantiated, find violations of that instrument attributable to a member state of the OAS, including the United States."[28]

Hence, according to the Commission, the American Declaration, though originally drafted as a mere declaration, now contains legally binding obligations for all OAS-Member States, including and especially those, who are not parties to the American Convention.

---

25 Meaning Articles 3 lit. l, 17, 106 and 145 of the actual OAS-Charter.

26 *Baby Boy v. USA*, Case 2141,., Report No. 23/81 (1981), Inter-Am. C.H.R, at para. 15-16.

27 See for example: *Roach vs. USA*, Case 9647, Report No. 3/87 (1987), Inter-Am. C.H.R; *William Andrews vs. USA*, Case 11.139, Report No 57/96 (1986), Inter-Am. C.H.R.; *Mary and Carrie Dann vs. USA*, Case 11.140, Report No. 75/02 (2002), Inter-Am. C.H.R.; *Rafael Ferrer-Mazorra et. al. vs. USA*, Case No. 9903, Report No. 51/01 (2001), Inter-Am. C.H.R; *Wayne Smith, Hugo Armendarit, et. al. vs. USA*, Case No. 12.562, Report No. 81/10 (2010), Inter-Am. C.H.R.

28 *Mary and Carrie Dann vs. USA*, Case 11.140, Report No. 75/02 (2002), Inter-Am. C.H.R., at para 163.

In its legal argumentation the Commission often refers to the Advisory Opinion OC-10/89 „Interpretation of the American Declaration of the Rights and Duties of Man Within the Framework of Article 64 of the American Convention on Human Rights“[29] rendered by the Inter-American Court of Human Rights in 1989. There, the Court pointed out that „to determine the legal status of the American Declaration it is appropriate to look to the inter-American system of today in the light of the evolution it has undergone since the adoption of the Declaration, rather than to examine the normative value and significance which that instrument was believed to have had in 1948.“[30] The Court then referred to the human rights provisions in the Charter of the OAS as well as to Artices 106 and 145 OAS-Charter (dealing with the functions and powers of the Commission) and stated: „Hence it may be said that by means of an authoritative interpretation, the member states of the Organization have signaled their agreement that the Declaration contains and defines the fundamental human rights referred to in the Charter. (...)“[31]

This view is strongly and persistantly objected by the US, for whom the Declaration constitutes a mere non-binding declaration of principles producing with political and not legal obligations. [32] So far, the question of the legal nature of the Declaration – even though dealt with by some scholars[33] - has not been subject of a profound legal analysis. The binding character of the American Declaration could be explained either by means of international customary law or by means of international treaty law, i,e. indirectly through interpreting the

29 Inter-American Court of Human Rights, Advisory Opinion OC-10/89, July 14, 1989. Series A No. 10.

30 Inter-American Court of Human Rights, Advisory Opinion OC-10/89, July 14, 1989. Series A No. 10, at para. 43

31 Inter-American Court of Human Rights, Advisory Opinion OC-10/89, July 14, 1989. Series A No. 10, at para. 43.

32 See for example the answer of the US in the case *Hugo Armendariz v. United States*, Case 526-03, Report No. 57/06 (2006), Inter-Am. C.H.R., at para. 21: „the State contends that the American Declaration does not create legally binding obligations on OAS member states and cannot be said to create rights or impose duties on the United States, and therefore any assertion that the United States has violated any of the Declaration's provisions has no validity“. See also: Response of the Government of the United States of America to the Inter-American Commission on Human Rights Regarding Jessica Gonzales Petition No. P-1490-05, p. 26, http://www.aclu.org/files/pdfs/womensrights/gonzales_govtresponse20060925.pdf.

33 See for example *Buergenthal*, The Revised OAS-Charter and the Protection of Human Rights, he American Journal of International Law, Vol. 69, No. 4 (Oct., 1975), 828-836, at 834.

OAS-Charter. For the means of this article, a deeper analysis of this aspect would be go too far, but it must be stated that it remains highly doubtful whether the Declaration as such has become legally binding for the OAS-Member States over the time. The US point of view appears to be more convincing[34] as it is a fundamental principle in international treaty law that states can only be bound by a norm if they agree to be bound.[35]

Since 1981, the Commission has found violations of the Declaration by the US in a large number of cases. Most cases deal with the application of the death penality in the US, especially to persons under the age of 18, a practice undertaken by some US States in the past.[36] The most recent case "Mark Anthony Stroman vs. US" dealing with the death penalty is of July 22, 2011. In that case, the Commission condemned the judicial execution of Mark Anthony Stroman, that took place on July 20, 2011, in Texas, in defiance of the precautionary measures[37] the Commission has granted earlier in favor of the applicant to protect his life and physical integrity Through the precautionary measures, the Commission asked the United States to refrain from carrying out the death penalty until the Commission had the opportunity to issue a decision on the petitioners' claims regarding the alleged violations of the American Declaration. Additionally, the Commission again reminded the US of its obligations to fully respect the human rights set forth in the American Declaration.

Furthermore, the Commission recently published a country report about US immigration law, finding a breach of various rights of the American Declaration

34 It may be true that some of the Declaration's core rights are also part of universal customary law, binding upon all States. Insofar, a comparison can be drawn to the Universal Declaration of Human Rights, of which it is held, that some of its core rights have become international customary law. For a deeper legal analysis of the problem of the binding nature of the Declaration see: *Gillich*, The American Declaration of the Rights and Duties of Man: A Legally Binding document or only a non-binding declaration of principles?, presentation held at American University, Washington College of Law on July 26, 2011, pending for publication.

35 Article 34 VCLT states: „A treaty does not create either obligations or rights for a third State without its consent."

36 See for example: *Roach and Pinkterton vs. USA*, Case 9647, Inter-Am. C.H.R., Report No. 3/87 (1987) and *Michael Domingues vs. USA*, Case 12.285, Inter-Am. C.H.R, Report No 62/02 (2002).

37 The authority of the IACHR to issue precautionary measures in respect of Member States of the Organization of American States (OAS) is provided for under Article 25 of the Commission's current Rules of Procedure,

(i.a. the right to asylum, the right to family life, etc).[38] Also, the situation of the Guantanamo detainees has been under review by the Commission. Beginning with the first report in 2002[39], only two months after the US began transferring individuals to Guantanamo Bay, the Commission granted precautionary measures requesting the US to take the „urgent measures necessary to have the legal status of the detainees at Guantanamo Bay determined by a competent tribunal“.[40] In the following years the Commission reiterated its precautionary measures and amplified them to address other human rights concerns that have arisen (including the possible infliction of methods of interrogation that constitute torture or other cruel, inhuman or degrading punishment or treatment and the transfer of detainees to third countries where there is a real prospect of such treatment.[41] Most recently, on August 2, 2011, the Commission approved a resolution urging the US to close the detention facility without delay and to arrange for the trial or release of the detainees.[42] The Commission also urged the US to reveal the identities of those detainees who have been cleared for transfer and to ensure that they are afforded an adequate, individualized examination of the factual basis for their transfer before an independent and impartial tribunal. Furthermore, the Commission reiterated its request to conduct an in-loco visit to Guantanamo Bay to interview any person detained there. The US has invited the Commission to visit Guantanamo in the past, but it indicated that personal interviews with the detainees would not be permitted, a condition that the Commission does not accept.[43]

---

38 Report on Immigration in the United States: Detention and due process, OEA/Ser.L/V/II. Doc. 78/10, 30 December 2010, available at: http://cidh.org/countryrep/USImmigration/TOC.htm.

39 Guantanamo Bay Precautionary Measures Communication of March 12, 2002 from IACHR President *Juan E. Mendez* to US Secretary of State *Colin Powell.*

40 Detainees in Guantanamo Bay, Cuba; Request for Precautionary Measures, Inter-Am. C.H.R. (March 13, 2002).

41 See for further references: *Tittemore*, Guantanamo Bay and the Precautionary Measures of the Inter-American Commission on Human Rights: A Case for International Oversight in the Struggle Against Terrorism, Human Rights Law Review 6:2 (2006), 378-402.

42 Resolution No. 2/11 Regarding the Situation of the Detainees at Guantanamo Bay, United States MC 259-02, available at: http://www.cidh.oas.org/pdf%20files/Resolution%202-11%20Guantanamo.pdf.

43 Inter-Am.C.H.R. press release No. 86/11.

IV. Conclusion

It has sometimes been argued that the Inter-American System was a purely South- and Central-American System and the American Convention is often riduculed as the „Latino Convention“. But, on the contrary: As shown above, the US plays an active and vital role in the Inter-American System of Human Rights. With the USA and Canada as Members States of the OAS, the OAS is a truly Inter-American organization.

The Inter-American Commission on Human Rights, with its dual role as an organ under the OAS-Charter as well as an organ under the American Convention, is the principal vehicle for the development and the protection of human rights in the Inter-American System. In its first years of operation, the Commisson considered more than 3,700 communications concerning alleged human rights violations in the Americas and it still faces a large number of human rights charges. In exercising its functions, the Commission has always interpreted its powers extensively. By this means, the Commission has contributed largely to the evolution of the human rights protection in the Inter-American System. However, the Commission's view of the legally binding character of the Declaration remains challenged by the US. This problem will certainly continue to be a matter of dispute between the US and the Inter-American Commission.

Gender-Neutral Language in U.S. Courts

*by Judith D. Fischer**

I. Introduction

Whether language should be gender-neutral has been a topic of discussion on both sides of the Atlantic.[1] Speakers of various languages who want to avoid biased wording confront unique problems.[2] In some languages, every noun is assigned a gender that must agree with associated words.[3] Three-gender systems, such as German or Dutch, employ feminine, masculine, and neuter genders that must be taken into account in addressing problems of gender bias.[4] By contrast, in English, most nouns are neuter, a noun's gender is determined by the sex of the referent, and there are fewer instances of required gender agreement. But English does present its own specific problems, as discussed below.

This article considers the problem of gender and language in a legal setting by presenting results of a study of U.S. judicial opinions, which are written in English. Part II presents background about gender-neutral language in English. Part III discusses graceful ways to accomplish gender neutrality. Part IV then presents the study's results through data from federal appellate judges' opinions.[5]

---

* Judith D. Fischer is an associate professor of law at the University of Louisville in Louisville, Kentucky, U.S.A. Her email address is judith.fischer@louisville.edu.

1 See *Deborah Cameron*, Feminism and Linguistic Theory 6 (2d ed. 1992) (stating that "the challenge to sexist language could and can be found among speakers of many languages, including French, German, Dutch, Italian and Japanese."); *Ann Weatherall*, Gender, Language and Discourse 11 (2002) (stating that sexist language has been an issue for speakers of many languages).

2 *Anne Pauwels*, Linguistic Sexism and Feminist Linguistic Activism 551, 556-59 in The Handbook of Language and Gender (Janet Holmes & Miriam Meyerhoff eds., 2003) (discussing specific difficulties in the use of gender-neutral terms in Dutch, German, French, and Spanish).

3 Id. at 557.

4 Id. at 557-59. A discussion of proposed gender-neutral solutions in those and other languages is beyond the scope of this article, but the topic has been amply covered elsewhere. E.g. id.

5 A full report of this study was published as Framing Gender: Federal Appellate Judges' Choices about Gender-Neutral Language, 43 U.S.F.L. Rev. 473 (2009).

II. Background on gender-neutral language

In this article, *gender-biased language*, which is sometimes called *sexist language*, means language that represents the male as the norm,[6] gratuitously identifies the sex of a referent, or demeans or trivializes women.[7] Its opposite, *gender-neutral language*, sometimes called *nonsexist language*[8] and *gender-inclusive language*,[9] avoids gender bias. These definitions focus on bias in favor of the masculine because, although gender-biased language can be directed against males, it is usually directed against females, who most often experience its negative effects.[10]

1. Gender as an attribute of language

Many of the world's languages employ grammatical gender systems.[11] The term *gender* has its roots in the Old French word *gendre*, which simply meant *kind.*[12]

---

6 See *Janet B. Parks & Mary Ann Roberton*, Explaining Age and Gender Effects on Attitudes Toward Sexist Language, 24 J. Language & Soc. Psychol. 401, 402 (2005) (citing studies showing that "sexist language can suggest that the masculine is the norm and the feminine is the exception."); *Anne Pauwels*, Women Changing Language 13 (1998) (stating that in sexist language, "practices and usage express a bias against women in favour of men."); *Bobbye D. Sorrels*, The Nonsexist Communicator 1 (1983) (stating, "Broadly defined, sexist communication precasts either females or males into roles on the basis of sex alone.")

7 See *Casey Miller & Kate Swift*, Words and Women 51 (1976) (arguing against "suffix words used to introduce an irrelevant sexual distinction"); *Parks & Roberton*, supra note 6, at 402 (defining sexist language as "words, phrases, and expressions that unnecessarily differentiate between women and men or exclude, trivialize, or diminish either gender") (citation omitted).

8 See *William B. Hill*, A Need for the Use of Nonsexist Language in the Courts, 49 Wash. & Lee L. Rev. 275, 276 (1992).

9 See *Cheryl B. Preston*, This Old House: A Blueprint for Constructive Feminism, 83 Geo. L.J. 2271, 2296-97 (1995) (using the term "gender-inclusive language").

10 *Janet B. Parks & Mary Ann Roberton*, Attitudes Toward Women Mediate the Gender Effect on Attitudes Toward Sexist Language, 28 Psychol. Women Q. 233, 233 (2004) (stating, "Although sexist language can be directed toward men, studies in English-speaking cultures have established that its deleterious and disempowering effects typically accrue to women.").

11 *Greville G. Corbett*, Gender 1-2 (1991).

For linguists, "Genders are classes of nouns reflected in the behavior of associated words."[13] While grammatical gender may have some connection to sex, the two categories are not coextensive,[14] and in some languages gender labels have little direct tie to sex.[15] In others, called "semantic" or "natural gender systems," grammatical gender is determined by the sex of the word's referent.[16] These differences mean that eliminating gender bias is fraught with its own special problems in each language.[17] Because this article covers U.S. judicial opinions, it focuses on the English language, which is a natural gender system.[18]

2. Gender bias in the English language

Gender-biased language appears in English in three settings. The first is through male-linked words that are used in a pseudo-generic sense.[19] This includes using nouns like *man* and *mankind* to refer to both females and males, as in the following sentence: "Man needs food."[20]

---

12 Id. at 1.

13 Id.

14 *Corbett*, supra note 11, at 1 (calling gender "the most puzzling of the grammatical categories").

15 *Pauwels*, supra note 6, at 37-38 (citation omitted)).

16 Id.

17 See *Cameron*, supra note 1, at 6 (2d ed. 1992) (stating that "the challenge to sexist language could and can be found among speakers of many languages, including French, German, Dutch, Italian and Japanese."); *Weatherall*, supra note 1, at 11 (stating that sexist language has been an issue for speakers of many languages); *Graham Martin*, When Is a 'Manageress' a 'Manager'? Approaches to Gender-Neutral Language Use in Five West European Languages, 40 Linguist: J. Inst. Linguists 80, 80-83 (2001) (discussing efforts at gender-neutral language in English, French, Spanish, Italian, and German); *Pauwels*, supra note 2, at 556-59 (discussing specific difficulties in the use of gender-neutral terms in Dutch, German, French, and Spanish).

18 *Pauwels*, supra note 6, at 37.

19 See *Francine Wattman Frank*, Language Planning, Language Reform, and Language Change: A Review of Guidelines for Nonsexist Usage 105, 119 in Language, Gender, and Professional Writing: Theoretical Approaches and Guidelines for Nonsexist Usage (*Francine Wattman Frank & Paula A. Treichler* eds., 1989) (using the term "pseudogenerics" to refer to male-linked terms that purportedly include persons of both sexes).

20 *Dale Spender*, Man Made Language 152 (2d ed. 1985) (citation omitted).

The pseudo-generic masculine also occurs in the gendered third-person-singular pronouns *he*, *him*, and *his*,[21] which cause what has been termed "the pronoun problem."[22] When these pronouns refer to identified persons, they are outside this article's definition of gender bias because they do not present the masculine as the norm. A problem arises, however, when a writer needs a pronoun to refer to a person of unspecified sex, as in this example: "A lawyer should state his argument clearly." This use of the masculine pronoun is inaccurate for the legal field, which in the United States is now composed of about one-third women.[23] It illustrates how pseudo-generic terms treat the masculine as the norm by omitting reference to the feminine. Women are thus "eliminated from language, and consequently from thought and reality."[24]

A second type of gendered language in English is gender-marked terminology. Gendered kinship terms like *mother* and *father* legitimately describe roles based on sex.[25] However, other words like *waitress*, *chairman*, and *chairwoman* are unnecessarily gender-marked.[26] When persons of both sexes perform the same functions, calling attention to their sex in this way is gratuitous.[27] Such gendered terms often "make women invisible, treat them as secondary, or have a trivializing effect on the linguistic portrayal of women."[28] These terms can be replaced with more neutral words,[29] like *server* and *chair*.[30]

---

21 *Dennis Baron*, Grammar and Gender 98 (1986) (pointing out that "gender agreement in English occurs not between adjective and noun but in the pronoun system, specifically in the third person pronoun"); *Graham Martin*, When Is a 'Manageress' a 'Manager'? Approaches to Gender-Neutral Language Use in Five West European Languages, 40 Linguist: J. Inst. Linguists 80, 80 (2001) (explaining that in English, a major focus of the language revolution has been on personal pronouns).

22 See *Beverly Ray Burlingame*, Student Essay, Reaction and Distraction: The Pronoun Problem in Legal Persuasion, 1 Scribes J. Leg. Writing 87, 87 (1990).

23 ABA Commission on Women in the Profession, The Unfinished Agenda: Women in the Legal Profession 14 (Executive Summary 2001).

24 *Spender*, supra note 20, at 157.

25 *Miller & Swift*, supra note 7, at 51.

26 Id.

27 See *Parks & Roberton*, supra note 6, at 401 (noting that terms like "drum major" and "majorette" are "hierarchic and separatist").

28 *Pauwels*, supra note 6, at 43. See also *Ann Weatherall*, Women and Men in Language, 25 Hum. Comm. Res. 275, 277 (1998) (stating that biased language "conceal[s] the existence and importance of women as a social group").

29 For further suggestions and resources on changing gender-marked language, see Part III, infra.

30 But see *William Safire*, On Language: Genderese, N.Y. Times Mag. (May 16, 1999), available at http://query.nytimes.com/gst/fullpage.html?res=9501E1D

A third type of gender-biased language arises from the user's own choice and sometimes consists of repeating old, formulaic phrasing. This includes references to men and women in nonparallel terms, as in the phrase "man and wife."[31] It may also involve referring to women in terms that demean or trivialize them, such as calling an adult woman "little girl" or "honey." As linguist Deborah Cameron has explained, when used by non-intimates, such terms "are inherently disrespectful. They are a unilateral declaration by the man that he need not trouble about the formalities expected of non-intimates."[32] Within recent memory, U.S. judges have addressed women in the courtroom with such terms.[33] But as law professor Deborah Rhode has observed, due to increased consciousness about demeaning language, the use of such trivializing terms is no longer common.[34]

3. The movement for gender-neutral language

Before the twentieth century, the gender bias in English was confronted only sporadically For example, in the late nineteenth century both Julia Smith[35] and Elizabeth Cady Stanton[36] rewrote the Bible in gender-neutral language A con-

---

9163AF935A25756C0A96F958260) (objecting to replacing "chairman" with "chair" because it "sounds four-legged").

31 See *Miller & Swift*, Casey Miller & Kate Swift, The Handbook of Nonsexist Writing 85-87 (1980).

32 *Cameron*, supra note 1, at 106. See also *Robin Lakoff*, Language and Woman's Place 25 (1975) (pointing out than calling an adult woman a "girl" suggests that she is immature and irresponsible). See also *Ann Bartow*, Some Dumb Girl Syndrome: Challenging and Subverting Destructive Stereotypes of Female Attorneys, 11 Wm. & Mary J. Women & L. 221, 259 (stating that calling an adult woman a "girl" indicates that she is subordinate).

33 See, e.g., *John C. Coughenour* et al., The Effects of Gender in the Federal Courts; The Final Report of the Ninth Circuit Gender Bias Task Force, 67 S. Cal. L. Rev. 745, 812 (1994) (reporting that some attorney respondents in a Ninth Circuit survey said federal judges had addressed them as "'young lady'" or "'little girl'"); *Nancy Blodgett*, "I Don't Think That Ladies Should Be Lawyers, A.B.A. J. 48 (Dec. 1, 1986) (reporting that a New York judge called a courtroom lawyer "little girl").

34 *Deborah L. Rhode*, The Unfinished Agenda: Women and the Legal Profession 20 (2001).

35 See *Frank*, supra note 19, at 128 (referring to Julia Smith's 1876 feminist Bible).

36 See *Tracy A. Thomas, Elizabeth Cady Stanton* on the Federal Marriage Amendment: A Letter to the President, 22 Const. Comment. 137, 153-54 (2005) (citing *Elizabeth Cady*

certed movement for widespread change arose only in the late 1960s, as the second wave of the women's movement gathered momentum.[37] Feminists in the United States became "trailblazers in both exposing sexist bias and proposing changes."[38]

The latter part of the twentieth century saw an increase in the trend toward gender-neutral language in English.[39] As professionals in various fields began to adopt it, gender-neutral language appeared in employment advertising, textbooks, the popular media, dictionaries,[40] and religious publications.[41] Studies showed a decline in the use of masculine nouns and pronouns as generics.[42] A 1993 news article reported anecdotal evidence that New York judges' choices of language were "a sign of how mainstream the cause of 'inclusive language' has become 30 years after the feminist movement of the 1960s."[43] One scholar observed, "We are becoming less and less able to envision females when male terminology is used."[44]

The movement for gender-neutral language has had its opponents.[45] They have argued that tradition should not be changed,[46] that sexist language is only a

---

Stanton, The Woman's Bible (1896) and recounting how *Stanton* rewrote the Bible "using a feminist lens").

37 *Cameron*, supra note 1, at 9 (stating that feminists began examining sexism in language "during the late 1960s and 1970s"); *Frank*, supra note 19, at 118 (stating, "The reawakening and growth of the feminist movement in the late 1960s and 1970s rekindled interest in the question of language and gender."); *Betty Lou Dubois & Isabel Crouch*, Linguistic Disruption: He/She, S/He, He or She, and He-She in Women and Language in Transition 28, 29 (*Joyce Penfield* ed., 1987) (stating, "by far the majority of writers before the 1970s did not worry about the use of pronouns.")

38 *Pauwels*, supra note 2, at 552.

39 Id. at 561.

40 *Pauwels*, supra note 6, at 203-09 (presenting documentation of changes in these areas).

41 Id. at 31 (noting that feminist theologian *Mary Daly* has had a significant impact on changing sexist language in religious expression.)

42 *Pauwels*, supra note 2, at 563; *Robert L. Cooper*, The Avoidance of Androcentric Generics, 50 Int'l. J. Soc. Language 5, 19 (1984)) (finding the greatest decline in androcentric generics in publications "addressed to women and the well-educated.")

43 *Deborah Pines*, When 'She' Replaces 'He' at Foley Square, 210 N.Y.L.J. 1, 1 (Nov. 1, 1993).

44 *Cheryl B. Preston*, This Old House: A Blueprint for Constructive Feminism, 83 Geo. L.J. 2271, 2296 (1995).

45 See *Maija S. Blaubergs*, An Analysis of Classic Arguments against Changing Sexist Language, 3 Women's Stud. Int'l Q. 135, 136 (1980) (listing arguments advanced against changing masculine generics); *Frank*, supra note 19, at 124 (stating that some negative reactions have "taken the form of ridicule and satire"); *Michael Levin*, Vs. Ms.

trivial issue,[47] that gender-neutral language is awkward,[48] and that it annoys readers.[49] The first two objections are countered in Section I-D below, which documents the importance of gender-neutral language. The third and fourth objections are countered in Section II, which presents a variety of techniques for writing graceful and unobtrusive gender-neutral language.

4. The importance of gender-neutral language

Scholars and commentators in several fields have shown that concerns about biased language are far from trivial. Language scholars and psychologists have demonstrated that biased language affects individuals' perceptions of themselves and the world. Meanwhile, legal professionals have articulated the importance of nonsexist language both to fairness in the law and to the clarity of legal documents.

Casey Miller and Kate Swift, influential proponents of gender-neutral language, alluded to a perhaps apocryphal research report entitled "Development of the Uterus in Rats, Guinea Pigs, and Men."[50] By implying that male humans have uteruses, that title dramatizes what language scholars' research has now

---

in Sexist Language: A Modern Philosophical Analysis 217, 222 (*Mary Vetterling-Braggin* ed., 1981) (asserting that nonsexist language reforms are "encroachments to resist."); *Parks & Roberton*, supra note 6, at 401-02 (citing participants on both sides of the debate about gender-neutral language.)

46 See *Frank*, supra note 19, at 124-25 (citing appeals to tradition by opponents of language reform); *Janet B. Parks & Mary Ann Roberton*, Contemporary Arguments against Nonsexist Language: Blaubergs (1980) Revisited, 39 Sex Roles 445, 448 (1998) (citing appeals to tradition by opponents of language reform).

47 *Paula A. Treichler & Francine Wattman Frank*, Guidelines for Nonsexist Usage 137, in Language, Gender, and Professional Writing: Theoretical Approaches and Guidelines for Nonsexist Usage (Francine Wattman Frank & Paula A. Treichler eds., 1989).

48 Justice *Antonin Scalia* recently opined that gender-neutral language often leads to awkward phrasing. *Antonin Scalia & Bryan A. Garner*, Making Your Case: The Art of Persuading Judges 119 (2008). See also Safire, supra note 30, (stating that gender-neutral language "can take the punch out of a good sentence," but acknowledging that sometimes proponents of nonsexist language "have indisputable logic on their side").
But see *Treichler & Frank*, supra note 47, at 141 (stating that "convoluted alternatives almost always signal a deeper problem and the need for further analysis in the writing or editing process.")

49 See *Parks & Roberton*, supra note 46, at 453 (noting study subjects' objection to using gender-neutral language because some do not approve of it).

50 *Miller & Swift*, supra note 31, at 9.

solidly shown: that supposedly generic male-linked words are often perceived as referring only to males.[51]

Language scholars thus argue that gender-biased language subtly creeps into the consciousness of both women and men, burdening them with stereotypes about the meaning of being female or male.[52] Such language "reinforce[s] sexist attitudes and behaviors,"[53] assigning females to "secondary status."[54] Linguist Anne Pauwels has concluded that gender-biased language "not only reflects but also helps to construct and perpetuate a sexist reality."[55]

Scholars from the fields of psychology and social scienc have corroborated language scholars' conclusions. Psychologists Laura Madson and Jennifer Shoda found that student subjects perceived pseudo-generic masculine words as gender-biased,[56] and Mykol Hamilton found that subjects hearing a story that used male-linked generics saw male images more than female ones.[57] Gender-biased language has even been shown to limit girls' views of their vocational options.[58] As feminist Dale Spender put it, language "determines the limits of our world, which constructs our reality."[59] Gender-neutral language more accurately reflects that reality.[60]

---

51 See *William R. Todd-Mancillas*, Masculine Generics=Sexist Language: A Review of the Literature and Implications for Speech Communication Professionals, 29 Comm. Q. 107, 115 (Spring 1981) (summarizing fourteen studies showing that subjects "perceive 'man'-linked words and third-person singular generics as referencing men more frequently than women."); *Pauwels*, supra note 6, at 71-73 (citing studies); *Janet Bing*, Penguins Can't Fly and Women Don't Count: Language and Thought, 15 Women & Language 11 (1992) (citing studies); *John Gastil*, Generic Pronouns and Sexist Language: The Oxymoronic Character of Masculine Generics, 23 Sex Roles 629, 630 (1990) (citing studies); *Parks & Roberton*, supra note 6, at 402 (citing studies).

52 *Miller & Swift*, supra note 7, at x; Parks & Roberton, supra note 6, at 402 (citing studies).

53 *Gastil*, supra note 51, at 630.

54 *Miller & Swift*, supra note 7, at x.

55 *Pauwels*, supra note 6, at 92. See also Bing, supra note 51, at 11 (arguing that language affects thought).

56 *Laura Madson & Jennifer Shoda*, Alternating Between Masculine and Feminine Pronouns: Does Essay Topic Affect Readers' Perceptions?, 54 Sex Roles 275, 284 (2006).

57 *Mykol C. Hamilton*, Masculine Bias in the Attribution of Personhood, 15 Psychol. Women Q. 393, 396-97 (1991).

58 *Parks & Roberton*, supra note 6, at 402.

59 *Spender*, supra note 20, at 139.

60 See *Cameron*, supra note 1, at 103 (stating that gender-neutral language is more "in line with the ways things really are.")

Legal professionals have also recognized the negative effects of gender-biased language. Beginning in the 1980s, a wave of gender task-force studies appeared in various U.S. jurisdictions, both state and federal.[61] Some of the published reports proposed the use of gender-neutral language in statutes, judicial opinions, and other legal writing.[62] Coverage of gender-neutral language also began to appear in legal writing textbooks.[63]

Increased focus on gender-neutral language in the U.S. legal profession has been prompted first of all by principles of fairness. As Judge William Hill stated, the legal profession "demands of its practitioners a reverence and respect for the power of the written and spoken word."[64] When lawyers' language excludes "more than one-half of the population," Judge Hill argued, "then surely something is awry."[65] He concluded that avoiding gender bias in legal discourse "is the right thing to do."[66] Numerous others have urged lawyers to use gender-

---

61 See *Michael B. Shortnacy*, Guilty and Gay, a Recipe for Execution in American Courtrooms: Sexual Orientation as a Tool for Prosecutorial Misconduct in Death Penalty Cases, 51 Am. U. L. Rev. 309, 320 n. 39 (2001) (citing studies); *Morrison Torrey*, You Call That Education?, 19 Wis. Women's L.J. 93, 93 n.1 (2004) (citing studies).

62 E.g., Ohio Joint Task Force on Gender Fairness, Final Report of the Ohio Joint Task Force on Gender Fairness 6 (1995) (proposing that gender-neutral language be used in "all rules, canons, jury instructions and other materials prepared by all participants in the justice system"); Gender Bias in the Courts of the Commonwealth Final Report, 7 Wm. & Mary J. Women & L. 705, 786 (2001) (stating that "most language in court publications [in Virginia] is gender-neutral," and recommending that "[a]ll court documents be reviewed periodically for gender-neutral language."); Missouri Task Force on Gender and Justice, Report of the Missouri Task Force on Gender and Justice, 58 Mo. L. Rev. 485, 658 (1993) (recommending that gender-neutral language be used in numerous specified publications and that judges and clerks be encouraged to use it); Wisconsin Equal Justice Task Force, Final Report: Gender Bias Task Force Report Summary, 6 Wis. Women's L.J. 173, 174 (1991) (recommending that jury instructions be written in gender-neutral language). A New York committee published a pamphlet recommending the use of gender-neutral language in the courts. New York State Judicial Committee on Women in the Courts, Fair Speech: Gender Neutral Language in the Courts 4 (2d ed. 1997) [hereinafter "Fair Speech"].

63 E.g., *Linda H. Edwards*, Legal Writing: Process, Analysis, and Organization 217-21 (4th ed., 2006); *Richard K. Neumann & Sheila Simon*, Legal Writing 250 (Aspen Pubs. 2008); *Laurel Currie Oates & Anne Enquist*, The Legal Writing Handbook: Analysis, Research, and Writing 157-58 (4th ed., 2006) (each recommending gender-neutral language and suggesting techniques for writing it).

64 *Hill*, supra note 8, at 275.

65 Id. at 276.

66 Id. at 275.

neutral language,[67] often stressing that the law conveys a society's norms, which should be fair to all its members.[68] Few have opposed these views.[69] As Judge Judith Kaye stated, "Why shouldn't lawyers lead others in promoting equality in every way possible?"[70]

Gender-neutral language can thus help construct a frame of the legal system that includes and empowers both genders.[71] It is also more exact.[72] When certain words sometimes mean males, sometimes mean females, and sometimes include both sexes, confusion may result.[73] Moreover, "many brief readers — male and female judges and their staffs — do notice and do care" whether lawyers use gender-neutral language.

67 E.g., *Terri Le Clercq*, Expert Legal Writing 127-33 (1995) (suggesting ways to incorporate gender-neutral language); *Burlingame*, supra note 22, at 87 (noting that generic masculine language is "now widely considered inherently sexist"); *Rick Bales*, Gender-Neutral Language, Bench & B. 40, 40-41 (May 2002) (stating that "Gender-neutral language has become both accepted and expected"); *Gerald Lebovits*, He Said–She Said: Gender-Neutral Writing, 74 N.Y. St. B.J. 64, 64 (2002) (stating that those who view the movement for gender-neutral language as a phase "are wrong").

68 E.g., *Lebovits*, supra note 67, at 64 (arguing that "discriminatory writing perpetuates discrimination"). See also *LeClercq*, supra note 67 at 127, 129 (1995) (arguing that lawyers should be concerned about sexist language partly because it "excludes much of its audience").

69 But see *Scalia & Garner*, supra note 48, at 123 (stating that Justice Antonin Scalia believes gender-neutral language often requires a sacrifice to the "second-best circumlocution.") At the insistence of his co-author *Garner*, who favors "invisible gender-neutrality," Scalia agreed that their book would be written in gender-neutral language. Id. at 116-17.
Another opponent of gender-neutral language in the law offered two main arguments. The first was based on the aesthetic argument that avoiding the generic masculine can lead to awkward phrasing. The second was based on the libertarian argument that authors should be free to choose their language. *Steven Shavell*, Comment, 82 Geo. L.J. 1777, 1777 (1994).

70 *Judith S. Kaye*, A Brief for Gender-Neutral Brief Writing, N.Y.B.J. 2, 2 (May 21, 1991). See also *Hill*, supra note 8, at 275 (arguing that the courts should use gender-neutral language because of their desire to "include all members of society as equal participants").

71 See *Spender*, supra note 20, at 139.

72 Fair *Speech*, supra note 62, at 4.

73 *Sorrels*, supra note 6, at 2.

III. Using Gender-Neutral Language in English

A writer who decides to use gender-neutral language in English has several ways to achieve that end. They have met with varying degrees of acceptance.

1. Pronouns

Some proposed substitutes for generic masculine pronouns employ cumbersome neologisms[74] like *heris* (for *her or his*)[75] or add punctuation to existing words to create forms like *s/he*, *he/she.*[76] A major problem with these terms is that, as William Safire has observed, they are "unspeakable."[77] Moreover, such dramatic departures from readers' expectations may cause readers to stumble, diverting attention from the writer's intended message.[78] Attempts to introduce such neologisms into wide use have thus far failed.[79]

A second solution to the pronoun problem is to use the plural forms *their*, *they*, and *them* to refer to singular antecedents. This expedient is now common in informal speech: "If you know anyone who's going to the game, tell them to call me." Some have promoted this singular *they* as a solution to the pronoun

---

74 See *Richard S. Neal*, The Definitive Solution to the Problem of Sexist Language: How and Why It Is Solved (2003). Under his guidelines for creating new words, id. at 17-19, the generic substitute for him and her would be hir, id. at 20-21, and the suffix –man would become -wan, id. at 31. Thus the word human would become huwan. Id. at 42. Neal believes such changes are unobtrusive and likely to be accepted. Id. at 41. I disagree. See text accompanying notes 77 to 78, infra.

75 *Todd-Mancillas*, supra note 49, at 113.

76 *Treichler & Frank*, supra note 47, at 161 (recommending that writers avoid forms that use slashes or parentheses).

77 *William Safire*, I Stand Corrected 179 (1984).

78 See *Joseph M. Williams*, Style: Ten Lessons in Clarity and Grace 28 (9th ed. 2007) (disapproving of he/she and s/he as clumsy); *Todd-Mancillas*, supra note 49, at 113 (predicting that "neologisms like 'heris' and 'herm' are less likely to find acceptance and permanent adoption than the less contrived alternatives such as pluralizing the subject."); *Treichler & Frank*, supra note 47, at 161-62 (stating that forms using brackets or parentheses are "difficult to pronounce and awkward in the possessive").

79 *Corbett*, supra note 11, at 223 (1991) (stating that, because few other languages use such terms, it is not surprising that these neologisms have not been widely accepted in English); *Baron*, supra note 21, at 212 (stating that these contrived epicene pronouns have not been widely adopted); *Sorrels*, supra note 6, at 20 (stating that such forms are not likely to achieve "widespread acceptance" in the near future.)

problem.[80] However, the lack of number agreement still causes the reader to stumble and can create confusion about whether the plural pronoun refers to a generic person or a group. Its informality and potential for confusion make it unacceptable in formal writing,[81] including legal writing.[82]

There are more graceful ways to avoid biased pronouns.[83]

- The writer can change an antecedent noun to the plural so that a plural pronoun is appropriate. Thus "A lawyer should file his brief on time" can become the gender-neutral "Lawyers should file their briefs on time."
- The writer can recast a sentence to avoid the pronoun altogether: "It is important to file briefs on time." Sometimes the articles *a* or *the* or the pronoun *who*[84] will help: "A lawyer should file a brief on time," or "A lawyer who files a brief late may be sanctioned."
- The passive voice may eliminate the need for a pronoun: "Briefs should be filed on time." Using the passive voice, of course, can create new difficulties, because passive constructions are often wordy, and the lack of an identified actor tends to make a sentence vague. Therefore, commentators suggest using this alternative sparingly.[85]
- Alternating pronouns is another way to avoid the generic masculine: "If a lawyer does not file his brief on time, a judge may lose her temper."

---

80 See *Ann Bodine*, Androcentrism in Prescriptive Grammar: Singular "They", Sex-Indefinite "He", and "He or She" in The Feminist Critique of Language 177 (*Deborah Cameron* ed., 1990).

81 *Treichler & Frank*, supra note 47, at 155-56 (stating that using "they with a singular antecedent is widely condemned within the scholarly community, [so] we do not advocate its use in writing.").

82 *Anne Enquist & Laurel Currie Oates*, Just Writing 206 (2d ed. 2005) (calling the singular they ungrammatical); *Burlingame*, supra note 22, at 103-04 (stating that the use of the singular they "in formal legal writing risks a significant loss of persuasiveness," and may lead some to "stigmatize the lawyer as illiterate.").

83 For lists of suggestions on how to avoid generic masculine pronouns, see *Val Dumond*, The Elements of Nonsexist Usage: A Guide to Inclusive Spoken and Written English 25 (1990); *Bryan A. Garner*, A Dictionary of Modern Legal Usage 800-01 (2d ed. 2001); *Miller & Swift*, supra note 7, at 158-64; *Oates & Enquist*, supra note 82, at 148-50; *Treichler & Frank*, supra note 47, at 153-80; *Burlingame*, supra note 22, at 99-108; *Richard B. Klein*, Make It A 'Brief,'" 8 Verdicts, Settlements & Tactics: A Personal Inj. Litig. Rep. 363, 366 (1990).

84 See *Treichler & Frank*, supra note 47, at 166 (suggesting the use of relative pronouns, which have no grammatical gender).

85 E.g., *Treichler & Frank*, supra note 47, at 172-73 (stating that the passive voice "can produce less than felicitous results" and recommending that writers use it to avoid the generic masculine only when there is no "more concise and graceful solution").

However, this can be confusing if a reader is trying to follow a discussion by tracing the participants' gender. Respondents in a study by psychologists Madson and Shoda found this option cumbersome,[86] but Treicher and Frank recommend it "if done carefully."[87] A careful approach would avoid the hazard of unintentionally engaging gender stereotypes, as occurred when one speaker used *he* for good students and *she* for a student who was hesitant to ask questions.[88]

- Paired pronouns can also avoid the generic masculine: "A lawyer should file his or her brief on time." Paired pronouns have the advantage of reflecting reality, and Madson and Shoda found that readers preferred this form over alternating pronouns.[89] However, this approach can be clumsy,[90] especially if repeated often.
- Repeating the noun can avoid the need for a pronoun altogether: "If a lawyer does not file a brief on time, the lawyer may be sanctioned."[91] A disadvantage of this option is that it may be both repetitive and wordy.
- Similarly, using a synonym can avoid the need for a pronoun: "The clerk keeps the court calendar. That is the person who can schedule your hearing."[92] This option can also result in wordiness. Moreover, it must be undertaken carefully, because it risks confusing readers. Referring to the same person or concept with different terminology can undermine clarity, which is especially important in legal writing.[93]

86 *Madson & Shoda*, supra note 56, at 284.

87 *Treichler & Frank*, supra note 47, at 160.

88 Id. at 161 (citation omitted).

89 *Madson & Shoda*, supra note 56, at 284 (reporting data showing that readers preferred paired pronouns over alternating pronouns).

90 See *Burlingame*, supra note 22, at 99 (offering a phonological explanation for why the pairs seem clumsy); *Sorrels*, supra note 6, at 20 (advising that, to avoid "distractions and inefficiency," writers should avoid using repeated paired pronouns).

91 See, e.g., *Miller & Swift*, supra note 31, at 43.

92 See Fair Speech, supra note 62, at 8 (suggesting replacing a pronoun with a synonym).

93 See *Barbara Child*, Drafting Legal Documents: Principles and Practices 319 (2d ed. 1992) (stating, "constant variation, sometimes derogatorily called 'elegant variation,' can be irritating and distracting in any context. In legal drafting, it is totally unacceptable because the shifts make a reader wonder whether there is some hidden difference in meaning or reference."); *Scalia & Garner*, supra note 48, at 107 (stating that in brief writing, "the same word should be used to refer to a particular key concept").

Because the last five methods can be cumbersome, especially on repeated use, commentators advise using them with care.[94] But taken together, the above suggestions provide writers with several solutions that can be unobtrusive.[95] Where a sentence is deftly constructed, the reader may never know that the writer consciously avoided using sexist pronouns.

2. Nouns

There are also graceful ways to change gender-biased nouns and noun phrases. For example, for the pseudo-generic masculine noun *man*, the writer can use *humans* or *persons*: "Humans breastfeed their young." Where words gratuitously identify the sex of a referent, a writer can choose neutral alternatives by, for example, replacing *waitress* with *server*, *policeman* with *police officer*, and *weatherman* with *weather forecaster*. The motivated writer can find suitable alternatives, perhaps by consulting one of the many lists of substitutes for sexist nouns.[96]

Where the gender-biased language arises from the writer's own choice, a writer can cultivate sensitivity to the problem. Avoiding non-parallel phrasing like *man and wife* and patronizing wording like *the gentle sex* requires that the writer be alert to the bias in such terms and seek gender-neutral alternatives. *Husband and wife* is an appropriate parallel phrase, and *the gentle sex* can be replaced with a word like *women*.

---

94 E.g., *Treichler & Frank*, supra note 47, at 159 (recommending sparing use of he or she), 160-61 (urging care in alternating pronouns), and 172-73 (recommending sparing use of the passive voice); *Burlingame*, supra note 22, at 105 (recommending sparing use of the passive voice).

95 *Bryan Garner*, for example, contends that gender-neutrality can be invisible. Scalia & Garner, supra note 48, at 116.

96 E.g., *LeClercq*, supra note 67, at 131; Fair Speech, supra note 62, at 5-6; *Miller & Swift*, supra note 31, at 109-113; *Pat Chew & Lauren K. Kelley-Chew*, Subtley Sexist Language, 16 Columb. J. Gender & L. 643, 667-68 (2007); *Carolyn Korsmeyer*, The Hidden Joke: Generic Uses of Masculine Terminology, in Sexist Language: A Modern Philosophical Analysis 116, 122 (*Mary Vetterling-Braggin* ed., 1981).

IV. The Study Results

1. The study sample and design

To determine the extent of federal appellate judges' use of gender-neutral language, my research assistant and I looked at several aspects of published judicial opinions. Our sample contained recent opinions by every female judge, including senior judges, who were sitting on the United States courts of appeals in June of 2007 and who had issued opinions in the previous eighteen months that were available on Westlaw. We also included male judges as a comparison.

To compose our main sample ("the Larger Sample"), we paired each female with a male judge from the same court whose birth date was closest to hers. We paired by age because we thought that persons born around the same time were likely to have been exposed to similar societal attitudes about gender and language during their formative years. This yielded 48 pairs, for a total of 96 judges in the Larger Sample. In June of 2007, the total number of active and senior federal appellate judges was 255.[97]

Second, we read a smaller sample of those opinions ("the Smaller Sample") more closely, checking for instances of gender-neutral and gender-biased language. Third, we compared data from the years 1965 and 2006. The methodology for each of these portions of the study is described below.

2. Methodology and findings

a. The Larger Sample

(1). Examination of gender-neutral pronoun pairs

To collect data on the use of gender-neutral pronoun pairs by judges in the Larger Sample, we conducted a Westlaw search of their opinions dated January 1, 2006 through June 30, 2007. This yielded a total of 4721 opinions, which we searched by computer for the gender-neutral pronoun pairs *he or she*, *him or her*, and *his or her*.[98] We examined each instance of these phrases. If a phrase

97 496 F.3d at vii-xiv.

98 We also searched for each pronoun pair with the feminine pronoun first: she or he, her or him, and hers or his. But when we found only two instances of those pairs in the sample for the year 2006, we dropped it from our formulation. We also dropped the phrase his or hers because it was so infrequent.

was part of a quotation or a close paraphrase from another source, we did not count it, because it did not represent a choice of wording by the judge being studied. Of course, there was some gray area in making these determinations. For example, one lengthy and commonly cited immigration statute is written in gender-neutral language.[99] Where a judge used a pronoun pair in referring to this statute, but not in a direct quotation, we made a judgment from the context whether that language should be attributed to the judge or to the statute's drafters.

(2). Results

After recording the data for each judge in the Larger Sample, we then expressed the subjects' use of gender-neutral pronoun pairs as percentages of the total number of opinions for each group, as shown in Table 1.

Table 1

The Larger Sample

	Occurrences of *he or she*	Occurrences of *him or her*	Occurrences of *his or her*	Total number of pronoun pairs	Total number of cases	Uses of pronoun pairs expressed as a percentage of the total number of cases
Female judges	141	26	201	368	2439	15%
Male judges	116	19	174	309	2282	13.5%
Total	253	45	367	665	4721	14%

Occurrences of gender-neutral pronoun pairs in a sample of opinions dated from January 1, 2006 to June 30, 2007

Certain caveats about these data must be acknowledged. Using paired pronouns is only one method of avoiding gender-biased pronouns; a writer may accomplish that end through various other methods. However, those methods, de-

99 8 U.S.C. § 1231 (2000).

scribed above,[100] are not easily identified. For example, use of *they* to avoid a gendered singular pronoun cannot easily be distinguished from other uses of *they* that are not related to gender neutrality. Nor can one definitively identify more creative restructuring of syntax to avoid a gender-biased word choice. Moreover, many opinions do not include any generic pronoun references,[101] so they present little occasion to use either gender-biased or gender-neutral pronouns. These caveats make it plain that a tally of a judge's gender-neutral pronoun usage is not a dispositive measure of that judge's commitment to avoid gender bias. Still, the aggregate data in this study show a trend toward gender neutrality through many appearances of gender-neutral pronouns pairs. As Table 1 shows, we found 665 of these pairs among the 4721 cases we reviewed.

The degree to which individual judges used these pairs varied. Among the women judges, ten used no gender-neutral pronoun pairs, and the highest numbers of pronoun pairs appeared in the opinions of Judges Sonia Sotomayor (56), Maryanne Barry (38), and Sharon Prost (32). Among the men, ten used no gender-neutral pronoun pairs, and the highest numbers of pairs appeared in the opinions of Judges Eric Clay (47), Robert Sack (33), and Ronald Gilman (33).

The data also showed a small difference between younger and older judges. We divided the female and male groups in half by birth year[102] and found that the use of gender-neutral pronoun pairs expressed as a percentage of total cases was slightly higher for the younger group (15.6%) than for the older group (14%). However, a linear probability model showed that this difference was not statistically significant as measured by Student's *t* test. Likewise, the difference between the women and men as a whole (shown in Table 1) was not statistically significant. Among the subjects of this study, then, both younger and older judges and female and male judges used gender-neutral pronoun pairs to a statistically similar degree.

We did find a notable difference among the circuits. Three circuit courts showed a statistically significant difference in the use of gender-neutral pronoun pairs. The judges in the samples from the Fifth and D.C. circuits were significantly *less* likely to use gender-neutral pronoun pairs than were judges in the entire sample, while judges from the Second Circuit were *more* likely to use gender-neutral pairs.

---

100 Supra part III.

101 See infra notes 106 to 108 and accompanying text.

102 Female judges in the older half were born in 1945 or earlier; males in the older half were born in 1943 or earlier.

There was also a notable difference based on the political party of the appointing president. Judges appointed by Democrats used an average of 9.84 gender-neutral pronoun pairs in the sampled opinions, while those appointed by Republicans used an average of 4.1.

b. The Smaller Sample

(1). In-depth examination of opinions

The suggestions for writing gender-neutral language, discussed above in section II, illustrate the varied choices available to a judge who wishes to avoid gender-biased language. Because some of those choices cannot readily be found by a computer search, to check for them, my research assistant and I closely read a Smaller Sample of opinions, which we developed by randomly selecting six female and six male judges from the Larger Sample.[103]

For these twelve judges, we read the newest five opinions dated before June 30, 2007 that were shown on Westlaw as appearing in either the Federal Reporter or the Federal Appendix,[104] for a total of sixty opinions. We recorded all uses of gender-biased and gender-neutral language that we could identify. As with the Larger Sample, we did not count pronouns that appeared in quotations and close paraphrases from other sources. Collecting these data again involved some gray area, because not all methods of eliminating gender-biased language are clearly identifiable.[105]

---

103 We developed this sample by listing each female judge by circuit and in alphabetical order within the circuit; we then chose every eighth judge from this list, for a total of six female judges. This yielded a list of the following women judges: from the Third Circuit, *Jane Roth*; from the Fifth Circuit, *Priscilla Owen*; from the Seventh Circuit, Di*ane Sykes*; from the Ninth Circuit, *Susan Graber*; from the Tenth Circuit, *Mary Beck Briscoe*; and from the D.C. Circuit, *Judith Rogers*.
We then added the male judges we had previously paired with those women: from the Third Circuit, *Walter Stapleton*; from the Fifth Circuit, *Carl Stewart*; from the Seventh Circuit, *Frank Easterbrook*; from the Ninth Circuit, *Richard Clifton*; from the Tenth Circuit, *Michael Murphy*; and from the D.C. Circuit, *Harry T. Edwards*.

104 We did not include opinions identified on June 30 as "slip opinions," even though we recognized that they might later appear in the Federal Reporter of the Federal Appendix.

105 See *Todd-Mancillas*, supra note 49, at 113 (pointing out that it will not be obvious where a writer has consciously used a plural noun in order to use the plural "they").

(2). Results

This reading illustrated an intuitive point: only some opinions present issues about gender-neutral language. An example of a case that did not is *United States v. Rankin*, a criminal case.[106] The opinion did not mention any general legal principles that included gendered pronouns, nor did it include any ready opportunities to use gender-biased nouns like *mailman*. The opinion's masculine pronouns referred to Rankin himself and were thus not sexist.[107] Feminine pronouns referred to a female officer.[108] This is illustrative of the many opinions that contained neither gender-biased nor obviously gender-neutral language.

We did, however, find both gender-biased and gender-neutral references to persons of unspecified sex in the Smaller Sample.

Table 2

The Smaller Sample

n = 60 cases

Gender-neutral pronoun use	Biased pronoun use	Generic use of a gendered pronoun fitting the sex of a relevant person	Gender-neutral noun use	Biased noun use
9	11	32	1	0

Occurrences of biased and gender-neutral terms[109]

As shown in Table 2, thirty-two of the gendered pronouns occurred in generic statements that had some relation to particular persons. Thirty of those pronouns were masculine. For example, in a case involving a male defendant, Judge Priscilla Owen referred to the required analysis by stating, "a defendant cannot fail to invoke [certain] factors in support of his motion."[110] Two of the gendered pronouns were feminine, used by Judge Carl Stewart and Judge Harry Edwards to state general principles that applied to women.[111] Because of their

106 487 F.3d 229 (5th Cir. 2007).

107 Id. at 230, 231.

108 Id. at 230.

109 The sixty opinions consisted of five recent opinions each by six female and six male judges. For further explanation, see supra note 103 and accompanying text.

110 *United States v. Wash.*, 480 F.3d 309, 317 (5th Cir. 2007).

111 *Greenwell v. State Farm Mut. Auto. Ins. Co.*, 486 F.3d 840, 843 (5th Cir. 2007) (stating, in a case where the plaintiff was a woman, "An employee merely alleging sickness as

close relation to actual persons in the cases, we did not classify these pronouns as sexist. Using a gendered pronoun this way — as part of a general statement that applies to a particular individual in the case — may be a reasonable way to use a gendered third-person pronoun without suggesting that the masculine is the norm.

However, there were eleven clearly biased pronouns in the Smaller Sample. Two were masculine pronouns in a general statement in *Decatur Ventures, LLC, v. Daniel*,[112] where Judge Frank Easterbrook stated, "[A] professional owes a duty of care only to his client plus any third party who the professional knows will see and rely on any opinion he renders."[113] As discussed above, it may be reasonable for a writer to express this kind of general principle with a pronoun of the same gender as a relevant person. However, the professional in question in *Decatur Ventures* was a woman.[114] We recorded this as gender-biased language.

A second example of biased pronouns appeared in a case concerning student transfers to other school districts.[115] Although there was no particular male student under discussion, in a single sentence Judge Mary Briscoe used masculine pronouns four times: "If a student transfers to a school district in which he is not a resident, he cannot compete in athletics for one year, unless the transfer is due to a bona fide change of residence by his parents, or he can demonstrate a legitimate hardship."[116] The controlling statute is written in gender-neutral language.[117]

We also looked for gender-biased nouns in the sixty cases, but the Smaller Sample was notably lacking in gender-biased terms like *mailman* or *founding fathers*. We did find instances where judges apparently intentionally framed points in nonsexist language. In one case concerning expert testimony, Judge Harry Edwards mentioned what "lay persons" can appropriately be expected to

---

the reason for her absence does not automatically provide sufficient FMLA-notice."); *Jochims v. NLRB*, 480 F.3d 1161, 1168 (D.C. Cir. 2007) (stating, in a case where it was alleged that a woman was a supervisor, "supervisory authority is not conferred on an employee merely by vesting her with a title.")

112 485 F.3d 387 (7th Cir. 2007).

113 Id. at 390.

114 Id. at 390.

115 *Christian Heritage Acad. v. Okla. Secondary Sch. Activities Assn.*, 483 F.3d 1025, 1027 n. 1 (10th Cir. 2007).

116 Id.

117 Ok. Stat. tit. 70, 8-103.2 (West Supp. 2006).

know.[118] This is a gender-neutral counterpart for *laymen,* which was in more widespread use in 1965, as discussed below.

And in an opinion concerning fiduciary obligations,[119] Judge Jane Roth used the plural noun *fiduciaries* in several places,[120] thus making a plural pronoun appropriate. Similarly, Judge Michael Murphy repeated the phrase *third party* several times, perhaps in order to avoid a gendered pronoun.[121] It seems likely that other judges avoided bias through deft phrasing that we could not detect.

Although the Smaller Sample produced numbers too small for meaningful statistical analysis, the low amount of biased phrasing in these cases suggests that many judges are framing their opinions in gender-neutral language. It further suggests that more blatantly biased wording, like calling an adult woman "little girl,"[122] has now become rare or nonexistent in federal appellate opinions.

c. Changes between 1965 and 2006

(1). Comparison of data from the two years

We also examined whether judges' use of gender-neutral language has changed over time. To analyze this, we chose the year 1965 as a benchmark because it immediately preceded the late 1960s, when U.S. feminists began their movement for gender-neutral language.[123] We used the year 2006 for comparison because it was the last complete year at the time we collected the data. We conducted a computer search of all federal court of appeals cases for both years,[124] searching for opinions that included the same pronoun pairs we counted in the Larger Sample. We also counted cases using the less common phrases *himself or herself* and *herself or himself,* which we had not examined in the Larger Sample

---

118 *Briggs v. Wash. Metro. Area Transit Auth.*, 481 F.3d 839, 846 (D.C. Cir. 2007).

119 *Wachtel v. Health Net, Inc.*, 482 F.3d 225, 226 (3d Cir. 2007).

120 Id. at 233.

121 *United States v. Andrus*, 483 F.3d 711, 716 (10th Cir. 2007) (including phrasing like the following: "Valid third party consent can arise either through the third party's actual authority or the third party's apparent authority.")

122 See supra note 32 and accompanying text.

123 See *Cameron*, supra note 1, at 9 (identifying "pressures to look at [gender-biased] language which arose, roughly, during the late 1960s and 1970s").

124 Interestingly, the total numbers of opinions for 2006 varied slightly depending on the date when we checked the database. *West's* research attorneys were unable to explain the cause of this difference. The totals reported for the year 2006 in this article were recorded from searches conducted on November 20, 2007.

because of their infrequency. Finally, we counted uses of selected nouns in both years.

Unlike our approach to the Larger Sample, we did not review each pronoun pair identified by this search; we simply recorded the gross number of cases that included gender-neutral pronoun pairs. We also checked uses of selected gender-neutral nouns like *mailman* and *postal worker(s).*

(2). Results

A comparison of 1965 opinions with those from 2006 shows a dramatic increase in the use of gender-neutral language over that period. Between 1965 and 2006, the total number of reported cases from the federal courts of appeals increased from 3661 to 28,086,[125] or 667%. At the same time, use of the three gender-neutral pronoun pairs *he or she*, *him or her*, and *his or her* showed a much greater increase, from 55 to 2361, or 4192%. On average, federal appellate judges in 2006 were much more likely than judges in 1965 to use these pronoun pairs. The difference was statistically significant at the 1% level.[126]

Comparisons of noun phrases also show a trend toward gender neutrality.[127] The increase in use of the terms *reasonable person*[128] and *police officer* was statistically significant at the 10% level. In the same period, there was a proportional decrease in cases using the gender-biased terms *reasonable man* and *layman* and its plural *laymen*, which were significantly less likely to be used in 2006 than in 1965. This comparison was also made at the 10% level of significance.

The other terms we compared occurred too infrequently for meaningful statistical analysis. But we did find that the number of cases including the gender-biased terms *founding fathers* (2 in 1965 and 2 in 2006) and *mailman* or *postman* (3 in 1965 and and 6 in 2006) remained essentially static despite the large

---

125 The totals for both years include cases with no opinion attributed to a particular judge — for example, per curiam and memorandum opinions. We did not attempt to identify and separate such cases from the totals.

126 Under a two-sample proportion test, the Z-score was equal to 26.50803.

127 We did not examine use of the term reasonable woman, because using that term is more than a linguistic choice. It reflects a different legal standard, which is outside the scope of this article. For a discussion of the "reasonable woman" standard for sexual harassment, see *Chew & Kelley-Chew*, supra note 96, at 672-75.

128 This finding comports with *Chew* and *Kelley-Chew's* finding that, partly because of the debate over the legal standard, federal judges now use the term reasonable person (instead of reasonable man) 96% of the time. *Chew & Kelley-Chew*, supra note 96, at 672.

increase in cases. The gender-biased *mankind* increased modestly (from 8 to 21), but not in proportion to the overall increase in cases. Meanwhile, there were increases in the gender-neutral terms *founders* (from 1 to 9), *mail carrier* (from 5 to 15), *postal worker* (from 0 to 31), and variations of *lay persons* (from 3 to 110).[129] There were no instances of *founding mothers* in either year and only one instance of *humankind.* Altogether, although these numbers are small, they suggest a trend toward gender-neutral language.

At the same time, though, the data show that some biased language still continues to appear. And interestingly, another recent study showed that the U.S. Supreme Court has some catching up to do.[130] Its author concluded that only Justice Alito's opinions could serve as models of gender-neutral language.[131] These results indicate a need for continued progress toward fairness.

V. Conclusion

Since this study's benchmark year, 1965, English-speaking professionals in various fields have recognized that gender-biased language makes women invisible and constructs an inaccurate world. Many U.S. judges have apparently taken note of these developments. This study found that both female and male judges are increasingly choosing nonsexist language, thus bringing the law closer to its broad goal of being fair to all citizens.

Still, the study revealed that some biased language continues to appear in federal court opinions.[132] This suggests a continued need for consciousness-raising about gender-neutral language, a need that may also be of interest to speakers of other languages as they confront the issue of gender bias in their own unique linguistic circumstances.

---

129 The term Postal Worker appeared in some cases as part of the name of a union. We did not include those cases in our total.

130 *Leslie M. Rose*, The Supreme Court and Gender-Neutral Language: Setting the Standard or Lagging Behind?, 17 Duke J. Gender L. & Pol'y 81 (Jan. 2010).

131 Id. at 127.

132 See also *Chew & Kelley-Chew*, supra note 96, at 668, 672 (concluding from an examination of noun phrases in various legal documents that progress toward gender-neutral language in the legal profession was disappointing, but noting that some "gender-neutral word options are now widely used in the legal community.")

US and EU: The Comparative Responses to the Global Economic Crisis

*by Lisa H. Nicholson**

I. Introduction

"The present regulatory system has failed to effectively manage risk, require sufficient transparency and ensure fair dealing."[1] Such was the preliminary finding of the United States Congressional Oversight Panel in January 2009, following another year where the lack of confidence that investor uncertainty breeds caused the credit markets to all but seize up. Globally, banks and insurance companies had written off more than €1 trillion between mid 2007 and the start of 2009 as the global stock markets lost more than €16 trillion (about 1.5 times the GDP of the European Union) since August 2007.[2] Governments and central banks around the world similarly echoed the Oversight Panel's sentiment as they repeatedly advanced stimulus and bailout packages in attempts to inject liquidity into the banking system and restore confidence in the capital markets.[3]

The environment that led to this crisis of confidence was fueled by the activities of those – bank and non-bank financial institutions, retail and institutional investors, among other market participants – seeking higher returns on their

* Professor of Law; University of Louisville, Louis D. Brandeis School of Law. The author wishes to thank Blake Chavis and Miran Vilas for their research assistance. Professor Nicholson visited the Johannes Gutenberg-University Mainz in 2007, 2009 and 2011.

1 Congressional Oversight Panel, Special Report on Regulatory Reform (January 2009) at 2, submitted under Section 125(b)(2) of Title I of the Emergency Economic Stabilization Act of 2008, Pub. L. No. 110-343 (the "Congressional Oversight Panel Special Report").

2 See *Jacques de Larosiere*, Chair, The High-Level Group on Financial Supervision in the EU (February 25, 2009) (the "de Larosiere Report") at 6.

3 See *de Larosiere* Report at 6 (noting that "the world's monetary authorities and its regulatory and supervisory financial authorities can and must do much better in the future to reduce systemic dangers and inter-connected vulnerabilities."). See also *Bertrand Benoit, Quentin Peel and Chris Bryant*, We All Want to Put the Global Economy Back on its Feet," Financial Times (March 27 2009) (reporting that German Chancellor Angela Merkel argued, "We were spending too much to create growth that was not sustainable. It isn't just that the banks took over too many risks. Governments allowed them to do so by neglecting to set the necessary [financial market] rules and [ ] by increasing the money supply too much.").

investments amid a climate of plentiful liquidity and low investment yields.[4] These market participants were aided by lax regulatory oversight; the unregulated or insufficiently regulated mortgage lending system; an increased reliance on complex securitization financing techniques; and the systemic over-affection for leveraging without sufficient capital reserves. The opaque trading activities of these market participants camouflaged the mis-priced risks as well as the poor quality of the assets underlying the financial products that were sold to investors.[5] When all was revealed, the entire house of cards came crashing down leading to the most epic economic crisis to strike worldwide in almost a century.

Globally, the market regulators[6] found themselves hamstrung in their ability to keep pace with the increased use of innovative financial products;[7] the rise in

---

4 See *De Larosiere*, J. et al., Report High Level Group on Financial Supervision in the EU, p. 7, 25 February 2009, available at http://ec.europa.eu/internal_market/financies/docs/de_larosiere_report_en.pdf (the "de Larosiere Report").

5 See id.

6 The following list of regulators had authority over their respective areas prior to the financial crisis and ensuing recession that hit countries around the globe. During the relevant period, the key U.S. bank and capital market regulators were: Securities & Exchange Commission ("SEC"), Commodity Futures Trading Commission ("CFTC"), Federal Reserve System (the "Fed"), Federal Deposit Insurance Corporation ("FDIC"), Financial Industry Regulatory Authority ("FINRA"), Office of the Comptroller of the Currency ("OCC"), National Credit Union Administration ("NCUA"), and Office of Thrift Supervision ("OTS"). Correspondingly, in the European Union, the key regulators were the European Central Bank ("ECB") and the level 3 committees: the Committee of European Banking Supervisors ("CEBS"), the Committee of European Insurance and Occupational Pensions Supervisors ("CEIOPS") and the Committee of European Securities Regulators ("CESR"). On the national level in Germany, the key regulators were the Bundesanstalt für Finanzdienstleistungsaufsicht ("BaFin"), the financial regulatory authority of Germany; and the Deutsche Bundesbank, the central bank of Germany and member of the European System of Central Banks.

7 The global capital markets of the last two decades have witnessed a marked increase in the introduction and use of the more complex financial products with names like mortgage-backed securities ("MBS"), collateralized debt obligations ("CDOs"), collateralized loan obligations ("CLOs"), asset-backed commercial paper, auction rate securities, credit default swaps ("CDS"), financial insurers, special purpose entities ("SPEs") and structure investment vehicles ("SIVs"). Regrettably, locally and on a global scale, the financial regulations and internal risk management requirements failed to keep pace with these new market products and investment vehicles. See Congressional Oversight Panel Special Report. See also de Larosiere Report at 7.

trading volumes;[8] the introduction of new market participants; the convergence of financial services and their providers; and the continued globalization of the financial industry.[9] These regulatory oversight failures set the stage for lots of finger-pointing and public outrage as well as numerous governmental pledges to redesign the regulatory landscape on both sides of the Atlantic.

This article examines the environment that sparked the meltdown and sets forth the regulatory responses undertaken by the United States, and the European Union – including the separate response undertaken by Germany. Regulatory reform requires better monitoring of both the financial activities and the financial markets in which these activities occur. The aim is to pinpoint and warn against the build-up of risky behaviors that have the propensity to devastate the entire capital market structure. This article considers the regulatory measures taken to increase supervision of those significant participants in the financial markets and questions whether future turmoil can be prevented by these measures.[10]

II. The Origins of the Global Economic Crisis

The first sign of trouble appeared in the U.S. during the summer of 2007. By mid-June 2007, two hedge funds[11] run by the U.S. investment banking giant, Bear Stearns Companies, Inc. ("Bear Stearns"), which had invested in some $20 billion in securities backed by mortgages, reportedly were in danger of collaps-

8 The dollar value of average trading volume in the U.S. capital markets, for example, which was approximately $87 billion a day in February 1999, sprang to $251 billion a day by February 2009. See SEC *Chairman Mary L. Shapiro*, Testimony Concerning Enhancing Investor Protection and Regulation of the Securities Markets (March 26, 2009) (the "Shapiro March 2009 Testimony").

9 See Congressional Oversight Panel Special Report.

10 While it is important to pinpoint and warn against the build-up of risky behaviors in the markets, it is equally important for regulators to address and possibly limit the type of activities that these significant market players can undertake in an effort to avoid devastating outcomes in the future. A separate and forthcoming article will address this aspect of the systemic risk problem, noting the roles of increased capital reserve requirements, leverage limits and the so-called "Volker Rule."

11 A hedge fund is an investment vehicle that is open to a limited range of professional and wealthy investors and is permitted to undertake a wide range of investment and trading activities. This market participant was largely unregulated during the run up to the economic crisis. As a result, such investment vehicles could engage in very aggressive trading strategies such as engaging in short selling, over-leveraging their investment portfolios, buying on margin, and investing heavily in the securities of a single issuer.

ing.[12] Two weeks after the disclosure of potential losses, both hedge funds filed for bankruptcy protection on July 31, 2007.[13]

While one would not ordinarily expect that the failure of two U.S. hedge funds could spark a contagion, it did. This supposedly isolated event exploded due to the nature of the investment product involved. The collapsed hedge funds had invested heavily in mortgage-related securities that were quite similar to what other big-named U.S. and European banks and non-bank financial institutions also were holding at the time. When Bear Stearns reported problems with its hedge funds, other entities began reviewing their holdings and panic quickly gripped the entire market. This phenomenon allowed phrases like *systemic risk* and *market contagion* to enter the world lexicon. Globally, we learned firsthand that a single private institution could pose a systemic risk if that entity is large enough or interconnected with other entities such that its failure would actually damage and drag down other counter-parties around the world.[14] Fear of a potential collapse led to market contagion. As will be illustrated, banks and non-bank financial institutions began to distrust their counter-parties' balance sheets.

The troublesome securities held by the two hedge funds as well as other major market participants are generically referred to as CDOs.[15] These complex investment instruments can be formed by purchasing stakes in a variety of previously existing bonds that were typically backed by residential mortgages with the goal of diversifying risk.[16] By mid-2007, the booming market for bonds that

---

12 The Bear Stearns Asset Management Group reportedly sent a letter to its investors informing them that its "High-Grade Structured Credit Fund" had lost more than 90% of its value, and its "High-Grade Structured Credit Enhanced Leveraged Fund" had lost virtually all of its investor capital. See Reuters, 2 Bear Stearns Funds Are Almost Worthless, NY Times (July 17, 2007). See also *Bethany McLean and Joe Nocera*, All the Devils are Here, at 285 (Penguin Group 2010).

13 See *Danny Fortson*, Bear Stearns Funds Enter Bankruptcy, The Independent (August 2, 2007).

14 See *Allan Sloan*, On the Brink of Disaster, Fortune at 82 (April 14, 2008); Kathleen A. Scott, Addressing the Conditions Leading to 'Systemic Risk' on a Global Basis, NYLJ, at 3 (Mar. 18, 2009).

15 See *Vikas Bajaj and Julie Creswell*, Bear Stearns Staves off Collapse of 2 Hedge Funds, NY Times (June 21, 2007).

16 Id. To better understand the CDO and its risk potential, an understanding of a close relative, the mortgage-backed security would be helpful. A MBS (at its core-) is a bond backed by the promise of a stream of payments from a portfolio of mortgages. While the MBS was sold as a relatively safe alternative to other investment options, if any of the homeowners were ever to miss their monthly payments or subsequently default on

were backed by the cashflows from residential mortgages began faltering, mainly because homeowners had started defaulting on their mortgages in larger numbers throughout the U.S.[17] Adding to the pressure of holding such securities, financial institutions, including Bear Stearns, were required by the U.S. accounting rules to mark the value of their investments to the price of similarly traded assets in the market.[18] This obligation proved onerous for many financial institutions because of the difficulty in valuing this esoteric investment vehicle, including the inability to unwind with certainty many of the more complex CDOS back to the underlying assets whose cashflows were supposed to support investor payouts.[19]

Following the announcements of the hedge funds' bankruptcy filings, other market participants slowly started acknowledging and revealing the extent of their exposure and projected losses, partly in order to restore confidence in the markets. The German bank IKB Deutsche Industriebank ("IKB") was among the first to go public with its August 2007 revelation that its full-year earnings would be "significantly lower" due to losses related to the faltering US mortgage market.[20] IKB, a small-company lender, was a leading investor in CDOs and other asset-backed securities. It also became the first international casualty of the financial crisis when its investments exceeded the bank's liquidity and equi-

---

any of mortgages that were pooled together to create the portfolio, the holder of the MBS would suffer.
This risk can be magnified in the case of the CDO, another type of asset-backed security that creates separate pools of pass-through payment rates or tranches for different classes of bondholders with varying maturities. The repayments from the pool of pass-through securities are used to retire the bonds in the order specified by the bonds' prospectus. For example, the investors in the CMO are divided up into three classes. They are called either class A, B or C investors. Each class differs in the order they receive principal payments, but receives interest payments as long as it is not completely paid off. Class A investors are paid out first with prepayments and repayments until they are paid off. Then class B investors are paid off, followed by class C investors. In a situation like this, class A investors bear most of the prepayment risk, while class C investors bear the least, Investopedia, available at http://www.investopedia.com/terms/c/cmo.asp. A trust is created to capture the mortgage cashflow payments and allocate those payments to each investor. The CDO is that trust.

17 See *De Larosiere* Report at pp. 7-9, 11.

18 See *De Larosiere* Report at p. 11.

19 See *De Larosiere* Report at pp. 8, 11.

20 See *Tobias Buck*, National Reputation Hangs on IKB Rescue, The Financial Times (2 August 2007).

ty capital levels.[21] To preserve trust in the German banking system, the national government sponsored a rescue package that required a $4.7 billion funding agreement and the takeover of the bank's $11 billion credit line.[22]

Like IKB and the two failed Bear Stearns hedge funds the summer before, Bear Stearns was rumored also to be over-leveraged and experienced liquidity problems in March 2008 due to its investments in mortgage-related securities.[23] Unable to secure short-term funding due to the market's inability to value its purported collateral, Bear Stearns faced its final trading day on March 14, 2008. It was subsequently swallowed by JPMorgan Chase ("JPMC") in a government-supported deal on Sunday, March 16, 2008.[24] The U.S. government defended its orchestrated attempt to save Bear Stearns from bankruptcy, saying it was important to ensure the orderly function of financial markets.[25]

The U.S. government's action did not stabilize the markets in the interim despite numerous efforts, however. Six months later, two other US investment banking giants faced collapse. Both held extensive positions in mortgage-related securities. While Merrill Lynch & Co. ("Merrill Lynch") was able to find a buyer in the Bank of America Corporation in September 2008,[26] Lehman Brothers Holdings, Inc. ("Lehman") was not as lucky. Despite round-the-clock efforts, there was no orchestrated rescue of Lehman. When Lehman subsequently filed for bankruptcy protection on September 15, 2008, market uncertainty turned to panic.[27] Indeed, financial markets around the world plummeted on news that a

---

21 See id. See also IKB Rescue Pushed Germany into Deficit in 2007, Reuters (22 October 2008, *Renee Schultes*, KFW Doubles Provisions for IKB Rescue, Financial News, (27 November 2007).

22 *Tobias Buck*, National Reputation Hangs on IKB Rescue, The Financial Times (August 2, 2007) (reporting that the rescue package put together by German banks to cover losses at IKB was designed not just to save the bank, but also the reputation of the German banking sector).

23 *Roddy Boyd*, The Last Days of Bear Stearns, Fortune at 86 (April 14, 2008) (noting that Bear Stearns reportedly had $11.1 billion in tangible equity capital supporting $395 billion in investments, a leverage ratio of more than 35 to 1).

24 JPMC completed its 2008 purchase after the Fed agreed to take control of a $30 billion portfolio of mortgage-linked Bear Stearns assets. See *Kate Kelly*, Bear Stearns Neared Collapse Twice in Frenzied Last Days, Wall St. J (May 29, 2008); *Landon Thomas, Jr.*, Aftershocks of a Collapse, With a Bank at the Epicenter, NY Times (March 18, 2008).

25 See Paulson Defends Bear Stearns Bailout, NY Times (March 16, 2008).

26 See *Phillip Inman*, Wall Street Crisis: Bank of America Buys Merrill Lynch, The Guardian (September 15, 2008) (reporting that Bank of America, the largest retail bank in the US, agreed to buy Merrill Lynch for around $50bn on September 14, 2008 in a deal that traders said could resolve the firm's funding crisis).

27 See *de Larosiere* Report at p. 12.

large money market fund's NAV dropped below $1 per share.[28] That the Reserve Primary Fund "broke the buck" due to its investments in Lehman commercial paper, started a chain reaction of concern and withdrawals.[29]

Numerous investment funds that relied on Lehman for day-to-day financing, like London-based hedge funds, reportedly found themselves unable to do business because their accounts with Lehman or Lehman's subsidiary were frozen.[30] Indeed, more than $210 billion was withdrawn from the markets over two day.[31] Before long, lenders, investors, banks and nonbank financial institutions were all paralyzed with fear. Market participants simply did not trust one another's positions, and neither wanted to lend nor trade with each other. Distrust and uncertainty caused these entities to hoard cash, delay production and lay-off workers. Credit markets worldwide seized up. By the end of 2008, the financial crisis had erupted into a global economic crisis. Market contagion had ensued. The markets needed reassurance. Something had to be done for stability and confidence to reign again.

III. The Global Response

1. Attempts to Stimulate the Economy

In the midst of the financial crisis, governments and central banks all over the world repeatedly worked to contain the hysteria that spread throughout the financial system and froze market activities by injecting stimulus funds into their respective banking and capital markets. On October 3, 2008, former President George W. Bush signed into law the Emergency Economic Stabilization Act of 2008 (the "EESA").[32] The Act authorized the expenditure of $700 billion for the purchase of illiquid mortgage-related assets (commonly referred to as "troubled assets") from financial institutions through the newly-created Troubled Asset

---

28 See *Justin Fox*, Three Lessons of the Lehman Brothers Collapse, Time Magazine (September 15, 2009).

29 See *Katie Rushkewicz*, Fund Times: Industry Leaders Want Money Market Reform, Morningstar News (March 13, 2009); *Justin Fox*, Three Lessons of the Lehman Brothers Collapse, Time Magazine (September 15, 2009).

30 Id.

31 Id.

32 Division A of Pub.L. 110-343, 122 Stat. 3765, enacted October 3, 2008.

Relief Program ("TARP").[33] The ever-changing financial system required an almost immediate shift in purpose to a direct injection of monies into the financial institutions to recapitalize them. Approximately $350 billion was allocated to U.S. bank and non-bank financial institutions in the final quarter of 2008.[34] On January 12, 2009, the second $350 billion was released for use to stabilize the US financial system.[35] Despite repeated attempts by the federal government, the U.S. economy remained stagnant by year-end 2010.

The European Council, similarly, approved the European Economic Recovery Plan (the "EERP") on December 11 and 12, 2008 which created a €200 billion fund that would permit EU member states to grant subsidized loans, guarantees, and direct aid up to €500,000 to individual enterprises.[36] This rescue fund, comprised of a combination of EU and national resources, amounted to 1.5% of the EU's GDP at the time. The European Commission (the "Commission") also announced on January 26, 2009 that, to improve the supervision of large banks and other financial institutions cross borders, it would allocate an extra €36.2 million to the national banking, insurance and securities industry supervisors – known as CEBS, CEIOPS and CESR, respectively, as well as the accounting and auditing bodies.[37]

On the national level the German government also approved a rescue package for the financial industry in October 2008, totaling €500 billion.[38] It included funds for the recapitalization of the banks and insurers, funds to purchase risky asset – if necessary, and funds to back up guarantees. Notably, Germany required banks that were beneficiaries of recapitalizations to engage in lending to

33 See id. See also Breakdown of the Final Bailout Bill, Washington Post (September 28, 2008).

34 See *Colin Barr*, Obama: Give Me the Money, CNNMoney.com (January 12, 2009).

35 See id.

36 See Communication from the Commission to the European Council, A European Economic Recovery Plan, COM(2008)800 final, 26 November 2008, available at http://ec.europa.eu/economy_finance/publications/publication13504_en.pdf; See also FAQs on the European Economic Recovery Plan, Memo/08/735 (26 November 2008), available at: http://europa.eu/rapid/pressReleasesAction.do?reference=MEMO/08/735.

37 See *Nikki Tait and Jennifer Hughes*, EU Financial Regulators to Receive €36.2m, Financial Times (January 26, 2009).

38 See *Gregory Viscusi*, EU Nations Commit 1.3 Trillion Euros to Bank Bailouts, Bloomberg (October 13, 2008). See also *Marcus Walker, Joellen Perry, Thomas Catan and Mike Esterl*, In Reversal, Germany Redies Its Own Bailout, Wall St. J. (October 11, 2008).

small and medium-sized enterprises.[39] A second stimulus package comprised of €50 billion in public investments and tax cuts for 2009 and 2010 was unveiled in January 2009.[40]

Chancellor Angela Merkel blamed the economic meltdown on a policy driven boom. She reportedly asserted that "It happened because we were living beyond our means [and that] governments encouraged risk-taking in order to boost growth" but such spending was not sustainable.[41] As such, the German response to the economic crisis was initially at odds with the US response. According to US columnist David Brooks, German and American political leaders engaged in an epic debate during the first half of 2010. American leaders argued that the economic crisis was so bad that governments should borrow billions to stimulate growth, while German leaders including German Finance Minister Wolfgang Schaeuble argued that a little short-term stimulus was sensible, but anything more was nearsighted.[42] What was needed was not more debt, but measures to balance budgets and restore confidence.

To that end, Germany spent about 1.5 percent of GDP on their stimulus, while the US reportedly borrowed an amount equal to 6 percent of GDP in an attempt to stimulate growth.[43] Bearing in mind that results from one quarter do not settle the stimulus/austerity debate, it appears that Germany was on the right

39 See *Marcus Walker, Joellen Perry, Thomas Catan and Mike Esterl*, In Reversal, Germany Redies Its Own Bailout, Wall St. J. (October 11, 2008).

40 See *Kate Connolly*, Germany Approves €50bn Stimulus Package, Guardian.Co.UK, (January 27, 2009).

41 See also *Bertrand Benoit, Quentin Peel and Chris Bryant*, We All Want to Put the Global Economy Back on its Feet, Financial Times (March 27 2009). See also *D.W. MacKenzie*, Economics Professor, A Responsible Response to the Financial Crisis, MonetaryCurrent.Com (April 10, 2009 (in comments praising Germany and Chancellor Merkel's response to the current crisis cited to the boom-bust theory that earned economist *F.A. Hayek* his Nobel Prize in economics. "Hayek's theory was that rapid increases in the money supply cause unsustainable investment booms. Increased money supply lowers interest rates, and lower interest rates cause businesses to invest more, especially in longer term projects. Low interest rates also cause households to put less money into savings, while focusing more on immediate consumption. It is obvious that the recent boom was driven largely by both a boom in household consumption and investment in new construction. The problem with all this consumer and business spending is that it is financed by increased money supply, rather than by real increases in economic productivity, and such monetary booms must lead to inflation.").

42 See *David Brooks*, US Could Learn From Germany's Long-term Response to Economic Crisis, Seattle Times (August 27, 2010).

43 Id.

track. By late 2010, the German economy reportedly had grown at a sizzling (and obviously unsustainable) 9 percent annual rate with unemployment at pre-crisis levels.[44] The U.S. economy, while steadily recovering, is at a slower pace.

2. The Enactment of Structural Regulatory Reforms to Curb Systemic Risk

The global financial crisis forced governments to review their regulatory system for the financial markets, including the rules governing financial products and services. Most importantly, the governments began to review existing regulations to determine where gaps existed that might threaten the stability of their banking systems. This article focuses on those measures undertaken by the U.S. and the European Union.

a) The United States

The regulatory failings in the U.S., for example, can be attributed to numerous shortcomings, including turf wars among the various regulators, funding shortfalls, an incomprehension of risk magnitudes, and the failure of regulations that considered the inter-connectedness of significant players in the financial system, to name a few.[45] The SEC, in particular, was both blameless and blameworthy in the financial crisis. The SEC had been hampered during the many years leading up to and through the financial crisis in its efforts to "protect investors, facilitate capital formation and maintain fair, orderly, and efficient markets"[46] because it remained significantly under-funded,[47] and understaffed[48] despite the many mar-

---

44 Id.

45 I believe that the regulatory failings in the U.S. also can be attributed to regulatory apathy, regulatory capture, or the subordination to a deregulatory leadership.

46 See U.S. Securities and Exchange Commission, Office of Inspector General, Semiannual Report to Congress, October 1, 2008 –March 31, 2009 at p. 5, (noting SEC's mission).

47 The SEC's operating budget had increased only incrementally during the period of 1999 through 2008, from $341 million to $906 million. See Frequently Requested FOIA Document: Budget History – BA vs. Actual Obligations, available at http://www.sec.gov/foia/docs/budgetact.htm. Specifically, its budget for the years 1999 through 2002 (the period preceding discovery of the wave of accounting scandals) was $341 million; $377 million; $423 million; $514 million, respectively; and only increased following calls for more funding in 2002 to $716 million in 2003; $812 million in 2004; $887 million in 2005; $888 million in 2006; $882 million in 2007 and $906 million in 2008. Id.

ket changes. Further, two significant legislative changes that were adopted more than a decade ago – the Gramm Leach Bliley Act of 1999 ("GLBA")[49] and the Commodities Futures Modernization Act of 2000 ("CFMA")[50] – re-arranged the regulatory landscape, leaving some market participants and some financial products without any regulatory oversight. As a result, the SEC was given neither the authority to regulate the trading of derivative securities (including asset-backed securities and credit default swaps), nor regulatory authority over the conduct of some of those market participants (including the investment banking holding companies, the hedge funds, and their investment advisors), who traded in the products that have been attributed to the economic crisis.

Nevertheless, the opportunity to regulate the then-five largest investment bank holding companies was both obtained and subsequently squandered by the SEC.[51] When Congress passed the GLBA, it created a significant regulatory gap by failing to give the SEC or any other federal agency the authority to regulate large investment bank holding companies. Consequently, there was no federal requirement following the enactment of the GLBA that these entities report and maintain sufficient capital reserves, liquidity levels or leverage limits. At the request of The Goldman Sachs Group, Inc., Morgan Stanley, Merrill Lynch, Lehman and Bear Stearns in 2004, however, the SEC created the so-called Con-

---

48 The SEC had a staff of 3,511 full time equivalents during fiscal year 2008. See U.S. Securities and Exchange Commission, FY 2010 Congressional Justification at p. 1 (May 2009). See also Testimony of Linda Chatman, Former SEC Director of Division of Enforcement, Before the U.S. Senate Committee on Banking, Housing and Urban Affairs Re: Maddoff Matter (January 27, 2009). The SEC had 80 fewer staffers than it had at its 2005 fiscal year peak. See Testimony of SEC Division Heads before House Comm. on Financial Services Subcommittee on Capital Markets (February 4, 2009). Nevertheless, it regulated and oversaw the activities of approximately 5,600 broker-dealers, over 11,000 investment advisors, 4,600 registered mutual funds, 12,000 public companies, 600 transfer agents, 11 stock and option exchanges, over five clearing agencies and ten credit rating agencies, among other financial intermediaries, through March 2009. See Shapiro March 2009 Testimony. See also U.S. Securities and Exchange Commission, Office of Inspector General, Semiannual Report to Congress, October 1, 2008 – March 31, 2009 at p. 5 (noting that the SEC also oversees the Public Company Accounting Oversight Board (PCAOB), the Financial Industry Regulatory Authority (FINRA), and the Municipal Securities Rule-making Board (MSRB)).

49 Pub.L. 106-102, 113 Stat. 1338, enacted November 12, 1999.

50 Pub.L. 106–554, 114 Stat. 2763, enacted December 21, 2000.

51 See *Stephen Laboton*, SEC Concedes Oversight Flaws Fueled Collapse, NY Times (September 26, 2008); *Daniel Indivigilio*, Is the SEC to Blame for Lehman's Failure? The Atlantic (April 20, 2010).

solidated Supervised Entities ("CSE") program, pursuant to which these five investment bank conglomerates voluntarily submitted to the SEC's oversight jurisdiction.[52] Until then, the SEC only regulated the broker-dealer entities of investment banks. It began with capital requirements for holding companies then added liquidity supervision.[53] The near-collapse of Bear Stearns and the subsequent bankruptcy of Lehman revealed that the SEC failed in its oversight of liquidity and capital requirements. Morgan Stanley and Goldman Sachs, the last two major U.S. investment banks, both announced on September 22, 2008 that they would become traditional bank holding companies regulated by the Federal Reserve.[54] Without investment bank participants, the CSE program subsequently ended in late 2008.[55]

In late March 2008, then-Treasury Secretary Henry L. Paulson introduced a plan to overhaul the way the US financial system was regulated. The *Blueprint for a Modernized Financial Regulatory Structure* was designed to promote "economic growth and stability in the United States" by reforming the regulatory structure applicable to the banking, securities, insurance and futures industry away from the current system of functional regulation.[56] The Treasury proposed a regulatory approach that would have established distinct regulators focused on one of three objectives: (i) market stability regulation; (ii) safety and soundness regulation (otherwise known as prudential regulation); and (iii) business conduct regulation.[57] This proposal also called for increased authority for the Federal Reserve and the consolidation of numerous federal regulatory agencies, including a recommendation to merge the SEC with the CFTC.[58] While the Blueprint introduced many ideas that were ultimately incorporated into the recent push for regulatory reform, it was a highly political document introduced during an election year. As such, little progress was made on the Blueprint's reform proposals.

---

52 See SEC Press Release, Chairman Cox Announces End of Consolidated Supervised Entities Program, (September 26, 2008).

53 See Testimony of *E. Sirri*, Testimony concerning the Consolidated Supervision of U.S Securities Firms and Affiliated Industrial Loan Companies, before the Committee on Banking, Housing and Urban Affairs, U.S. Senate (October 4, 2007).

54 Wall Street in Crisis: Last Banks Standing Give Up Investment Bank Status, The Guardian, September 22, 2008.

55 SEC Press Release, Chairman *Cox* Announces End of Consolidated Supervised Entities Program, (September 26, 2008).

56 The Department of the Treasury, Blueprint For a Modernized Financial Regulatory Structure (March 2008), w.w.w.treasury.gov (the "Blueprint").

57 See, the Blueprint.

58 See, the Blueprint.

A little over a month after taking office in 2009, President Barack Obama outlined his "core principles" for reforming the current financial regulatory system with bipartisan leaders of the House Financial Services and Senate Banking committees. According to the President, "strong financial markets require clear rules of the road, not to hinder financial institutions, but to protect consumers and investors, and ultimately to keep those financial institutions strong."[59] He noted the need for greater accountability and transparency; stricter oversight of financial institutions to prevent systemic risks; gap-filling regulatory restructurings; and more uniform supervision and oversight of financial products marketed to consumers and investors based on actual data of how actual people make financial decisions.[60] President Obama also acknowledged the need for greater cooperation with global U.S.-counterparts.

Although details of the Administration's proposal would not be made publicly available until many months later, Treasury Secretary Timothy Geithner repeated many of these key regulatory reform principles during an appearance before the House Financial Services Committee on March 26, 2009.[61] The primary focus of Secretary Geithner's congressional testimony, however, concerned the manner in which systemic risk could be addressed. To that end, he called for the creation of a systemic risk regulator, increased capital and risk management standards; the registration of all hedge fund advisers who manage assets over a certain threshold; the comprehensive regulation of the OTC derivatives market; and the strengthened regulation of money market funds. Perhaps the most forward-thinking proposal was the idea of providing the government with so-called "resolution authority" over systemically important[62] non-bank

---

59 Speech Transcript, *Obama's* Remarks on Regulation in the Financial Sector, Washington Post (February 25, 2009), available athttp://projects.washingtonpost.com/obama-speeches/speech/131/. See also White House Briefing Room, Blog, posted by Macon Phillips (February 25, 2009).

60 Id.

61 See Treasury's Regulatory Reform Proposal Press Release (March 26, 2009); Secretary *Timothy Geithner's* Testimony before the House Financial Services Committee on Regulatory Reform (March 26, 2009).

62 Systemically important firms "would not be limited to banks or bank holding companies (BHCs), but could include any financial institution that was deemed to be systemically important in accordance with legislative requires. In defining such firms, the following characteristics should be taken into account: (1) the financial system's interdependence with the firm; (2) the firm's size, leverage (including off-balance sheet exposures), and degree of reliance on short-term funding and (3) the firm's importance as a source of credit for households and business, and governments and as a source of liquidity for the financial system." See Treasury's Regulatory Reform Proposal Press Release (March

financial institutions that fall outside the FDIC's existing resolution regime. Such authority would have enabled the orderly liquidation of Lehman, thereby avoiding market panic associated with the uncertainty that accompanies a bankruptcy filing.

The Treasury Department subsequently released a detailed white-paper of the new Administration's recommendations for regulatory reform, entitled *Financial Regulatory Reform – A New Foundation: Rebuilding Financial Supervision and Regulation*, on June 17, 2009.[63] This proposal signaled a restructuring of the federal regulatory system. It was designed to meet five key objectives:

- Promote robust supervision and regulation of financial firms;
- Establish comprehensive supervision and regulation of all financial markets;
- Protect consumers and investors from financial abuse;
- Improve tools for managing financial crisis; and
- Raise international regulatory standards and improve international co-operation.[64]

Specifically, the Treasury proposal called for a partial restructuring of regulatory jurisdiction with the creation of four new entities: (i) the Financial Services Oversight Council ("FSOC"), chaired by the Treasury and including the heads of the principal federal regulators of the financial industry; (ii) the Consumer Financial Protection Agency ("CFPA"), an independent agency; (iii) the Office of National Insurance, to be housed within the Treasury; and (iv) the National Bank Supervisor, a single agency (with status separate from the Treasury) responsible for all federally chartered depository institutions and all federal branches and agencies of foreign banks.[65] While the FDIC and the NCUA would continue in existence – with the former supervising and regulating state-chartered banks and the latter, supervising credit unions, this Treasury proposal also contemplates the merger of the OTS and the OCC into the National Bank Supervisor.[66]

26, 2009); Secretary *Timothy Geithner's* Testimony before the House Financial Services Committee on Regulatory Reform (March 26, 2009).

63 Department of the Treasury Financial Regulatory Reform – A New Foundation: Rebuilding Financial Supervision and Regulation (June 2009), www.financialstability.gov/docs/regs/FinalReport_web.pdf ("The New Foundation").

64 See The New Foundation.

65 Id.

66 As of June 2009, four different federal agencies had roughly the same (or at least overlapping) jurisdiction and authority over depository institutions. Indeed, the OCC had oversight responsibility for national banks, while the OTS had responsibilities for sav-

On the issue of systemic risk, the Treasury proposal also called on the Federal Reserve to have responsibility for macro-prudential consolidated supervision over those firms that could pose a risk to the entire financial system and the FSOC to monitor firms and markets for micro-prudential risks.[67] The FSOC's chief obligation would be to identify emerging micro-prudential risks and inform the Fed where such risks could pose a systemic threat. It also would be tasked with facilitating and coordinating information sharing; filling gaps in supervision, and providing a forum for jurisdictional disputes among regulators.[68]

The Administration also proposed establishing new threshold regulations for any financial institution whose combination of size, leverage and interconnectedness could pose a systemic threat if it should fail. These so-called "Tier 1 FHC" would become subject to the Fed's supervisory oversight regardless of whether it owned a depository institution.[69] This proposal would expand the Fed's power since the GLBA limited the Fed's authority over functionally regulated subsidiaries of financial holding companies. Under the Treasury's proposal, consolidated supervision of Tier 1 FHCs would allow the Fed to regulate the parent company and all subsidiaries – without regard to whether the entity was foreign or domestic, or whether the entities had been regulated or unregulated in the past. Once declared a Tier 1 FHC, that entity would be subject to higher capital, liquidity and risk management standards than other firm.[70] Correspondingly, all banks and bank holding companies also would have to strengthen their capital reserves and other prudential standards as well.[71]

The Treasury further proposed to unveil the increased activities in what has become the shadow banking system[72] by proposing more robust reporting re-

---

ings and loan associations, the Fed has responsibility for the member banks of the Federal Reserve System, and the FDIC had responsibility for all federally insured depository banks and state non-member banks. The goal of the Treasury proposal is to have the National Bank Supervisor supervise and have oversight authority over all federally-chartered depository institutions.

67 Micro-prudential supervision focuses on the actions of individual institutions and the protection of the institution's customers. By contrast, macro-prudential supervision focuses on the system as a whole, and "seeks to protect the overall economy from significant losses. The two are by necessity intertwined. See de Larosiere Report at p. 38.

68 The New Foundation.

69 The New Foundation.

70 The New Foundation.

71 The New Foundation.

72 Over the last decade, there has been a growth in financial activity outside of the traditional banking system, with more borrowing and lending and risk management occurring through securitizations. Initially, this process was designed to reduce credit risk by

quirements on issuers of asset-backed securities and by requiring loan originators and securitization brokers to retain a financial interest in the performance of those products. The Treasury also proposed legislative changes to reduce investor and regulatory reliance on credit-rating agencies. Finally, throughout the process, the U.S. reform plan called for a harmonization of regulations and goals of the SEC and the CFTC, as well as greater safeguards on payment and settlement systems and more oversight in the OTC derivatives market.[73]

The U.S. Congress worked on competing regulatory reform bills from December 2009 through mid-2010. The Senate passed its version of a financial overhaul bill (SB 3217) by a vote of 59-39 in May 2010, while the House passed its version (HR 4173) much earlier by a vote of vote: 223 – 202 in late 2009.[74] As the finalized bill emerged from conference in late June 2010, President Obama stated that the bill included 90 percent of the Treasury proposals.[75] The Se-

---

spreading it more widely to those entities with better resources to manage it. Unfortunately, the removal of the links between actual borrowers and lenders led to the erosion in lending standards, which was greatly revealed when the housing boom dampened and housing prices fell. See generally, The New Foundation.

73 The New Foundation.

74 "Bill Summary & Status - 111th Congress (2009 - 2010) - H.R.4173 - THOMAS (Library of Congress)". Available at Library of Congress, http://thomas.loc.gov/cgi-bin/bdquery/z?d111:HR04173:@@@L&summ2=m&#major%20actions. The Senate bill's major provisions included: (i) giving federal regulators new authority to seize and break up troubled financial firms without taxpayer bailouts; (ii) creating a Consumer Financial Protection Bureau within the Fed with rulemaking and some enforcement power over banks and non-bank financial institutions who provide consumer financial products or services such as credit cards or mortgages; (iii) requiring that most derivatives trading be executed on a public exchange and that large commercial banks who have access to the Fed's Discount Window be required to divest their derivatives trading business to wholly separate entities; (iv) establishing a nine-member Financial Stability Oversight Council to monitor and address system-wide risks to the financial system; (v) increasing capital requirements for banks with more than $250 billion in assets based on higher-risk and size; (vi) requiring loan originators and securitizers to hold a portion of that risk on their balance sheets; and (vii) requiring hedge funds that manage more than $100 million in assets to register with the SEC. See *David M. Herszenhorn*, Bill Passed in Senate Broadly Expands Oversight of Wall Street, NY Times (May 20, 2010).

75 See Remarks by the President on Wall Street Reform (June 25, 2010), available at: http://www.whitehouse.gov/the-press-office/remarks-president-wall-street-reform-1.

nate voted 60 to 39 to approve the conference bill on July 15, 2010 following passage by the House on June 30, 2010 by a 237-192 vote.[76]

On July 21, 2010, President Obama signed into law the Dodd-Frank Wall Street Reform and Consumer Protection Act[77] – the most significant overhaul of U.S. financial regulations since the 1930s. The Act mandates new regulations to monitor and control large and systemically significant financial institutions. The Dodd-Frank Act also mandates establishing a new consumer protection bureau at the Fed, restricts proprietary trading by banks, sets mortgage lending and securitization standards, enhances the SEC's enforcement powers, and requires greater transparency and oversight of the derivatives markets, hedge funds and their advisors, credit rating agencies.[78]

To deal with systemic risk, Title I of the Dodd-Frank Act, in relevant part, establishes the Financial Stability Oversight Council to oversee all financial institutions – both bank and non-bank.[79] The Council is chaired by the Treasury Secretary, and includes the Chairman of the Board of Governors of the Federal Reserve System, the Comptroller of Currency, the Director of the newly-created Consumer Financial Protection Bureau ("CFPB"), the respective chairpersons of the SEC, FDIC, CFTC, NCUA, the director of the Federal Housing Finance Agency, and an independent member (to be appointed by the President) having insurance expertise as voting members. The Council is required to meet at least once each quarter and to monitor the U.S. financial markets in order to identify systemic financial risks, promote market discipline and respond to emerging threats.[80]

---

76 "Bill Summary & Status - 111th Congress (2009 - 2010) - H.R.4173 - THOMAS (Library of Congress)". Available at Library of Congress, http://thomas.loc.gov/cgi-bin/bdquery/z?d111:HR04173:@@@L&summ2=m&#major%20actions.

77 Pub. L. 111-203, "Bill Summary & Status - 111th Congress (2009 - 2010) - H.R.4173 - THOMAS (Library of Congress)". Available at Library of Congress, http://thomas.loc.gov/cgi-bin/bdquery/z?d111:HR04173:@@@L&summ2=m&#major%20actions.

78 Pub.L. 111-203, "Bill Summary & Status - 111th Congress (2009 - 2010) - H.R.4173 - THOMAS (Library of Congress)". Available at Library of Congress, http://thomas.loc.gov/cgi-bin/bdquery/z?d111:HR04173:@@@L&summ2=m&#major%20actions

79 Pub.L. 111-203, "Bill Summary & Status - 111th Congress (2009 - 2010) - H.R.4173 - THOMAS (Library of Congress)". Available at Library of Congress, http://thomas.loc.gov/cgi-bin/bdquery/z?d111:HR04173:@@@L&summ2=m&#major%20actions

80 Pub.L. 111-203, "Bill Summary & Status - 111th Congress (2009 - 2010) - H.R.4173 - THOMAS (Library of Congress)". Available at Library of Congress,

To assist the Council, the Act provides that bank holding companies with $50 billion or more in assets and nonbank financial companies that are supervised by the Fed (i) must submit plans for their orderly liquidation in the event of material financial distress (the "Living Wills); (ii) are subject to credit exposure limits (under certain circumstances); (iii) may be subject to the Fed's limit on the amount of short-term debt that may be accumulated; (iv) is subject to higher minimum leverage capital requirements; (v) could be subject to debt-to-equity ratio limits of no more than 15 to 1; and (vi) is required to take off balance sheet activities into account when computing capital for purposes of determining whether capital requirements are met, among other requirements.

Finally, the Act also establishes a procedure for placing distressed financial institutions and systemically significant non-bank financial institutions into receivership under the mandated "Resolution Authority" provisions in Title II of the Act. Had this procedure been in place, it could have dealt more effectively with the problems at Bear Stearns and Lehman. This authority allows the government to break financial contracts, like CDS in the resolution process and avoid paying out monies to undeserving managers or counter-parties.

b) The European Union

The disruption in the U.S. credit markets spread through the financial institutions in Europe, many of whom had also invested in mortgages and mortgage-related securities. Highly leveraged and faced with liquidity issues, many turned to their respective governments for assistance. However, the EU found itself faced with an inadequate crisis management infrastructure. The lack of coordination between Member States posed serious problems.[81] One nation's financial policies have had negative spillover effects on other countries. Additionally, the EU suffers from a lack of harmonization of its core rules governing bank and non-bank financial institutions. In other words, Member States have different bankruptcy laws, different reporting obligations different risk management assessments, and different definitions of economic capital, to name a few.[82]

National rules and regulations are significantly different from one country to the next, encouraging regulatory arbitrage and competitive distortions. Commentators argue that this diversity is the product of the EU's common directives.

---

http://thomas.loc.gov/cgi-bin/bdquery/z?d111:HR04173:@@@L&summ2=m&#major%20actions

81 See *de Larosiere* Report at pp. 10-11, 27-29.

82 See *de Larosiere* Report at pp. 27-29.

[83] More precisely, EU members are given options in the enforcement of the EU's common directives. Too often Level 1 directives are left to a wide range of national options; thereby creating a maze from which the Level 3 committees are to create a single solution. The crisis revealed just how interconnected Member State's financial institutions were and how difficult it was to conduct crisis management in cases of cross-border institutions.

On February 25, 2009, the High-Level Group on Financial Supervision in the EU, headed by Jacques de Larosiere, introduced its proposal (the "de Larosiere Report"),[84] to the European Commission (the "Commission") to overhaul the regulation of the EU's financial markets and its participants in an effort to avoid future contagion. The High-Level Group noted that the existing supervisory system failed on both the micro and macro level.[85] Moreover, "[E]ffective macro-prudential supervision must encompass all sectors of finance and not be confined [solely] to banks." [86] Among the 31 recommendations proposed in the de Larosiere Report,[87] the High-Level Group proposed that an enhanced Euro-

---

83 See *de Larosiere* Report at pp. 27-29.

84 See *de Larosiere* Report. Jacques de Larosiere was a former Banque de France governor.

85 See *de Larosiere* Report at p. 11 (noting "Regulators and supervisors focused on the micro prudential supervision of financial institutions and not sufficiently on the macro-systemic risks of a contagion of correlated horizontal shocks.").

86 See *de Larosiere* Report at p. 39.

87 The *de Larosiere* Report also made recommendations about the functioning of the derivatives market, including development of appropriate risk-mitigation techniques and transparency measures. Similarly, the Commission revealed in its March 4, 2009 "Communication for the Spring European Council" that it also had been considering issues relating to capital reserves. To that end, it proposed amendments to the Capital Requirements Directive, which came into force in 2006. Specifically, the Commission proposed that:
Banks generally would be restricted from lending to other banks more than 25% of their capital base;
The criteria for determining whether hybrid capital should be eligible to be counted as part of a bank's Tier 1 capital (for purpose of establishing capital adequacy requirements) would be set EU-wide;
EU regulated financial institutions must ensure that originators and sponsors of securitized products retain at least 5% of the risks; and
National banking supervisors would be required to consider the impact that their decisions have on the wider EU sector.
The Commission also considered establishing higher capital requirements for certain complex structured credit products and strengthening the capital requirements for proprietary trading exposures of structured credit. To become effective, of course, all of

pean financial supervisory framework be adopted,[88] based on two pillars structured as follows:

- The EU should create a system of committees with more supervisory authority, along with the establishment of a European Systemic Risk Council ("ESRC"), which would be chaired by the president of the ECB, to deal with inter-connected macro- and micro prudential issues. On the one hand, the ESRC would be responsible for overall "macro-prudential" policy, employing risk warnings as inputs to EU supervisors and giving them direction based on comparisons across member states, harmonizing national regulations on capital adequacy requirements, supervisory standards and deposit guarantee schemes to name a few.
- Housed under the ESRC, the EU also should establish a European System of Financial Supervision ("ESFS") consisting of three new committees to deal at the micro-prudential level with banking, insurance and securities supervision; thereby replacing the old Lamfalussy Level 3 Committees. As proposed, the new committees – a European Banking Authority, a European Insurance Authority and a European Securities Authority (collectively the "European Authorities") would have an expanded role and binding authority to coordinate the application of supervisory standards. Specifically, the European Authorities (in cooperation with the ESRC) would be responsible for conducting *legally binding* mediations between national supervisors, the adoption of *binding* supervisory standards, the adoption of *binding* technical decisions applicable to individual institutions, oversight and coordination of colleges of supervisors, licensing and supervision of specific EU-wide institutions, including credit rating agencies.[89]

The ESFS would be reviewed no later than three years after its establishment and additional responses might then be considered, including establishing two authorities – one responsible for banking and insurance prudential issues

---

these amendments would have to be approved by the European Parliament and the Member State. Thereafter, if all goes as planned these amendments would have to be implemented by the Member States by October 31, 2010 and would take effect in early 2011.

88 At the EU level, there were three primary financial services committees for micro-financial supervision – the Committee of European Banking Supervisors ("CEBS"), Committee of European Insurance and Occupational Pensions Committee ("CEIOPS") and the Committee of European Securities Regulators ("CESR"), collectively known as the "Lamfalussy level 3 Committees. Problematically these committees only had advisory powers. There was no single body in Europe with macro-prudential responsibilities to monitor systemic risks. See *de Larosiere* Report.

89 See *de Larosiere* Report at p. 46-48.

and financial stability and the other responsible for the conduct of business and market issues, and empowering the ESFS with wider supervisory duties at the European level. The Group stopped short of recommending the transfer of supervisory responsibilities of financial firms from member-states to the European level.[90]

Less than a week after the publication of the de Larosiere Report, the Commission revealed in its March 4 release its Communication for the Spring European Council entitled, *Driving European Recovery* that it intended to propose by May 2009 a new European financial supervision package based in large measure on the de Larosiere Report, for decision by the European Council by June, with the newly-adopted structure in place by 2011.[91] The Commission also proposed to develop measures to address gaps in European and national regulations on consumer protection, hedge funds, derivatives, executive compensation, and credit rating agencies, to name a few, between April and June 2009.

The Commission subsequently released its *Communication, European Financial Supervision* on May 27 in which it outlined its proposal to reform the financial supervision system to help restore confidence and also proposed a new system to warn against future financial crisis.[92] The Commission endorsed the two pillar structure (the ESRC and ESFS) recommended by the de Larosiere Report, including the creation of the European Authorities.

Under the Commission's proposal the ESRC would (i) collect and analyze all information relevant for monitoring and assessing potential threats to financial stability that arise from macro-economic developments and from developments in the entire financial system; (ii) identify and prioritize such risks; (iii) issue warnings where risks appear to be significant; (iv) give recommendations on measures to be taken in reaction to identified risks; (v) monitor the follow-up to warnings and recommendations; and (vi) liaise effectively with the IMF and the Financial Stability Board (created during the G-20 meeting in April 2009) and third-country counterparts.

The ESRC warnings would be channeled through the ECOFIN Council, which is part of the European Council. Its warnings and recommendations, while not legally binding on the recipients, are expected to be acted upon and any inaction must be adequately justified. Public disclosures of these recommendations or warnings will be determined by the ESRC on a case-by-case ba-

---

90 See *de Larosiere* Report at p. 46-48.

91 See European Commission, Driving European Recovery, COM(2009) 114 Final (4 March 2009).

92 See European Commission, European Financial Supervisors, COM(2009) 252 Final (27 May 2009).

sis. The ESRC would be accountable to the European Council and the European Parliament. Membership in the ESRC is open to the ECB president and vice president, the governors of the 27 national central banks, chairperson of the three European Authorities and a member of the Commission.

According to the Economic and Monetary Affairs Commissioner Joaquin Almunia, "The financial sector was one of the main drivers of growth since the creation of the single market in the early 90s, but it also nearly brought the economy to a halt . . . the [European Systemic Risk Council] would for the first time equip the EU with a pan-European macro-prudential supervision system."[93]

The ESFS, as proposed, would supervise individual financial institutions with a network of national financial supervisors (who would have day to day supervisory authority of those institutions within its borders) working in tandem with the new European Authorities. The European Authorities would (i) ensure a single set of harmonized rules; (ii) ensure consistent application of EU rules – acting as mediator when needed; (iii) ensure common supervisory culture and consistent supervisory practices; (iv) exercise full supervisory authority over credit rating agencies and EU central counter-party clearing houses, to name a few; (v) ensure a coordinated response in crisis situations by facilitating cooperation and the exchange of information between authorities – again acting as mediator when necessary; (vi) collect micro-prudential information by establishing and maintaining a central European database; and (vii) undertake an international role. Its decisions, as well as those of the Commission will be reviewable by EU courts.

On June 18-19, 2009, the European Council published its support of the recommendations of both the de Larosiere Report and the Commission's Communication, European Financial Supervision." The macro-prudential regulator (earlier referred to as ESRC) is now the European Systemic Risk Board ("ESRB"). The ESRB would be based in Frankfurt and chaired by the President of the European Central Bank ("ECB") for an initial term of 5 years. The ECB will oversee the day-to-day operations of the ESRB, providing staff and support.

On September 20, 2010, the European Parliament – following agreement by all Member States – voted through the new supervisory framework proposed by the Commission. This was confirmed by the ECOFIN Council on November 17, 2010. The three European Supervisory Authorities were established in January 2011.

93 Press Release, Brussels, 27 May 2009.

IV. Conclusion

Both the US and the EU are off to a good start, notwithstanding the compromises that each had to make to enact the current regulatory reform. Nevertheless, there is still a lot of work yet to be concluded before a true assessment of whether future crises can be averted by the regulatory structural changes in the EU and US. Although each jurisdiction has enacted meaningful legislation, the regulatory framework is still in skeletal form.

In the US, much of the detailed regulations that will set the parameters for the enforcement of obligations are yet to be written. The SEC[94] and Fed are tasked with this responsibility, with the SEC bearing the greater burden. Specifically, the SEC is required to issue 95 new regulations, complete 17 one-time studies and 5 on-going reports.[95] In the EU, the individual new entities – including the ESA will have to determine what regulations should be enacted to fill in the gaps left by the earlier regulations.

While neither resulting pieces of legislation rectify the too big to fail problem of large interconnected bank and nonbank financial institution, each provides tools to monitor such institutions and sound warning bells before their collapse infects the entire financial system. Their ability to ably regulate all financial institutions will, of course, depend upon the will of the independent regulatory entities as well as the strength any regulation promulgated under these key pieces of legislation. Whether the regulators can ignore the powerful lobbyist who prefer the status quo will also be determinative. Only time will tell.

94 The SEC is tasked with promulgating regulations to improve and standardize practices by loan originators, underwriters and credit rating agencies.

95 See *Zachary A. Goldfarb*, As Financial Reform Becomes Law, SEC Emerges with New Powers and Duties, The Washington Post (July 22, 2010).

Preparing Students to Practice Law in 2010 and Beyond: The Call for Skills Training in the United States and Germany

*by Susan Hanley Duncan**

The two types of legal knowledge – the theoretical and the practical – are complimentary. Each must have a respected place in legal education.

The Carnegie Foundation for the Advancement of Teaching

I. Introduction

Academics, policy makers and the public at large in the United States and Germany seek to improve the competence of those entering the legal profession, especially their proficiency in lawyering skills. While these countries share a common national interest, the structure for training new lawyers differs radically between the two countries. In the United States, a law degree is a post graduate degree typically involving three years of academic study followed by a state bar exam. Admission to law school in the United States is contingent upon taking a standardized admissions test (LSAT) and is quite competitive. In contrast, German students receive their legal training as undergraduate students and take no admissions test.[1] Unlike the American system which focuses primarily on the theoretical study of legal doctrine for three years with limited practical experiences, the German system involves two stages of training with the first four years involving academic study followed by a comprehensive exam (Erste Staatsexamen) and the second stage involving practical training (Referendariat) followed by a second exam (Zweite Staatsexamen). Although the American and German systems follow very different paths, neither country's legal professionals seem satisfied with how legal education is being delivered today.

The criticism of American legal education is nothing new.[2] However, recent American studies strongly criticizing United States law schools for not doing an

---

* Associate Professor of Law, Louis D. Brandeis School of Law.

1 *Stefan Korioth*, Legal Education in Germany Today, 24(1) Wisconsin International Law Journal 85, 90 (2006)

2 *Andreas Bucker and William A. Woodruff*, The Bologna Process and German Legal Education: Developing Professional Competence Through Clinical Experiences, 9 (5) German Law Journal 575, 584-586 (2008) (discussing articles finding problems with a law curriculum based on the case method).

effective job of integrating theory with practice brought the issue back to the forefront.[3] Many lawyers and professors acknowledge that American law students are not adequately prepared to practice law and would not entrust new graduates with a legal matter for their own families.[4] They point to a lack of "skills, attributes, and values that effective legal professionals command."[5] The American Bar Association which accredits law schools took notice of these complaints and is presently exploring what would be a major sea change to its standards requiring schools to shift from a teaching regime to a learning regime. These new output measures would seek to assess whether law graduates have acquired appropriate fundamental lawyering skills and evaluate whether they understand legal theory as well as their professional and ethical responsibilities.

Similar complaints concerning the German system exist on the other side of the Atlantic.[6] In particular, the long duration of the education, often over six years of study, and the broad compulsory contents continue to be criticized as too burdensome.[7] Learning this great amount of material is made even more difficult by the overcrowding of the classes caused by the policy that no students can be denied admission to the study of law.[8] In addition, the oral and written exams are very challenging with many students not passing them.[9] Some critics, similar to ones found in America, also find fault with the division of theory from practice by the two level system.[10] And prior to reforms made in 2002, the practical training stage had little focus on some important lawyering skills including negotiation, advocacy, legal advice, etc.[11]

Recently, however, a movement in Europe seeking to standardize European higher education has added a thorny dimension to the debate concerning how

3 *William M. Sullivan* et al., Educating Lawyers: Preparation for the Profession of Law (Jossey-Bass 2007); *Roy Stuckey* et al., Best Practices for Legal Education: A Vision and a Road Map (Clin. Leg. Educ. Assn. 2007).

4 *Earl Martin & Gerald Hess*, Developing A Skills and Professionalism Curriculum – Process and Product, 41 U. Tol. L. Rev. 327, 327 (2010).

5 Id.

6 *Stephan Leibfried, Christoph Mollers, Christoph Schmid, & Peer Zumbansen*, Redefining the Traditional Pillars of German Legal Studies and Setting the Stage for Contemporary Interdisciplinary Research, 7(8) German Law Journal 661, 677 (2006); *Jutta Brunnee*, The Reform of Legal Education in Germany: The Never-Ending Story and European Integration, 42 Journal of Legal Education 399 (1992).

7 *Korioth*, supra n. 1, at 103.

8 Id. at 104.

9 Id.

10 Id. at 105.

11 Id. at 98.

best to train lawyers in Germany. The Bologna Process' mandates seeking to harmonize bachelors degrees to just three years for all European countries presents major problems for legal education in Germany which has always required two stages of education extending well beyond three years. Thus both German legal educators and their American counterparts are now faced with new initiatives largely brought by external forces that seek to change how legal education is delivered in each of their countries. The challenge for legal educators in both countries is how best to ensure students develop the skills, competencies and values required in the legal profession. German schools may be required to do this in a completely different format than their past traditions while American schools may need to engage in major curriculum reform to infuse more of this in legal education.

Both the American Bar Association and the Bologna process appear to be pushing law schools to engage in curricular reform to make sure their graduates have more than just black letter knowledge of the law but also be proficient in skills.[12] These directives respond directly to the repeated calls for reform in legal education bubbling up in both countries and have the potential to dramatically change how legal education is delivered in the United States and Germany. As these countries have not seen much innovation in their legal education for decades no wonder these proposals have met some opposition. Part Two of this Article examines the proposed changes to the ABA's accreditation standards and what they will mean practically for American law schools. Part Three briefly explores the challenges the Bologna Process' mandates may impose on German legal education. Part Four suggests ways both countries might approach skills training as they face impending change to their systems including identifying specifically what skills should be developed, determining where in the legal training these skills are developed and how these skills should be assessed. Even if no external organization requires this formal change the law schools should engage in this reform regardless because it makes sense and will result in better students and lawyers.

II. United States

Since 1952, the Department of Education has recognized the American Bar Association (ABA) as the national agency for the accreditation of programs leading to the first professional degree in law. At its first meeting in 1878, the ABA

12 *Bucker*, supra n. 2, at 578.

formed the Committee on Legal Education, which was renamed in 1893 to the Section of Legal Education and Admissions to the Bar.[13] The ABA instructed the Committee and later the Section to work with the admitting authorities, usually the highest court of each state, to assist in establishing the legal education requirements for admission to the bar.[14]

As a result, the Section established the first standards and interpretations of these standards for law schools in 1921 and began publishing the names of the schools which met the standards. These ABA Standards reflected efforts to improve the competence of individuals entering the legal profession. In addition, the standards relieved the admitting authorities from the burden of evaluating the quality of an applicant's educational experiences.[15]

In September 2008, the Council of the Section of the Legal Education and Admissions to the Bar began a comprehensive review of the *ABA Standards and Rules of Procedure for the Approval of Law Schools.*[16] This review, which is required of all agencies approved by the U.S. Department of Education, has the potential to greatly change how legal education is delivered. To date not many proposals have been sent to the Council since it is very early in the process, which is expected to take three years.

The Standards Review Committee developed a schedule and a statement of goals and objectives, which are available on the Committee's website at http://www.abanet.org/legaled/committees/comstandards.html. The website also has drafts of proposed changes to the standards, interpretations and rules of procedure as they become available. Following the postings on this site is very informative for anyone interested in the future of American legal education.

The review is a dynamic process and therefore the drafts change frequently undergoing continuous revisions as subcommittees obtain feedback from interested parties. Consequently, this article will most likely be outdated when published; however, it will be useful in memorializing what was happening at least at this moment in time providing a context for the eventual changes.

Law school professors and administrators are paying the most attention to the proposed changes to Chapter Three, "Program of Legal Education," which is

---

13 James P. White, History of the Administration of the American Law School Accreditation Process, 21 J. Leg. Ed. 438, 439 (2001).

14 Id.

15 Id. at 440.

16 *This* review *is required of all agencies approved by the United States Department of Education. See 34 C.F.R. § 602.21 (2009).*

being spearheaded by the Student Learning Outcomes Committee, a subcommittee of the ABA's Section on Legal Education and Admission to the Bar's Standards Review Committee. The subcommittee's work has been guided by the Report of the Outcome Measures Committee. In conducting its research, that special committee examined relevant literature in the legal education field including the Carnegie Foundation's report on legal education and the Best Practices Report published by Roy Stuckey and others, which pointed to the value of incorporating outcome measures into the accreditation criteria.[17]

In addition, the special committee reviewed literature and heard testimony about how other fields of professional education (medicine, pharmacy, architecture) used outcomes measures in their accreditation process.[18] Finally, general literature reflecting the trend towards outcome measures in undergraduate higher education influenced the special committee, which ultimately recommended that the standards be revised to more heavily rely on output measures, shifting the focus in legal education from teaching to learning.[19]

Drawing on the special committee's report and input from various interested parties, the Student Learning Outcomes subcommittee currently proposes revising the Standards and Interpretations to shift from a teaching centered regime to a regime focusing on student learning as well as shifting from a curriculum focus to an outcomes focus.

The Student Learning Outcomes subcommittee has developed multiple drafts to date and continues to make revisions making it difficult to analyze the actual language of any revised standard; however some guiding principles seem to be surfacing around the outcome measures issue. The subcommittee's changes to Chapter Three of the standards centers upon a four-fold approach that would require law schools to: (1) identify outcomes; (2) offer a curriculum so student achieves outcomes; (3) assess outcomes; and, (4) assess the assessment. These strategies reflect an instructional design method invented by Grant Wiggins and Jay McTighe known as "backwards design" as discussed in their book

17 ABA Sec. Leg. Educ. & Admis. To Bar, Report of the Outcome Measure Committee 6 (July 27, 2008) [hereinafter Outcomes Measure report](available at http://www.abanet.org/legaled/committees/subcomm/Outcome%20Measures%20Final %20Report.pdf).

18 Id. at 6.

19 Id.; see also Sherrill B. Gelmon et al., Assessing Service-Learning and Civic Engagement 1 (Campus Contact 2001). This push for outcome measures is not new but it appears for the first time to be gaining some serious traction. See Gregory S. Munro, Outcomes Assessment for Law Schools (Institute for L. Sch. Teaching 2000).

Understanding by Design.[20] The circular nature of the model begins by articulating what a teacher (or a program) wants students to learn and then planning experiences and instruction to aid students in their learning. The circle continues by gathering evidence to determine if these learning objectives have been met and then using those results to improve teaching and learning.[21]

If the Council approves these new standards law schools would need to develop specific, measurable learning outcomes. Next, faculties would need to examine both the curriculum as a whole and individual course content to ensure students can achieve the identified learning outcomes. As a result, faculties will need to engage in both macro and micro review of the full course of study and individual courses to find where the possible gaps are between the desired outcomes and the course coverage. The law school would then be required to assess learning outcomes using a variety of formative and summative assessments methods across the curriculum to provide meaningful feedback to students. Finally, law schools would be expected to assess the achievement of those goals and use the results to improve programs and services and inform planning and resource allocation decisions.

The switch to a learning-outcomes approach will likely positively impact legal education. Although any change brings its challenges, this change has the potential to make us better teachers, help students learn better, and make our institutions more efficient and more accountable. This shift from a teaching-driven method of instruction ("if we say it they will learn it") to a learning-based method will require law professors to more explicitly identify outcomes and develop assignments and learning experiences to help students meet these outcomes.

This necessarily will require a shift to incorporating more practical skills into the law curriculum. This shift will not come easy for most schools. Since 1870 most law schools have given short thrift to teaching of practical skills preferring to rely on the case method developed by Christopher Columbus Langdell at Harvard. The case method views legal education as more of an academic exercise which seeks to develop analytical thinking skills by examining appellate court opinions. The academy taught students how "to think like a lawyer" and left to the bar the job of actually teaching young lawyers how to practice law.[22]

---

20 *Grant Wiggins & Jay McTighe*, Understanding By Design (highlighted& notations ed., Assn. for Supervision & Development 1998); see *also Patricia L. Smith & Tillman J. Ragan*, Instructional Design (3d ed., Josey-Bass 2005).

21 *Linda Suskie*, Assessing Student Learning 4 (Anker Publg. Co. 2004).

22 *Bucker*, supra n. 2, at 581.

This divide between the Academy and the Bar lessened somewhat when law schools approved clinic opportunities for their students.[23] However, even with this explosion of clinics students are still not adequately prepared to practice law because the clinics are generally not required for graduation.[24] In addition, most students even if they participate in one clinic or externship do not get the repeated exposure they need to become proficient in lawyering skills. Clinicians advocate for students to take several professional skills courses and be required to take a clinic or a field placement program. They would like to see clinical offerings expanded in the law schools.[25]

Whether simulations is an acceptable way to teach students lawyering skills is subject to debate. The ABA sub-committee (Student Learning Outcomes Sub-Committee) charged with looking at this issue proposed a new standard that would include simulations as an example of a learning experience that would provide law students with opportunities to reflect on their experiences and on the values and responsibilities of the legal profession, and develop a student's ability to assess his or her performance and level of competence. The Committee on Clinical Skills filed a comment with the ABA arguing that although simulations "may be excellent vehicles for teaching the law of professional responsibility and some aspects of professionalism, the absence of a real client and a real matter deprives students of the opportunity to develop a crucial part of a lawyer's professional identity: learning how to take responsibility for the emotional and human consequences of our actions as lawyers."[26] In their opinion, simulations have value in the law school curriculum but not as the sole means for teaching professional skills.

The ideal approach is to not have an either-or approach but to teach skills through real client experiences in addition to integration of skills through simulations in the traditional classroom setting.

Re-examining what we do from the top to the bottom, focusing on what students will be able to do upon graduation and making sure they can do those things when they graduate is long overdue and will greatly improve legal education. Yet the reactions among American law professors have been mixed. Many

---

23 Id. at 586-589 (excellent discussion of the rise of popularity of clinics in American law schools).

24 Id. at 605.

25 *Roy Stuckey*, Best Practices for Legal Education 167 (2007).

26 Comment of Clinical Skills Committee,http://www.abanet.org/legaled/committees/Standards%20Review%20documents/SRC%20Comments-ClinicalSkillsCommitteeOctober2009.pdf.

groups including legal writing professors, clinicians, librarians and doctrinal professors applaud and endorse the suggested revisions. Others remain skeptical arguing that the standards will stifle innovations and be too costly.

II. Germany

While American legal educators struggle over whether to replace inputs with outputs, German legal educators have been engaged in their own debate over the directives found in the Bologna Declaration of 19 June 1999. The Bologna Process began over 12 years ago when ministers of four European Union countries signed a written understanding.[27] The ministers declared their intent to harmonize the degrees and cycles between the European countries in an effort to strengthen the higher education system of Europe as a whole.[28] This movement grew from the four original countries to 45 countries participating in the process and has focused on adoption of three cycle degree systems, cooperation in quality assurance and the recognition of degrees and periods of study.[29]

Despite the relative success of the Bologna Process it has encountered some tensions with the German system of legal education. [30] These tensions mostly surrounded one important aspect of the Bologna Process, the three cycle degree system. The first cycle would end with the awarding of a bachelor's degree, the second with a masters and the third with a doctorate. In most cases the bachelors would take three years, the masters two years and a doctorate three years. This model mirrored the English and Irish system more so than the system Continental Europe had used.

German legal educators strongly opposed this bachelor's-masters Bologna Process reform and have thus far refused to allow a bachelor's degree alone to

27 Joint Declaration on Harmonization of the Architecture of the European Higher Education System by the Four Ministers in Charge for France, Germany, Italy, and the United Kingdom, May 25, 1998, available at http://www.bologna-berlin2003.de/pdf/Sorbonne_declaration.pdf.

28 Id.

29 The European Higher Education Area: Achieving the Goals Communique of the Conferences of Ministers responsible for Higher Education in Bergen on 19 & 20 May 2005,p. 2, available at http://ec.europa.eu/education/policies/educ/bologna/bergen.pdf.

30 *Laurel S. Terry*, Living With The Bologna Process: Recommendations to the German Legal Education Community from a U.S. Perspective, 7(11) German Law Journal 863, 873 (2006).

qualify a person to be a lawyer.[31] The new bachelor's-masters model raises serious questions for German legal educators about how practical skills could be delivered in such an abbreviated program.[32]

Perhaps German legal educators can stand firm and not alter the structure of legal education. However, practical reasons exist that may make this impossible. In her article, exploring the impact of the Bologna Process on German legal education Professor Terry suggests three potential sources of pressure which may make it impossible or ill-advised for German law schools to resist change.[33] These include:

- Pressure from other departments in their own universities;
- Pressure from the German legal community concerned about becoming isolated from the rest of Europe;
- Pressure from the German government which wants favorable ratings on its compliance with the Bologna Process.

Rethinking how legal education is delivered in Germany and perhaps melding the theoretical and the practical components has been discussed before. In fact, "in 1998 a broad majority of the Länder ministers of justice favored a proposal according to which theoretical and practical legal education should have been integrated in one course of study; classes at university were to be linked with stages of practical training in courts, law firms etc.; after this integrated course, a single final exam should have been the overall qualification for any legal profession."[34] Support for this proposal, however, dwindled. Perhaps the Bologna Process will revive this discussion much like the Carnegie Report and the Best Practices report did in the United States.

Unlike the United States, however, Germany at least up to this moment in time has not broadly implemented clinical education. Professor Richard J. Wilson offers several reasons Western European countries have held out in accepting clinical education including that many of these countries already have pre-existing apprenticeships.[35] The problem with the apprenticeship model as it presently exists is the lack of meaningful feedback the students get and the absence

31 Id. at 878-879.

32 *Bucker*, supra n. 2, at 577.

33 *Terry*, supra n. 30, at 879-883.

34 *Johannes Riedel*, The Reform of Legal Education In Germany available at http://elfa-afde.eu/Documents/LEGALEDUCATIONINGERMANY.pdf

35 *Richard J. Wilson*, Western Europe: Last Holdout in the Worldwide Acceptance of Clinical Education, 10 (7) German Law Journal 823, 832 (2009).

of any concrete connections to their academic studies.[36] In addition, how the apprenticeship period is designed gives students little experience learning some of the skills thought to be essential for lawyers.[37] This absence of meaningful training with the necessary skills makes the apprenticeship a solid idea for skills training in principle but not in practice.

IV. Next Steps

Whether the ABA passes the new accreditation standards or the Bologna Process ultimately forces Germany to change how legal education is delivered is impossible to know. But law educators in both countries should pay attention to these debates and discussions and incorporate many of their suggestions regardless if they become mandates or not. Engaging in serious curricular reform focusing on the development of lawyering skills ultimately benefits not only current students but also future lawyers and the public. Reflecting on what skills should be developed, where in the legal training they are developed and how they are assessed should be addressed no matter if these skills are incorporated in the academic study or in a separate apprenticeship model. To this end, I offer several suggestions for how this may be done.

1. Identify the fundamental skills considered necessary for the effective practice of law.

In the United States, the Association of Legal Writing Directors (ALWD) and other organizations concerned with student learning carefully follow the ABA's comprehensive review process often submitting comments on its proposed standards. In its September 2010 comment, ALWD urged the Council to specifically state and require certain fundamental skills of competent beginning lawyers.[38] Although ALWD appreciated the desire to craft standards that allow for flexibil-

36 Id. at 833.

37 Id.

38 Comment from Association of Legal Writing Directors to ABA Section of Legal Education & Admissions to the Bar (September 30, 2010) (available at http://www.abanet.org/legaled/committees/Standards%20Review%20documents/Outcome%20Measurements/Comment%20-%20outcome%20measures%20-%20ALWD%20-%20September%202010.pdf).

ity and innovation, it believed certain skills remain so fundamental that they must be explicitly included in the accreditation standards to ensure all law schools will allocate proper resources and coverage to these skills. ALWD proposed taking these skills out of an interpretation of Standard 302 and instead placing them directly in Standard 302 as follows:

Standard 302.

. . .

b. The learning outcomes shall include competency as an entry-level practitioner in the following areas:

. . .

(2) competency in the following skills:

(i) legal analysis and reasoning, critical thinking, legal research, problem solving, written and oral communications in a legal context, client interviewing, client counseling, negotiation, and fact development and analysis;

(ii) the ability to recognize and resolve ethical and other professional dilemmas; and

(iii) a depth and breadth of other professional skills sufficient for effective, responsible, and ethical participation in the legal profession.

Both countries should identify the most important skills necessary for its new graduates to have and require all providers of legal education to develop a plan for training students in these skills. The MacCrate report in America and two reports in Europe, The Council of Bars and Law Societies of Europe and the European Law Faculties Association's QUAACAS (Quality Assurance, Accreditation and Assessment Committee) committee's tuning report give law schools a blueprint of the skills, knowledge and competencies necessary to become a lawyer.[39] The ABA in the United States and the government in Germany should identify skills from these reports that all law schools must teach and not leave it up to individual law schools to decide which if any skills to incorporate into legal education.

39 *Wilson* supra n.35, at 840-842.

2. Engage in curriculum mapping in each law school to determine where the skills are being learned in the course of legal study.

Curriculum mapping is a deliberate process to design curricula that actually identifies and supports student achievement of learning outcomes. Curriculum mapping is defined as:

"A process by which all teachers document their own curriculum, then share and examine each other's curriculums for gaps, overlaps, redundancies, and new learning, creating a coherent, consistent, curriculum within and across schools that is ultimately aligned to standards and responsive to student data and other school initiatives."[40]

The term curriculum mapping was first introduced in the 1980s by Fenwick W. English. He used this term to describe the taught curriculum and not the written curriculum. The idea was to find a conceptual way to indicate that the actual curriculum taught in the classroom may be different than the one put to paper by curriculum developers. In the 1990s Heidi Hayes Jacobs broadened the term curriculum mapping to the definition above which involves a multi-phase process.

K-12 educators have engaged in this process for years. Law schools are relatively new to this process although some schools throughout the United States are already doing this. For example, Nova Southeastern, Charlotte School of Law, Denver and Dayton School of Law have all engaged in curriculum mapping.

These law schools take seriously whether they offer a curriculum that is designed to produce graduates who have attained competency in the learning outcomes they have identified by asking their professors to document the content and skills they teach and provide opportunities for their faculty members to talk to one another about their real classroom teaching and how those practices affect their students.

Multiple benefits result from engaging in such a process including empowering professors, improving student learning and achievement, informing planning and resource allocation decisions. One study of curriculum mapping in higher education found curriculum mapping empowers professors by helping the faculty to "grow as a collaborative community, to connect with each other to

---

40 *Susan Udelhofen*, Keys to Curriculum Mapping: Strategies and Tools to Make It Work (Corwin Press 2005).

decrease isolation." [41]It helps to promote a supportive, collaborative culture. By analyzing their practices and making decisions about curriculum professors learn from each other. This process reflects an African Proverb: "To go fast, go alone. To go farther, go together"

Engaging in curriculum mapping helps make sure we are really thinking about what students are learning and not just what we are teaching. Sharing the maps helps students understand how their courses help meet the learning objectives. Without curriculum mapping law schools risk delivering an uncoordinated course of study that might not support students to demonstrate and achieve the desired results. Having time to reflect helps the faculty create and revise the curriculum. Engaging in this process helps make sure the legal education program is consistent and coherent.

This graphic shows how the process actually works.

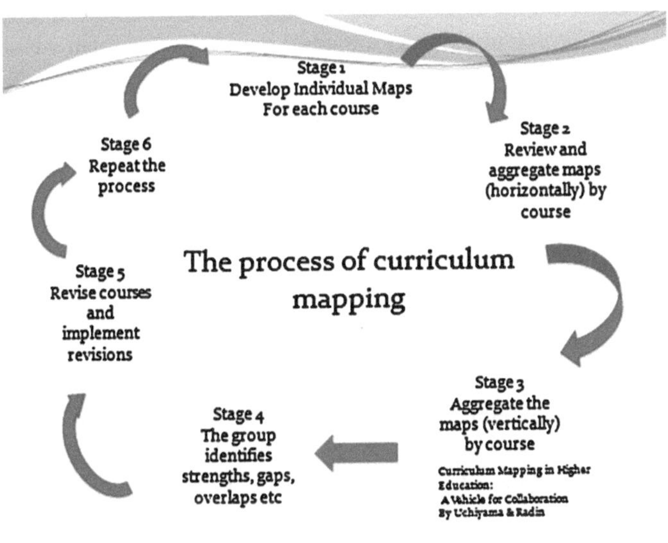

The first stage is to create individual maps. At this stage the decision needs to be made whether to engage in backwards mapping or forward mapping. Forward mapping "requires teachers to record their planned content, skills, and assessments for the entire school year." Some teachers may find this difficult es-

41 *Kay Pippin Uchiyama & Jean L. Radin*, Curriculum Mapping in Higher Education: A Vehicle for Collaboration, 33 Innov. High Educ. 271, 279 (2009).

pecially if they do not record lesson plans. Backwards mapping takes longer because it asks teachers to document the content, skills and assessments at the end of each month throughout the year.

When reviewing the maps Susan Udelhofen in her book *Keys to Curriculum Mapping* suggests teachers look for:

1) A clear connection between content, skills and assessment
2) Clear and concise skills. Are the skills listed as action verbs?
3) A variety of assessments. Is there a balance of assessments and is there required documentation of observation-type assessments?
4) The possible gaps in content and skills
5) The meaningless redundancies - are there topics that are taught multiple times at multiple points that are redundant
6) Repetitions in the content and skills. Does a curriculum reflect a repetition of content and skills that build or spiral?[42]

The later stages of the process include developing an action plan which includes deciding on timetables and who is responsible to address the specific issues. In summary, the faculty should be asking three critical questions during the process:

- Who is doing what?
- How does the work align with the learning outcomes identified by the law school?
- Are we working efficiently and effectively?

To get started faculties should use existing meetings to explain the process, offer professional development activities and disseminate handouts and articles to educate the faculty. Both American and German law schools can be engaging in this process now to determine how the graduates are receiving skills training. The schools may be surprised after mapping the curriculum how little skills students do get exposed to and learn, whether that be in the traditional American model or the apprenticeship model in Germany.

42 *Udelhofen*, supra n. 40,

3. Require both valid and reliable formative and summative assessment methods.[43]

Many different types of assessment exist with only one of them being the traditional method of measuring student learning, grading.[44] Assessments focusing on improving a student's learning or improving a professor's teaching often are referred to as formative assessments while assessments focusing on giving a grade are called summative assessments.[45] Although grades play a role in measuring student learning they cannot be the sole indicator because grading and assessment criteria may differ, grading standards may be vague or inconsistent, and grades alone may give insufficient information on student strength and weaknesses.[46] In addition, formative assessment unlike grades can help teachers determine what works and what does not helping improve the quality of their courses.[47]

This fundamental difference will not be the only concept law faculties need to understand. For these new standards to work law schools will need to educate their faculty on good assessment practices and how to implement them.[48] Multiple options for choosing an assessment strategy exist as well as assessment

43 Much of the content for this section comes from a previous article I wrote, *Susan Hanley Duncan*, The New Accreditation Standards Are Coming to a Law School Near You, What You Need to Know About Outcomes and Assessments, 16 JOURNAL OF THE LEGAL WRITING INSTITUTE 605 (2010).

44 *Mary J. Allen*, Assessing Academic Programs in Higher Education 17 (Anker Publg. Co. 2004). Legal educators need to become familiar with the assessment vocabulary and assessment procedures which will most likely require trainings and support.

45 *Michael Hunter Schwartz* et al., Teaching Law By Design: Engaging Students from the Syllabus to the Final Exam 137, 154 (Carolina Academic Press 2009). Other authors use the terms "traditional measurements" for describing traditional tests compared to "performance measurements" which requires students to "do" something to show their level of mastery. Allen, supra n.44, at 7-8.

46 *Linda Suskie*, Assessing Student Learning 6-8 (Anker Publg. Co. 2004). For a good discussion of the differences between grading and assessment see Allen, supra n.44, at 11-13. For example, she makes an excellent point that a grade point average from a class does not tell the professor which learning objectives are being mastered.

47 *Allen*, supra n.44, at 11.

48 *Trudy W. Banta, Elizabeth A. Jones & Karen E. Black,* Designing Effective Assessment (Jossey-Bass 2009).

tools.[49] Some of these tools will be familiar to law faculties, especially direct measures such as exams, papers, and interaction with a client.[50]

Other indirect measures encouraging reflection of students or alumni about their learning may not be as familiar to law faculties.[51] Some of these measures may include conducting surveys, focus groups and interviews.[52] Other ways to get students to reflect include minute papers, journals, and self-ratings.[53] The purpose of these measures, often referred to as formative measures, is to help students learn not to assign a grade.[54]

No matter which assessments are chosen legal educators should design several assessments and vary them.[55] When using summative assessments to assign a grade this is particularly important because no research finds that giving one exam at the end of the semester will adequately assess a student's knowledge.[56] External variables (student is sick, something is going on in student's life) may prevent a student from doing well on a particular day. In addition, a student may do better with one type of assessment compared to another.[57]

If law faculties take seriously the research that variety and quantity matter with assessments, more work will be demanded than writing one exam. In their book, Professors Schwartz, Sparrow & Hess offer a helpful checklist for law professors to ask themselves when designing assessments. This list includes:

- What is the rationale for this assessment?
- What do you want students to do?
- How much time will it take for students to complete?
- Will the assessment be completed in or outside of class?
- What is the assessment's content?
- Is there a particular format students should use?
- How much can students collaborate on the assessment?
- How will you provide feedback?[58]

---

49 *Suskie*, supra n. 46, at xii.

50 *Barbara E. Walvoord*, Assessment Clear and Simple 3 (Jossey-Bass 2004).

51 Id.

52 *Suskie*, supra n. 46at 223.

53 Id. at 168-184. Minute papers involve "giv[ing] students just a couple of thought-provoking questions and ask them to write no more than one sentence in response to each."

54 *Schwartz*, supra n.45, at 137.

55 *Schwartz*, supra n.45, at 154-158.

56 Id. at 155.

57 Id. at 157.

58 Id. at 163.

The book also provides helpful commentary for each one of these questions which can aid any professor planning his or her course.[59]

In recognizing that more assessments and more intentional design of assessments is contrary to most law school's practice and culture, the authors also encourage law professors to develop clear grading criteria through checklists, rubrics or samples to help save time.[60] In addition, students appreciate knowing exactly what was expected of them in advance.[61] Assessment literature strongly urges educators to develop a scoring guide to evaluate assessments.[62] To that end many resources exist to help law faculties develop for the first time or improve existing rubrics.[63]

In summary, law professors need to assess student attainment of the learning outcomes through multiple measures. These assessments need to be ongoing and focused not only on outcomes but experiences. They should be designed using best practices and the latest research on learning and teaching. In addition, designing effective rubrics requires professors to focus on the learning outcome or objective that students are expected to achieve and work backwards defining possible criteria that students need to demonstrate to show competency. These rubrics also provide students valuable feedback about their progress in achieving learning outcomes.

Assessment must also be at the institutional level and not just the professor level.[64] "Assessment is about learning" and that is why an integral part of this process involves assessing the assessment and making changes based on the information received.[65] Mary J Allen in her book *Assessing Academic Programs In Higher Education* offers an excellent definition of program assessment as "a framework for focusing faculty attention on student learning and for provoking meaningful discussions of program objectives, curricular organization, pedagogy, and student development."[66]

---

59 Id. at 139-143.

60 Id. at 147. See also *Sophie M. Sparrow*, Describing the Ball: Improve Teaching By Using Rubrics Explicit Grading Criteria, 2004 Mich. St. L. Rev. 1.

61 *Schwartz*, supra n.45, at 158.

62 *Suskie*, supra n.46, at 123.

63 Id. at 123-151; See also *Dannelle D. Stevens & Antonia Levi*, Introduction to Rubrics An Assessment Tool to Save Grading Time, Convey Effective Feedback, and Promote Student Learning (Stylus 2005).

64 *Allen*, supra n.45, at 4.

65 *Catherine A. Palomba & Trudy W. Banta*, Assessment Essentials: Planning, Implementing, and Improving Assessment in Higher Education 15 (Jossey-Bass 1999).

66 Id.

A uniform set of measures to assess institutional effectiveness will not be possible since effectiveness measures will be dependent on the unique mission of each law school. However, certain characteristics should be present for any effective assessment. These include processes that are useful, cost-effective, reasonably accurate and truthful, carefully planned, and organized, systematic, and sustained.[67]

Any assessment of institutional effectiveness will need to be proceeded by the law school defining clearly articulated institutional goals and implementing strategies to achieve those goals. Only after these first two steps is the law school able to assess the achievement of those goals and use the results to improve programs and services and inform planning and resource allocation decisions.

In his *Best Practices* book Roy Stuckey list six principles underlying best practices for assessing institutional effectiveness specifically in law schools.[68] These include:

- *The school regularly evaluates the program of instruction to determine if it is effective at preparing students for the practice of law.*
- *The school uses various methods to gather quantitative and qualitative information about the effectiveness of the program of instruction.*[69]
- *The school uses student performance and outcome assessment results in evaluation of the educational effectiveness of the school's program of instruction.*[70]
- *The school's processes of conducting assessments of student performance and educational outcomes meet recognized standards for conducting assessments in higher education.*[71]
- *The school solicits and incorporates opinions of its alumni as well as other practicing judges and lawyers who hire and interact with graduates of the school.*[72]
- *The school demonstrates how educational outcomes data is used to improve individual student and overall program performance.*[73]

---

67 E.g. Middle States Commission on Higher Education, Assessing Student Learning and Institutional Effectiveness Understanding Middle States Expectations (2005), http://www.msche.org/publications/Assessment_Expectations051222081842.pdf.

68 *Roy Stuckey et al.*, Best Practices For Legal Education (2007).

69 Id. at 266-270.

70 Id. at 270-271.

71 Id. at 271-272.

72 Id. at 272.

73 Id. at 272-273.

The best way for a law school to begin assessing the assessment is to engage in an assessment audit.[74] The purpose of this audit is to determine what is already being done and what is being planned or desired in the future.[75] Collecting centralized data about what is being done will involve collecting both classroom and institution wide assessment measures currently being used.[76] In addition, the audit should determine how this data relates to the various goals and learning objectives. Another critical part of the audit is to articulate how the assessment is used to make changes.[77] Finally, the audit needs to make recommendations for improving the assessment process.[78] In her book, *Assessment Clear and Simple,* Barbara Walvoord provides several charts for various disciplines to illustrate what a completed assessment audit may look like.[79]

Assessments can be staggered over several years and do not need to be completed on all students every year.[80] In addition, faculties can be selective about which learning objectives to assess and might consider assessing only a small amount of learning objectives at first.[81] The main point is to do some type of assessment every year instead of just waiting for the year before a site visit.[82] In her updated book Linda Suskie offers other ideas for keeping the assessment process simple including keeping paperwork minimal and looking at samples to evaluate outcomes instead of each student's work.[83] Additionally, Suskie urges work plans to reflect the time commitment it takes to lead and participate in assessment efforts.[84]

---

74 *Walvoord*, supra n.50, at 34.

75 Id.

76 Id. at 54-55.

77 Id. at 58.

78 Id. at 59.

79 Id. at Appendix F.

80 Allen, supra n.45, at 6.

81 Id. *Linda Suskie* suggests starting with no more than three to six. *Suskie*, supra n. 46, at 87.

82 *Linda Suskie*, Assessing Student Learning A Common Sense Guide 89 (2d Ed. *Josey-Bass* 2009).

83 Id.. This 2009 edition offers many current recommend readings at the end of each chapter which should be an invaluable resource for law professors interested in learning more about understanding assessment, planning for assessment success and using assessment results.

84 Id. at 88.

V. Conclusion

Both German and American legal educators struggle with how to make sure their graduates have acquired appropriate fundamental lawyering skills and evaluate whether they understand legal theory as well as their professional and ethical responsibilities. Recently the ABA in the United States and the Bologna Process in Europe are bringing this debate to the forefront of discussions on legal education reform. Both countries' law schools should engage in this curricular reform whether or not a mandate requires them to do it. Reflecting on what skills should be developed, where in the legal training they are developed and how they are assessed will benefit students and eventually new lawyers. This debate presents an opportunity for both countries to re-evaluate how they have traditionally delivered legal education and ascertain whether better methods exist for accomplishing their goals and objectives.

Öffentliches und Internationales Recht

Herausgegeben von Udo Fink, Dieter Dörr und Rolf Schwartmann

Band 1 Tim Schönborn: Die Causa Austria. Zur Zulässigkeit bilateraler Sanktionen zwischen den Mitgliedstaaten der Europäischen Union. 2005.

Band 2 Marc Torsten Hausmann: Das Cotonou-Handelsregime und das Recht der WTO. 2006.

Band 3 Hortense Ute Demme: Hegemonialstellungen im Völkerrecht: Der ständige Sitz im Sicherheitsrat der Vereinten Nationen. 2006.

Band 4 Theofaneia Rizou: Zugang zu Gerichten im Umweltrecht. Eine vergleichende Studie des deutschen und griechischen Rechts. 2006.

Band 5 Matthias Meyer: Die Bewertung parafiskalischer Abgaben aus der Sicht des europäischen Beihilferechts. 2007.

Band 6 Moritz Maus: Der grundrechtliche Schutz des Privaten im europäischen Recht. 2007.

Band 7 Roman Ringwald: Daseinsvorsorge als Rechtsbegriff. Forsthoff, Grundgesetz und Grundversorgung. 2008.

Band 8 Christine Heer-Reißmann: Die Letztentscheidungskompetenz des Europäischen Gerichtshofes für Menschenrechte in Europa. Eine Untersuchung zum Verhältnis von EGMR und EuGH in Menschenrechtsfragen unter Berücksichtigung des Verhältnisses des BVerfG zum EuGH. 2008.

Band 9 Caroline Volkmann: Die Strafverfolgung des Völkermordes nach dem Weltrechtsprinzip im internationalen Strafrecht und im Völkerstrafrecht. Untersucht am Beispiel der deutschen Rechtsordnung. 2009.

Band 10 Tobias O. Keber: Der Begriff des Terrorismus im Völkerrecht. Entwicklungslinien im Vertrags- und Gewohnheitsrecht unter besonderer Berücksichtigung der Arbeiten zu einem „Umfassenden Übereinkommen zur Bekämpfung des Terrorismus". 2009.

Band 11 Michael Kühn: Unilaterale präventive Gewaltanwendung. Eine Untersuchung zur „präventiven Selbstverteidigung" im Völkerrecht. 2009.

Band 12 Axel Groth: Die Dienstleistungskonzession im europäischen Vergabe- und Beihilfenrecht. 2010.

Band 13 Jürgen Bröhmer (ed.): The German Constitution Turns 60. Basic Law and Commonwealth Constitution. German and Australian Perspectives. 2011.

Band 14 Christine Kulwicki: Verfassungswandel. Die Wechselwirkung zwischen Grundrechten und informationstechnischen Ermittlungsmethoden. 2011.

Band 15 Dieter Dörr / Udo Fink / Russel Weaver / Tobias Keber (eds.): Brandeis meets Gutenberg. German-American Conversations on Law, 1991-2011. 2012.

www.peterlang.de

Johan D. van der Vyver

Implementation of International Law in the United States

Frankfurt am Main, Berlin, Bern, Bruxelles, New York, Oxford, Wien, 2010.
309 pp.
Legal Policy Symposium.
Edited by Gerhard Robbers and Bernd von Hoffmann . Vol. 9
ISBN 978-3-631-59880-1 · hb. € 60,80*

Even though the Constitution proclaims treaties entered into by the United States to be part of the supreme law of the land and authorises prosecution of offences against the law of nation in federal courts, the United States has had a checkered record in ratifying human rights instruments, in upholding decisions of international tribunals, and indeed in submitting itself to the jurisdiction of such tribunals. It refused to uphold judgments of the International Court of Justice within its municipal legal system, terminated the competence of the ICJ to adjudicate international disputes to which it is a party, and attempted to undermine the functioning of the international criminal court. It engaged in armed conflicts in blatant violation of international humanitarian law and subjected belligerent detainees to unbecoming interrogation techniques. There are clear indications that the Obama administration is setting the United States on a new course of international comity and *Völkerrechtsfreundlichkeit*.

Content: American foreign policy · Prosecuting offences against the law of nations · Ratification of international human rights instruments · A juvenile justice system that violates international standards of rights of the child · A hostile attitude toward jurisprudence of international tribunals · American exceptionalism and the international criminal court · Military interventions in Kosovo, Afghanistan and Iraq

FSC
www.fsc.org
MIX
Papier | Fördert
gute Waldnutzung
FSC® C083411

Kolibri 360 GmbH
Ferdinand-Jühlke-Straße 7
99095 Erfurt, Deutschland
produktsicherheit@kolibri360.de